RESTORATION 1989

Chicago Elects a New Daley

Restoration 1989

Chicago Elects a New Daley

Edited by
Paul M. Green and Melvin G. Holli

LYCEUM
BOOKS, INC.

59 E. Van Buren St.
Chicago, IL 60605

For Harry Welstein, who would have enjoyed the
RESTORATION

© Lyceum Books, Inc., 1991

Published in the United States by
LYCEUM BOOKS, INC.
59 East Van Buren, Ste. 703
Chicago, IL 60605

Composed and produced by
Publishers Services, Inc.

Library of Congress Cataloging-in-Publication Data

Restoration 1989 : Chicago elects a new Daley / edited by Paul M.
  Green and Melvin G. Holli.
        p.   cm.
    Includes bibliographical references and index.
    ISBN 0-925065-10-2 (hdbk.)   ISBN 0-925065-09-9 (pbk.)
    1. Mayors—Illinois—Chicago—Election. 2. Chicago (Ill.)—
Politics and government—1951– 3. Elections—Illinois—Chicago.
I. Green, Paul Michael.   II. Holli, Melvin G.
JS718.3.R47   1991
324.9337'11033—dc20   90-25042
                                                                       CIP

CONTENTS

Contributors

PAUL M. GREEN is director of the Institute for Public Policy and Administration at Governors State University. He is author and coauthor with Melvin G. Holli of several books on Chicago politics. Green also writes a monthly column on Chicago politics for *Crain's Chicago Business* and serves as an election analyst for WGN Radio.

EDWARD M. BURKE is the 14th Ward alderman and Democratic committeeman. A powerful and controversial city council member for over two decades, he now serves as chairman of the council's crucial finance committee.

JORGE CASUSO recently became Chicago *Tribune* bureau chief in Los Angeles. Previously, as a citywide reporter for the *Tribune*, he specialized in covering the political and economic aspirations of Chicago's growing Hispanic population. Casuso has a wide knowledge of Hispanic community and neighborhood organizations.

GREG HINZ is political reporter for the Lerner community newspapers on the city's North and Northwest sides. He is a recognized expert on the independent and gay political movements along the city's north lakefront.

MONROE ANDERSON served as Acting Mayor Eugene Sawyer's press secretary and political confidant. Formerly a reporter with the Chicago *Tribune* and *Newsweek*, Anderson is now director of station services at WBBM (CBS) Television in Chicago.

DON ROSE is a long-time leading political consultant and media advisor on the Chicago scene. Rose played a key role in Jane Byrne's stunning and surprising upset victory over Michael Bilandic in the 1979 Democratic mayoral primary. In recent years, Rose has worked for independent Democratic and Republican candidates in Chicago, Illinois, and around the country.

DAVID FREMON is a freelance political columnist for various periodicals and newspapers in the Chicago area and the author of the recent well-received book *Chicago Politics: Ward by Ward*.

RICHARD DAY is a nationally known pollster who specializes in Illinois and Chicago politics. In 1983, Day, working as ABC-TV's polling expert, was the first pollster to predict the upset victory of Harold Washington in the Democratic mayoral primary.

MELVIN G. HOLLI is a professor of history at the University of Illinois at Chicago and coauthor with Paul M. Green of *Bashing Chicago Traditions: Harold Washington's Last Campaign*. He is recognized as an expert on the impact of ethnicity and immigration on urban history.

Introduction

In 1989, Cook County State's Attorney Richard M. Daley was elected mayor of Chicago. The son of the city's most famous and longest-serving chief executive, Richard J. Daley (1955–1976), Richard M. won two hard-fought contests (Democratic primary and general election) to win the right to serve out the unexpired four-year term of the 1987 mayoral winner, Harold Washington.

The key to this book is understanding the politics of mayoral succession that followed Washington's death in November 1987. The sudden departure of the city's first black mayor shocked the African-American community in Chicago and left its citizens emotionally stunned and politically divided. The charismatic Washington had become a god-like figure to black Chicago and, like most deities, had not ordained his successor (a situation quite similar to the political aftermath of the death of Mayor Richard J. Daley in 1976). The ensuing internal conflicts in the African-American political community over which apostle would replace Washington as Chicago's black leader is the chief underlying cause for Rich Daley's election in 1989.

Contributing authors to this book reflect a mixture of academicians, journalists, and frontline political players. Like Chicago politics itself, this book is filled with conflicting opinions and contradicting interpretations of many events. The editors made a conscious effort to be fair to all sides, but we have not attempted to present a unified and harmonious analysis of the 1989 elections. There is seldom a single answer or explanation for political happenings anywhere in America, and that is especially true in Chicago. On completing this book, the reader will have to decide which scenario presented seems the most accurate and plausible. However, one fact will remain unchallenged—politics in the Windy City is not a game for the timid, and in the immortal words of Mr. Dooley, "It [still] ain't beanbag."

In part one, Paul Green lays out the big picture of both 1989 mayoral primaries (yes, there is a Republican party in Chicago) and the general election. In the first chapter he provides the groundwork for understanding the events that led to the selection of Alderman Eugene

Sawyer (6) to succeed Harold Washington as acting mayor. He reveals the depth of division in the African-American political community and argues that without this civil war, "Rich Daley and his brilliant campaign strategists would never have had the opportunity to contest, let alone win, the office of mayor of Chicago."

In discussing Daley's primary victory, Green discloses the near picture-perfect campaign put together by the state's attorney. According to Green, "Daley's grand strategy was to isolate Sawyer and Alderman Tim Evans (4) within the black community." Daley and his shrewd advisors carefully constructed a solid coalition of the remaining voting blocs in the city to implement this electoral strategy. This chapter also reveals how Daley, "the boy from the working-class Southwest Side Bridgeport neighborhood," expanded his philosophical and political base to the lakefront. In an ironic twist to Chicago's historic battles between lakefront reformers and ethnic machine supporters, young Daley in 1989 won over both constituencies and in doing so united the "bungalow and the condo" behind his candidacy.

Green describes Daley's victory in the general election over Evans and former alderman Edward Vrdolyak as a near reenactment of his primary win. Daley recognized that the split in the black community remained except that this time Evans's backers were wooing Sawyer's supporters to join their campaign. Unsure of his base vote, Evans was forced to spend much of the short campaign period trying to energize and consolidate his black support, which left him little time for any coalition building. Daley's campaign tactics were structured so that he would not become a unifying symbol for Evans in the black community. Daley downplayed his rhetoric and campaign style in dealing with Evans. As for Vrdolyak, the frontrunning Daley dismissed him as a minor "fringe candidate."

Richard J. Daley often said, "politics is a game of addition." In winning the general election young Daley, according to Green, followed his father's advice "by reaching out to add new voters and voting blocs to his campaign while his opponents ignored the old rule and engaged in the politics of subtraction."

In part two, the book examines the activities of various Chicago voting blocs in the 1989 mayoral elections.

Alderman Edward Burke (14) analyzes ethnic Chicago's response to the Daley campaign. Burke, a long-time political powerhouse on the city's Southwest Side and a leading city council critic of the Washington administration, argues that Daley's family name and recent city history "provided white ethnic voters with an easy choice (in 1989) and provided committeemen (elected local party leaders) in white ethnic wards with an easy task in getting out the vote."

Burke, briefly a mayoral candidate himself, congratulates Daley on his strategy of (1) "staying above the fray," and (2) providing a meaningful alternative to white voters tired and frightened of ongoing infighting in the black community. As a party man, Burke is hopeful that racial divisiveness inside the Chicago Democratic party will end and that the party organization will once again become a potent force in national and local elections. As for Daley's future, Burke believes he will play it clean, safe, and straight in his shortened first term (next election 1991) and the alderman guarantees that political analysts who predict a return to patronage politics under the new Daley will be proven wrong. "Those days," writes Burke, "are gone forever."

In Chicago's recent racially charged mayoral elections, Hispanics have been one of the two swing voting blocs in the city (the lakefront has been the other). Though not large in raw vote numbers, Hispanics have been courted heavily for their ability to tip (or at least tilt) the balance of power one way or the other in mayoral elections.

Jorge Casuso, a Chicago *Tribune* reporter and long-time observer of the Hispanic community, reveals how one ambitious and aggressive Hispanic politician, Alderman Luis Gutierrez (26), became a big-time player in Daley's run for city hall. In recapturing the dynamics and impact of Gutierrez's endorsement of Daley, the author also explains the recent dual evolution of Hispanics in Chicago life. Casuso discusses differences between young, liberal second-generation Hispanic activists (such as Gutierrez), who were drawn to Washington's candidacy and philosophy, and older, more conservative Hispanics, "who view themselves as part of an immigrant American tradition."

The future direction of Hispanic politics in Chicago is uncertain, but with Gutierrez allying himself closely with Daley, it is Casuso's view that other Hispanic politicians must decide whether to join the Daley train "or wait by the tracks for (another) one that may not come."

Chicago's north lakefront is made up of six wards (called by some the "East 40s"—they are wards 42, 43, 44, 46, 48, and 49) and, like the city's Hispanic voters, lakefront residents also have been courted heavily by recent mayoral contenders. Conventional wisdom describes lakefront voters as being liberal, independent, and nonaligned in the city's race-dominated politics. Greg Hinz, a columnist for the leading community newspaper on the lakefront, rips apart the "mythology" associated with the East 40s. Hinz calls the lakefront "an integrated microcosm of the city as a whole," with different racial, ethnic, economic, and lifestyle constituencies making up parts of all six wards.

Hinz weaves a story of how the Daley campaign sought out such diverse lakefront groups as gays, social liberals, and economic conservatives, as well as Jewish voters angered over the hesitancy of black leaders to denounce blatant anti-Semitic statements made by a member of Mayor Sawyer's administration. Hinz concludes that most lakefronters went with Daley for a variety of reasons, but in the words of the winner's chief media advisor, David Axelrod, key to Daley's lakefront landslide were his views "on the quality of life"—in short, bread and butter triumphed over political philosophy.

In part three, the most critical and controversial section of this book, African-American politics in post-Washington Chicago is analyzed and debated. Monroe Anderson, a former newspaperman and Mayor Sawyer's press secretary and confidant, reveals the extent of the split in the black community. Writing from a strong pro-Sawyer perspective, Anderson defends his friend's city council selection as acting mayor, attacks Sawyer critics such as Alderman Evans and Alderman Dorothy Tillman (3), and defends Sawyer's record as mayor. In the truest sense of Chicago's rough-and-tumble political tradition, Anderson "lets it all hang out" in going after Sawyer's critics, many of whom he labels as "saboteurs, malcontents, and misfits."

Anderson also attempts to place Sawyer in a political perspective. Calling his boss a nice man who was not particularly ambitious or articulate, Anderson believes the heat surrounding his selection on the chaotic night in December 1987 placed him in a precarious political situation. "If he was to continue as Chicago's second black mayor," writes Anderson, "he (Sawyer) had to shore up his (black) base" while attempting to be mayor of the entire city. Sawyer's enemies, both black and white, would not let that happen.

Anderson's insight and opinions make his chapter one of the liveliest discussions of Chicago politics in recent years.

Don Rose and James Andrews, two advisors to Alderman Tim Evans, cover much of the same ground as Anderson in their chapter, but with far different conclusions. The authors admit that "the Evans campaign . . . had no coherent strategy or perhaps too many strategies, few of which were executed adequately." Rose and Andrews dismiss Mayor Sawyer as "a gentleman placed by fate into a maelstrom where his will would never have taken him," and describe Daley's victory as the coming of age of a new high-tech political machine that will be fueled by "pinstripe patronage"—contributions from "law firms, financial organizations and developers."

Without apologies, Rose and Andrews lament the impact of Daley's victory on Chicago and its politics. They see it as "unraveling" the progressive black-white coalition so crucial to Washington's two victories and at least temporarily ending "political unity within the black community."

Like Anderson on Sawyer, Rose and Andrews on Evans take no prisoners in attacking or defending the major players and issues that shaped Chicago's political scene. From racial politics to campaign-insider stories, the authors tell it as they saw it.

Part four deals with the role of the media and polling in the 1989 mayoral elections. David Fremon, a well-known author/reporter of

Chicago politics, chastises the local Chicago newspapers for being almost totally in Daley's corner from the outset of the campaign. He also suggests that, except for black radio in Chicago, almost all television and radio stations in the city also favored Daley.

Fremon's critique of the political coverage also reveals how Daley and his advisors fostered and pushed their media advantage. Quoting noted Chicago television talk show host John Callaway that Daley "mastered the medium better than his rivals," Fremon maintains that "Chicago's press made no pretense as to its choice in the mayoral election"—it was Daley.

Richard Day and his associates examine thoroughly the impact of various polls on the primary and general elections. They present convincing early poll data depicting Daley's high and near-unbeatable "esteem" ratings among white and Hispanic Chicago voters. They also chart the rising political fortunes of Mayor Sawyer in the black community in his fight against not only Daley but also fellow black Tim Evans.

Daley's primary victory over Sawyer set the pattern for his triumph over Evans and Vrdolyak in the general election. Lower-than-expected black voter turnout had doomed Sawyer, and though black support began to solidify behind Evans, the black/white turnout differential factor remained the same.

According to Day, in both contests "voters in the predominantly black areas were . . . less likely to go to the polls than voters in the primarily white areas." As for the long-shot Vrdolyak candidacy, Day suggests that "surveys showed that [Vrdolyak] was never a factor." Which was proven on election day.

The book concludes with a chapter that provides a historical overview of Chicago politics from Richard J. Daley to Richard M. Daley. Author Melvin Holli relates how Chicago's changing demographics have affected its politics. His short and snappy summation of the trends and movements that gave the city its first woman mayor (Jane Byrne, in 1979) and its first black mayor (Harold Washington, in 1983) reveals the awakening of political reform and black political consciousness in the city.

Holli chronicles the red-hot racial and social issues that turned Chicago into "Beirut on the lake" in the 1980s, and how young Daley took advantage of his opportunity to lead an exhausted city during a desired cooling-off period. "It seemed clear," writes Holli about Daley's April 1989 general election victory, "that the old Byrne-Washington-Vrdolyak piss and vinegar had been drained at least temporarily out of Chicago politics."

In sum, this book is more than a story of raw urban politics, intra- and interracial tensions, and a parade of fascinating campaign characters. No—this book deals with a strange mayoral restoration of a name many thought had been sentenced to the historical archives and old-timer's memories. A *new* mayor Daley has returned to the fifth floor of Chicago's city hall and is now sitting in the same chair occupied by his dad for twenty-one years. Though the city has changed greatly between the eras of the two Daleys, many observers await eagerly to see if there will be many similarities. How Rich Daley balances the politics of his father's memory with the realities facing Chicago in the 1990s will determine how long his remarkable restoration will last.

PART ONE

The Mayoral Campaigns

It should be noted that in taking hold of a state, he who seizes it should examine all the offenses necessary for him to commit, and do them all at a stroke, so as not to have to renew them every day. . . . For injuries must be done all together, so that, being tasted less, they offend less; and benefits should be done little by little so that they may be tasted better.

Niccolo Machiavelli, *The Prince* (1513)

It has been my philosophy all my life that good government is good politics.

Richard J. Daley, Inaugural Address (1955)

Organizing the Sawyer campaign was like plastering a wall during an earthquake.

Larry Horist, Eugene Sawyer's campaign spokesman (1989)

"I wisht th' campaign was over," said Mr. Dooley. "I wisht it'd begin," said Mr. Hennessy. "I niver knew anything so dead. They ain't been so much as a black eye give or took in th' ward an' its less thin two months to th' big day."

Martin J. Dooley, *Mr. Dooley's Philosophy* (1902)

Chicago, it seems, has a way of leaving its imprint upon those who live in it. . . .

Richard Wright, Introduction to St. Clair Drake and Horace Cayton's *Black Metropolis* (1945)

No white ethnic politician can hope to take Richard J. Daley's place with comparable political and governmental power.

Milton Rakove, *Don't Make No Waves—Don't Back No Losers* (1975)

CHAPTER 1

The 1989 Mayoral
Primary Election

Paul M. Green

On October 15, 1987, Harold Washington delivered his final budget message as mayor of Chicago. City council members heard an upbeat and positive mayor tell them that although Chicago faced its most serious economic and social challenges in recent history, through "new efficiency and new productivity" and by working together the city would overcome any hurdle.[1]

In less than six weeks Harold Washington would die of a massive heart attack and the city that was enjoying a post–council wars cease-fire would be thrown once again into political chaos.

Following a brief period of intense general mourning and intense political maneuvering, 6th Ward Alderman Eugene Sawyer was chosen as Chicago's acting mayor. His selection in the early morning of December 2, 1987, by the Chicago city council planted the seed of disunity within the fragile Washington coalition (in his four mayoral victories, the 1983 and 1987 primary and general elections, Harold Washington never received more than 54 percent of the vote) that would eventually sprout into open warfare in the deceased mayor's bedrock constituency, African-American Chicago. Moreover, the cumulative effect of these intraracial battles within the city's African-American community would be to propel a nonblack, State's Attorney Richard M. Daley, directly into Washington's mayoral chair.

In one of the most ironic circles of events to occur in Chicago political history, young Daley's 1989 mayoral victory would be similar to Washington's historic 1983 mayoral triumph. Both men competed on a tilted political playing field because their opposition was divided hopelessly by personal animosity and hunger for power. According to one long-time North Side alderman, "Divide and conquer worked for Harold in '83 and it worked for Rich in '89."[2]

If December 2, 1987, was the Pearl Harbor of the 1989 Chicago mayoral contest, most of 1988 was hit-and-run guerrilla warfare between the eventual combatants and their supporters. To national media types observing the unfolding mayoral battles, especially those reporters from eastern time zones, Chicago politics seemed to be a cross between a western shoot out and "Animal House." However, a close examination of the 1989 "run for the hall" reveals that these events reflected ongoing, even historic, political and economic themes (some of which had been modified by Washington's two victories and recent socioeconomic changes in the city) that affected and constrained the campaigns of all the candidates.

These basic themes are:

1. In Chicago more than most other cities politics reflects demographics. Ethnicity, religion, and race have long been determining issues in city politics.

2. Chicago has a weak mayor/strong council form of government. This fact has forced past mayors who sought to wield citywide power to move heavily and often into the political trenches.

3. Once known as the "city of the big shoulders," Chicago now finds its shoulders drooping. Chicago's suburbs are challenging the big city for the high-paying and high-skilled service economy jobs.

4. As is true in many other cities, Chicago's middle class is being squeezed. Economic segregation threatens to turn Chicago into a metropolis of strictly separated "haves" and "have nots."

5. Chicago is a city of neighborhoods. Community or ward loyalty often has superseded loyalty to the city as a whole. Thus, for decades Chicago has been, not one huge city, but rather a collection of little villages tied together politically but not culturally.

6. Chicagoans believe in the concept of "reverse federalism." Local is more important than national or state. "Mayor" is a more sought-after title than "president" or "governor."

7. Although race and the rise of black political awareness has dominated recent Chicago politics, the so-called black political movement is not a monolith. Black leadership is split between the players (Democratic party–oriented blacks) and the nonplayers (black leaders who rose from community and not party organizations).

8. Most Chicagoans know politics will not solve or even alleviate their problems or concerns, but that does not dampen their ardor for the mayoral game. Like rooting for the Cubs, Chicago politics is a spectator sport that can lift your spirits or break your heart, even though your lifestyle will change very little no matter who wins. It's the chase that counts.

9. A mayoral election in Chicago is a magic time in the city. The only rule is, "there are no rules." All chips are dropped on the table.

And although big money and media politics have altered campaign strategy, having a well-coordinated field operation to get out your vote still counts mightily in Chicago.

10. More than most cities, Chicago has had a tradition of "rule or ruin" politics. Intraparty politics has always been far more brutal then interparty rivalries. In recent years, the "rule or ruin" philosophy has surfaced in intraracial rivalries for power.

In 1988 and 1989 all ten themes intertwined to give Rich Daley a relatively easy path to victory. From the moment he announced his candidacy, the campaign was Daley's to lose. And to his credit, the son of Chicago's legendary six-term mayor, Richard J. Daley, made almost no mistakes on his march to city hall. Still, without the civil war within the black community, Daley and his brilliant campaign strategists would never have had the opportunity to contest, let alone win, the office of mayor of Chicago.

SAWYER TAKES OVER: THE BATTLE RAGES ON

Mayoral succession in Chicago has never been pretty. In the twentieth century only two Chicago mayors, Carter Harrison II and Fred Busse, have ever given up their offices voluntarily by refusing to run for reelection. Both times previously in this century when a mayor died in office (Anton Cermak in 1933 and Richard J. Daley in 1976) power politics and not governmental process dominated the ensuing council replacement selection process. In 1933, newly selected mayor Ed Kelly was able to satisfy Cermak's power base by pledging fidelity to the Democratic organization; in 1976, however, Michael Bilandic never was able to replace Daley in the minds and hearts of Democratic party workers trying to maintain their crumbling political machine.

Sawyer's governmental options were limited as he took power. For political and personal reasons he had to win over a good chunk of black Chicago, which saw his selection as more of an insult to the now-deified Washington than a fair-fight council victory over fellow black Alderman Tim Evans (4). The new mayor was a life-long loyal Democrat, a player, but this experience taught him that he would have great difficulties maintaining his council selection majority (which was heavily white and anti-Washington) if he wanted to improve his standing in the black community. Thus the Sawyer dilemma: how to govern through a white-based governmental coalition in the council while winning over politically skeptical black voters in the community. The one thing Sawyer needed more then anything else was time, something his enemies would not allow him.

On February 16, 1988, Aldermen Robert Shaw (9) and William Henry (24), two of Sawyer's reliable black allies in the council, suggested publicly that there was no need for a special Chicago mayoral election in 1989. They argued that Sawyer's status as acting mayor gave him the power to serve out the rest of Washington's term because there were no regular city elections scheduled until 1991. Sawyer's backers disregarded the arguments that Washington's term was less than one-half over and that state law required a special election in such circumstances.

Alderman Evans's supporters rejected Sawyer's political strategy of waiting until 1991. They wanted to challenge the acting mayor while the memories of Washington and the December 2nd council selection process were still fresh in the minds of the black community and before Sawyer had time to solidify his position in city hall. In early April, Evans allies filed a lawsuit in Cook County Circuit Court to force the Chicago Board of Elections Commissioners to schedule a special election in 1989. Following a series of lengthy legal maneuvers involving Chicago Republicans, who for cost-saving reasons favored the 1991 election date, the Chicago Board of Elections, the city clerk, the State Board of Elections, and finally the Illinois Supreme Court, the 1989 special mayoral election was duly ordered.

It is important to note that the overwhelming beneficiary of the 1989 mayoral election movement was State's Attorney Daley. It would have been impossible for him to file this critical lawsuit, because it would have been perceived by crucial interests in Chicago only in racial terms. Thus, Evans and his core of supporters resembled earlier Daley partisans, whose attacks in late 1982–83 on then Mayor Jane Byrne opened up the door for Harold Washington.

As for Mayor Sawyer, he was a walking series of political and governmental contradictions. Though a Democratic ward committeeman for over two decades (his 6th Ward was the top vote-producing ward in the city) Sawyer appeared to be a reluctant warrior in dealing with his diehard political opposition. It took him seven months to oust his aldermanic enemies from key council committee chairmanships. Finally, calling his foes "obstructionists," Sawyer dumped them in mid-July, claiming that finance committee chairman Alderman Evans and budget committee chairman Larry Bloom (5) were blocking his affordable housing plans and tax increases needed "to keep this city operating."[3] Most Chicagoans understood Sawyer's action. They wondered, however, why it took him so much time to do it.

Sawyer's friends and allies responded to criticisms of the mayor by saying simply, "Sawyer is a nice man." Well educated, soft-spoken, and laid back, Sawyer seemed more like a genial and gentlemanly mayor of a southern midsize town than a hard-charging and tough-minded leader of a major northern city.

His seeming indecisiveness was compounded by several issues of personal integrity that strained his nice-guy image. First, there was the mysterious $30,000 fee he received from a lawyer in 1978. Sawyer claimed that the money reflected his work on a land deal (he reported it on his income tax return) but critics scored points by charging that this substantial sum reflected possible Sawyer involvement in various zoning deals. Second, his close relationship with consultant Erwin France caused him much public damage. France, a shrewd Chicago political veteran who carried heavy political negatives in many parts of the black community, appeared to many to be Sawyer's Cardinal Richelieu. According to the Chicago Sun-Times, "Sawyer paid France over $200,000 to advise him on transitional and other city matters."[4]

By far the most devastating event to Sawyer's image was his handling, or mishandling, of the Steven Cokely affair. Cokely, an aggressive and articulate black nationalist, worked for Sawyer as a liaison to the African-American community. Sawyer used the sharp-tongued Cokely as an effective weapon against pro-Evans spokespersons who were attacking the mayor in both white and black media. However, Cokely became a citywide mayoral liability once his virulent and often childish anti-Semitism (e.g., charging that Jewish doctors were injecting black children with the AIDS virus) became known throughout Chicago. Sawyer needed to drop Cokely quickly from the city payroll. Unfortunately, the mayor procrastinated. Torn between his desire to stand tall in the black community and to show sensitivity to Chicago's Jewish community and other fair-minded citizens, Sawyer appeared timid and weak. His final termination of Cokely came too late. Sawyer made few points with blacks by dumping Cokely, and he lost almost all potential support among the city's Jewish and independent voters by not firing Cokely immediately.

Battered in the black press, reeling from polls that showed Evans to be the overwhelming favorite of black voters, and finding white allies cooling to his administration, Sawyer nonetheless pressed on. Incumbent mayors in Chicago have one great advantage over most potential rivals—they can raise money. By September 1988, Sawyer had over $2 million in the bank; his main black rival, Evans, had less then $100,000.

Despite claims that he had failed to develop a reliable constituency or taken a firm grip on city hall, a defiant Sawyer struck back at his opposition. He pointed with pride at the reorganization of the Chicago Housing Authority under the leadership of his dynamic appointee Vincent Lane; he spoke boldly about his plans for trash recycling and Navy Pier redevelopment; although it had taken considerable tax increases, the mayor praised his city budget and fiscal policies (a view that later would prove bogus); and he made several key appointments of Asians, Hispanics, and whites to show that he was, "the only candidate of the entire city." The latter dagger was aimed directly at the heart of his main nemesis and rival, Alderman Tim Evans.

THE EVANS CAMPAIGN: THE POLITICS OF MEMORY

On October 30, 1988, (almost a month before the Illinois Supreme Court mandated a 1989 special mayoral election) 4th Ward Alderman Tim Evans announced his candidacy for the Democratic mayoral nomination. Evans had spent a very uncomfortable year jousting with Sawyer over who was the rightful heir to the Harold Washington legacy. A shrewd political infighter, Evans, like Sawyer, was a product of the Democratic organization. He had served his apprenticeship in the 4th Ward under the guidance of legendary black alderman Claude Holman. Ironically, many of Evans's most fanatical mayoral supporters were liberal Hyde Parkers (residents of the University of Chicago area that made up the southern part of his 4th Ward) who had opposed him in his aldermanic campaigns as late as 1987. Evans, who had been Washington's floor leader, had to play his "Harold card" quickly, even if it meant a slight reinterpretation of his political past. Without igniting black voters by using the politics of memory, Evans had little to no chance defeating Sawyer's politics of clout.

Evans's mayoral announcement took place in the same hotel (the Hyde Park Hilton) where Washington had made his city hall intentions known in 1982. Casting himself as a progressive and reformer, Evans called for "a crusade to advance the dream of fairness in this city once again."[5] Evans was not content to limit his rhetoric to advocating the restoration of a Harold Washington–type leadership in city hall. For reasons that probably were more personal than political, the 4th Ward alderman turned his mayoral announcement press conference into a bitter personal attack on "acting" Mayor Sawyer.[6] "The Acting Pharaoh," Evans argued, "is building a golden calf to lure us back into bondage even as the Pharaoh makers prepare to install the son [Rich Daley] of the old Pharaoh [Richard J. Daley] in his chair."[7] The biblical reference carried heavy significance in black neighborhoods, which for years had their churches and religion serve as their main source of community strength and pride. Evans had put his cards squarely on the table—he was challenging the mayor in the democratic mayoral primary and there was no chance of any reconciliation between him and Sawyer.

The Evans campaign hit the ground crawling. A few influential black journalists and community leaders claimed his campaign would "revive the Washington spirit," but Evans, hard-pressed for campaign cash, had to resort to a reactive hit-and-run campaign posture against Sawyer. He and his allies overplayed politically the first anniversary of Mayor Washington's death by trying to turn the solemn occasion into a series of Evans political rallies. However, the most colossal blunder of Evans's fledgling campaign was committed, not by the candidate, but by his most outspoken ally, 3rd Ward Alderman Dorothy Tillman. In a highly publicized campaign rally attended by Evans, Tillman called Sawyer "a shuffling Uncle Tom."

Tillman's accusation unleashed a hailstorm of protest across the city, but especially in the black community. The Reverend B. Herbert Martin, executive director of the city's Commission on Human Relations and the late mayor's pastor, led the condemnation of Tillman's remark, arguing that such language discredited Washington's memory. Sawyer soft-pedaled his anger by maintaining only that Evans ought to ask Tillman to retract the statement. Evans refused. Although many blacks still felt betrayed by Sawyer's selection as mayor, there was a growing feeling of sympathy and admiration for him in black Chicago.

Enter the Reverend Jesse Jackson. The Sawyer-Evans verbal warfare had turned mean and was getting meaner. Jackson, a much better king than king maker in Chicago's black community, told both camps to "stop the name calling" and offer the people "hope, not attack." Throughout the month of December, Jackson worked the media, trying to convince Sawyer or Evans to drop out of the February primary. In a spectacular display of political wizardry and personal diplomacy, Jackson brought Sawyer and Evans along with him on his annual Christmas Day visit to Cook County Jail. Jackson's message was clear— the chances of either man winning the February primary were slim if they both stayed in the race.

In the eyeball-to-eyeball showdown between the two black candidates, it was Evans who finally blinked. On December 29, 1988, Evans announced his withdrawal from the February Democratic primary. Clearly not happy with his political predicament, Evans put the best face possible on his decision. The 4th Ward alderman said he would give Sawyer a "clean shot" at the nomination. However, no matter what the primary outcome, he (Evans) would run as the candidate of the soon-to-be-formed Harold Washington party in the April general election.

Evans also made a fateful declaration that he would *not* endorse anyone in the Democratic primary. Rather, he told his cheering supporters, many of whom wore buttons that read "Harold Washington Party/Get Down for the Showdown April 4," "I am endorsing Tim Evans in the general election."[8] The bridge of no return had been crossed, and despite massive efforts in the next three months to achieve black unity, the split remained wide open.

RICHARD M. DALEY: THE SON ALSO RISES

From November 1988 through April 1989, Rich Daley's path to city hall resembled more the "divine cosmos" of Greek mythology then the traditional campaign uncertainties of Chicago politics. Almost every political development or public policy issue broke Daley's way. However, key to his remarkable three landslide victories in a period of five months[9] was his mastering of one of the oldest political axioms in American politics. "He (Daley) saw his opportunities . . . and he took 'em."

Running for a third term as Cook County state's attorney, Daley kept a low profile during most of the 1988 political maneuverings. He and his closest advisors saw clearly the widening split in Chicago's post-Washington black community, but before he could make any overt moves, three things had to happen. First, Daley had to trounce Terry Gainer, his GOP opponent in the November state's attorney contest; second, the courts had to call definitively for a 1989 special mayoral election based on the lawsuit brought forth by Alderman Evans supporters; and third, Daley had to make sure he would be the only major white ethnic mayoral candidate in the 1989 race. The last point was as critical as the first two for Daley, because many Northwest and Southwest Side ethnics held him accountable for splitting the white vote in the 1983 Democratic primary, thereby causing the incumbent mayor, Jane Byrne, to lose to the black candidate, Harold Washington.

All three critical events took place exactly the way Daleyites had hoped. On November 8th, Daley demolished Gainer by a 2-to-1 margin while winning reelection by a staggering 650,000-vote plurality. In late November, the Illinois Supreme Court ended all speculation and judicial appeals by ordering a special mayoral election in 1989. Publicly playing it cautious, Daley announced that he would take two weeks to examine his potential mayoral candidacy. However, privately he and several high-powered political and financial leaders were pressuring other ethnic mayoral candidates to drop out. They all would.

Even before he announced his decision to run for mayor, it was leaked (in Chicago politics there are "secret-secrets" and "leakable secrets") that Daley's noncampaign had hired David Wilhelm as campaign manager. Appointing Wilhelm, an experienced thirty-one-year-old political operative with close ties to Illinois U.S. Senator Paul Simon and liberal reform causes, was a major Daley strategy shift from his losing 1983 mayoral run. In that race, Daley circled his political wagons around his 11th Ward home base, the blue-collar Bridgeport neighborhood, and did little to reach out to Chicago's other major constituencies. 1989 would be different.

Even more important than Wilhelm was Daley's increasing reliance on Chicago media consultant David Axelrod. A former Chicago *Tribune* political reporter, Axelrod was in simple terms the hottest political consultant in the city. In 1984 he had masterminded Simon's upset victory over U.S. Senator Charles Percy, and in 1987 he worked as media advisor for Mayor Harold Washington. A tough protagonist in open debate and a clever strategist behind closed doors, Axelrod had close ties to many influential people in the critical lakefront wards of Chicago. Hired by Daley to handle the media for his state's attorney reelection campaign, Axelrod stayed on the job after the elections as a Daley confidant and spokesman.

As more and more pieces fell into place, the '89 Daley was clearly different from the '83 Daley. More lakefronters and independents rallied behind him. Paul Stepan, a wealthy political activist, agreed to serve as finance chairman; John Schmidt, a noted progressive Loop attorney, was earmarked for a major role in the upcoming campaign; and Assistant State's Attorney Julie Hamos, prominent in women's causes, was slated for deputy campaign manager. To be sure, Daley's closest advisors remained his brother Bill, a nationally known Democratic strategist who had worked in the 1984 and 1988 presidential campaigns, and his Bridgeport neighbor State Senator Timothy Degnan, a shrewd Springfield-wise politician, but the message was clear—candidate Daley no longer was tied to his Bridgeport roots.

On December 5th (the precise deadline day he had given two weeks earlier) Daley announced his candidacy for the Democratic mayoral nomination. Unlike the sluggish and disorganized campaigns of his mayoral rivals, Daley's campaign hit Chicagoans with the force of the battleship Missouri and the speed of a German blitzkrieg. He took the high road immediately, claiming he had made "no deals" with anyone and that he was not worrying about who else was running for mayor. "I don't need anyone in or out," a confident Daley said, ". . . I'm going to win."[10]

Daley left immediately on a traditional whirlwind political campaign tour of the city. Lost in the excitement of his well-organized first day of campaigning was a Daley staff announcement that the state's attorney had made a $200,000, ten-day television advertising buy to tell Chicagoans about his plans for a nonconfrontational mayoral campaign. If Daley's instant dropping of big bucks on media did not shake his rivals (especially other white candidates), his announcement of his new press secretary finished the job. Two days after announcing his mayoral campaign, Daley startled most Chicagoans, especially the political insiders, by naming Avis LaVelle (a well-respected, popular black city hall reporter for the city's most listened-to radio station, WGN) as his press spokesperson.

LaVelle's appointment would prove to be the single most brilliant political move in the entire campaign by Daley or, for that matter, anyone else. In selecting LaVelle, whose professional abilities and talent were recognized by all, Daley told Chicagoans, "My hiring her sends out a message that the bickering and arguing has ended."[11]

To be sure, this move was described as an appeal to the city's black voters to reconsider the '89 Daley campaign, but in reality the prime Daley targets were liberal-minded lakefronters and the city's Hispanics. The LaVelle selection was a reinforcing and visible political reminder to these swing voters that this Daley campaign would be far different from the 1983 version. Also, Daley's strategists wanted to isolate his two main black mayoral rivals within the black community. The LaVelle action was a major step in that direction, as it received overwhelming praise across the city—especially in the targeted non-ethnic and nonblack neighborhoods. By naming LaVelle, Daley also reminded his last remaining potential white ethnic rival, Alderman Ed Burke (14), that it was time for him to get out.

Ed Burke, like Daley a Southwest Side political leader, had little option but to fold his tents. Though he had made some deft and heart-felt political moves to change his confrontationist image (along with former alderman Edward Vrdolyak, Burke had led the anti-Washington forces during the council wars) by (1) apologizing to all Chicagoans for making "many mistakes" during his public career; (2) hiring Jesse Jackson's campaign manager, Jerry Austin, as his media consultant; and (3) supporting gay rights in the city, Burke knew the game was over. He simply could not out-ethnic Daley or match the state's attorney's arsenal of big-gun fund raisers. One week after Daley's announcement, Burke withdrew his candidacy and endorsed Daley. Though another white candidate remained in the Democratic primary field (5th Ward liberal Alderman Larry Bloom), Daley's ethnic path had been cleared and he now had a free hand to win over the city's Hispanics and independent lakefronters.

THE REPUBLICAN ALTERNATIVE

Observing the Chicago Republican party select a mayoral candidate, according to one old-time diehard GOP supporter, "is like watching a continuous 50-year train wreck . . . you know it is going to be a disaster . . . but morbid curiosity compels you to keep looking."[12]

In 1989 the Chicago Republicans outdid themselves in making their party look both irrelevant to the election process and embarrassingly foolish.

As city Democratic heavyweights lobbed political grenades at one another during the late part of 1988, Republican leaders sought out a single electable candidate. In 1987, Donald Haider, the eminent Northwestern University management professor, had run a respectable citywide mayoral campaign as the GOP nominee, but on election night he garnered only 4.3 percent of the vote (a figure that would be considered lofty in 1989).

In late 1988, under county chairman James Dvorak's direction, the GOP started wooing former Democratic mayor Jane Byrne and Democrat-turned-Republican former alderman Ed Vrdolyak. Resembling more a used car salesman or flea market dealer than a party chairman, Dvorak believed the only chance Republicans had in 1989 was to run a well-known turncoat Democrat.

For several weeks in public and private meetings Dvorak hinted at an immediate announcement of either a Byrne or Vrdolyak candidacy. Byrne, who had run a strong Democratic primary race against the late Mayor Washington in 1987, seemed to be the best hope. For all of her political attributes, Byrne's most attractive quality to city Republicans was her open hatred of Rich Daley and his allies. The Byrne-Daley feud had dominated Chicago politics during the early 1980s, and many believed that Byrne would do anything to prevent Daley from ever occupying city hall.

Despite several newspaper headlines and much speculation on radio and TV talk shows of a Byrne or Vrdolyak GOP candidacy, neither big gun entered the mayoral contest. As the filing deadline passed, the Republicans were left with eleven "political nobody candidates," and Chairman Dvorak was left to utter the understatement of the year: "I'm obviously disappointed."[13]

Perhaps most distressing to the city GOP was a *Sun-Times* editorial that called Chicago "still a one-party town," claiming that instead of a partridge in a pear tree, the GOP was left with eleven pipers piping. It also quoted Dvorak's comment on the process: "It beats the hell out of me."[14]

What happened? Neither Byrne nor Vrdolyak trusted Dvorak or other big-time statewide Republicans, such as Governor Jim Thompson. The latter did little to hide his friendship for Daley. Also, both Byrne and Vrdolyak were on losing streaks and figured one more loss might end any chance of a future political comeback. Finally, Daley's mayoral campaign organization looked like a political and financial juggernaut, and neither Byrne nor Vrdolyak wanted to give Daley the personal satisfaction of beating them.

SAWYER VS. DALEY: THE BATTLE IS JOINED

As the new year dawned, the battle lines inside the Chicago Democratic primary seemed firm. Daley, the challenger, was the clear favorite. His financial war chest would soon surpass Mayor Sawyer's own substantial campaign total. Mark Hornung, political writer for *Crain's Chicago Business*, observing the Daley fund-raising apparatus, wrote, "his [Daley's] team reads like a 'Who's Who' of political players in local and national Democratic politics."[15] Moreover, whereas the split in the black community remained wide open, Daley's own political organization was crisp and professional and the city's media were effusive in their praise for the state's attorney. The only blemish on his silky smooth operation was Daley's ongoing legal problem stemming from the unsuccessful 1986 nonpartisan mayoral petition campaign.

In the summer of 1986, allies of Daley had attempted to collect signatures for a November 1986 referendum to make the 1987 Chicago mayoral election nonpartisan. Conventional wisdom at that time suggested that the only way to prevent the 1987 reelection of Mayor Washington was to eliminate the partisan primary process that had propelled him to victory in 1983. In a nonpartisan system, unless a candidate received 50 percent of the vote plus 1 on election day, the top two finishers would face each other in a runoff. Because Daley foe Jane Byrne already had announced her unretractable candidacy for the Democratic mayoral nomination, Daleyites saw the nonpartisan process as the only way to get their man one-on-one with Washington.

The 1986 petition drive resembled a Keystone Kops movie. Allegations quickly surfaced concerning the validity of petition signatures. The courts ruled that the entire petition referendum drive was irrelevant because of some fancy Washington administration nonreform footwork (the mayor's city council majority placed three referendums [the legal maximum] of their own on the November ballot, thereby making the nonpartisan effort moot), but the charges of illegality remained an open issue. Daley's state's attorney office was responsible for investigating the accusations of petition illegality and forgery. In late December 1988, allies of Sawyer and Evans charged Daley with foot dragging in the investigation because some of the allegations of wrongdoing concerned Daley employees. Daley foes clamored for the appointment of a special prosecutor to take charge of the investigation. After some delay Daley concurred, former U.S. Attorney Dan Webb was appointed, and the issue soon disappeared into the scrap heap of political insignificance. As one leading Democrat suggested privately, "Daley's campaign was like rolling thunder powering down the highway—the petition controversy was a tiny pothole."[16]

THE SAWYER CAMPAIGN: UNITY FUTILITY

Gene Sawyer realized that without unified black support he could not hope to defeat Rich Daley. The abuse he had received from pro-

Evans black politicans and community leaders had shaken his confidence, hurt his pride, and wounded his conscience. Thus, the battle cry of "unity in the community" was not only a Sawyer political slogan, it also was a personal plea from a man who believed his soul needed redemption.

Prominent black clergymen, such as his own pastors Addie and Claude Wyatt and Bishop Louis Ford from the Church of God in Christ, came out strong for Sawyer. Loyal black political leaders, such as Illinois State Comptroller Roland Burris, Cook County Commissioner John Stroger, and several Chicago aldermen, such as Anna Langford (16), wrapped their arms around the mayor. It was Langford, a tough and experienced reform-minded black independent who had lost a legislative race to the organization-backed Harold Washington in the 1970s, who put the much-debated events of Sawyer's selection into the best political light for the mayor. "It was Sawyer," she argued "who took the heat to save the seat," and she charged further that, "Evans never had the votes to win."[17] Langford's logic and rhetoric were the heavy artillery of Sawyer's campaign to convince black Chicagoans that he was the only person who could have and did prevent a white from becoming Mayor Washington's successor.

Sawyer also sought close associates of Mayor Washington to endorse his black solidarity campaign. When he officially announced his candidacy in December 1988, Sawyer was flanked by the late mayor's brothers Ramon Price and Roy Washington. In early January, Congressman Charles Hayes (1), Harold Washington's hand-picked successor in the 1st Congressional District and a supporter of Evans's third-party candidacy, urged his constituents to support Sawyer in the primary, arguing, "My main thrust is to stop Daley."[18] However, a good chunk of Washington allies, especially in the Near South Side wards (2, 3, 4, 5), remained anti-Sawyer and pro-Evans. Although their negative rhetoric against the mayor cooled towards primary day, Sawyer remained unacceptable to these black leaders.

The biggest boost for Sawyer in the black community came from the Operation PUSH crowd. Founded and organized by the Reverend Jesse Jackson, PUSH served as a socioeconomic and political lightning rod for the black community. Its Saturday service attracted citywide media attention, and most black and "progressive" white and Hispanic candidates welcomed an invitation to address a PUSH meeting during an election campaign.

First onto Sawyer's bandwagon was former PUSH executive director Thomas Todd. Recognized as a black nationalist, Todd told black Chicagoans that the split between Sawyer and Evans must be subordinated "to the principle of what is in the best interest of the black community." He urged his audience to stand behind Sawyer in the primary. However, it was PUSH's main man, Jesse Jackson, who gave Sawyer the image boost he needed so desperately among black voters. Late in the campaign, Jackson was everywhere, speaking to and cajoling black voters on behalf of Sawyer. "It's not the time to worry," said Jackson "about what may happen in the general election, it is a must that we get out the vote for Sawyer."[19] And on the subject of black apathy towards the Sawyer campaign, Jackson laid it on the line, saying, "A non-vote in the primary is a vote for Daley . . . anytime we do not vote Daley's campaign grows stronger."[20]

Sawyer paid a heavy price for concentrating so much effort and attention on unifying the black community behind his candidacy. Even if his efforts had proved successful, a united black vote for Sawyer by itself would not have defeated Daley. Sawyer needed allies elsewhere in the city, and to get them he had to have an effective citywide campaign organization. Because of lack of attention, political naivete, or a combination of both, Sawyer's campaign flopped in Chicago's ethnic, Hispanic, and lakefront neighborhoods.

Clearly Sawyer faced significant campaign hurdles. All of the white aldermen who supported his December 1, 1987, selection were now pro-Daley. (Incredibly, Sawyer's reelection campaign was now opposed by most of the city council, a majority of whom had selected him as acting mayor in the first place). Other white and Hispanic politicians were cool to Sawyer's candidacy, thus leaving the mayor with limited access to political advice from outside the African-American community. Despite his long political experience, Sawyer had never run for any office outside of his home 6th Ward— let alone citywide. Finally, Sawyer's city hall staff operation was heavily sprinkled with pro-Evans diehards who, although mouthing loyalty to the acting mayor, actually were working for his defeat. This organizational confusion and lack of political direction exploded in Sawyer's face with the publication of the "Rochon memo" in early January 1989.

Reynard J. Rochon, a New Orleans political consultant, was Sawyer's campaign manager. In an October 11, 1988, memo, Rochon told Sawyer that leading members of his administration were committing "internal sabotage" by working secretly against his reelection. Moreover, Rochon criticized senior Sawyer advisors such as Monroe Anderson, the mayor's press secretary, Erwin France, Sawyer's chief confidant, and Elizabeth Hollander, city planning commissioner, for not doing a better job of promoting mayoral accomplishments. The memo was significant, not because of its accuracy, but because (1) its contents were leaked by someone in Sawyer's inner circle, and (2) in the words of one Sawyer insider, "it was written at all . . . you don't put that kind of crap on paper."[21] Many pols loyal to Sawyer who had questioned the mayor's choice of an outsider such as Rochon for campaign manager in the first place began spreading rumors that Rochon was a double agent. Although none of these stories panned out, Rochon's effectiveness and impact for the rest of the primary campaign were negligible.

Despite all of his campaign's disorganization and internal chaos, Sawyer displayed almost stoic dignity as he continued to plow headlong into battle. But the political pinpricks that plagued him throughout his short administration continued to puncture his dignified campaign. Sawyer admitted that he had not filed his federal income tax returns on time in 1986 and 1987; he refused to release detailed information concerning his personal finances; and it was revealed that one of his key fund raisers had been convicted of embezzlement and bank fraud charges a decade earlier. Still, Sawyer aides believed that the mayor could win significant white ethnic support because he was an unthreatening candidate (unlike Washington and, to a lesser degree, Evans) and because they believed some non-Irish white ethnics did not want to see a Daley machine reestablished.

As the campaign entered the home stretch, Sawyer worked the city's heavily Polish Northwest Side. According to one Sawyer strategist, "The mayor was doing far better among East Europeans than West Europeans, and we thought we could snare 20 percent of the total white ethnic vote . . . ."[22] Sawyer and his advisors were proved wrong as Daley received over 90 percent of the ethnic vote, but Sawyer's ethnic campaigning had a soothing impact on a city long divided by racial politics.

Events moved rapidly for Sawyer in the closing days of the campaign. Jackson's unity message was getting through to the African-American community; Alderman Bloom, recognizing reality, withdrew from the race and endorsed Sawyer; and city Republicans saw Ed Vrdolyak emerge not only as a write-in mayoral primary candidate, but also as a potential primary vote taker from Daley. The mayor's TV commercials (with the exception of the two silly negative spots that questioned Daley's intelligence) were getting the point across that the mayor was indeed "Gentleman Gene" (an image that was reinforced by the mayor's splendid and classy performance in dedicating the new Richard J. Daley public library branch in Bridgeport less than a month before primary day); and the polls showed the gap between him and Daley closing. However, the mayor was never able to parlay this momentum into a serious threat to Daley, despite some uncharacteristic political slips on the latter's part.

Why? Evans remained unmoved—he adamantly refused to endorse Sawyer. Facing Daley's efficient money-raising machine, Sawyer's own fund-raising efforts lagged, forcing the mayor to reduce or cancel TV ads in the campaign's crucial last days. Political snafus and errors in mayoral judgment continued to plague Sawyer until the very end. For example, in the campaign's closing days, Sawyer was placed on the defensive trying to explain away airport concessions given to fund-raising friends whose companies were judged to be unqualified by his own internal staff review. Finally, racial politics worked against him more than it did Daley as cries for black unity revealed that racist rhetoric was a two-way street.

At an Operation PUSH campaign rally held ten days before the primary, Congressman Gus Savage (2) jolted the Sawyer campaign by using unabashed racial slurs in attacking Daley. Savage, an avowed Evans supporter who allegedly had convinced Sawyer and Jackson that his comments would be totally supportive of the mayor, told the PUSH audience that he would vote for Sawyer over Daley, though both came from the Democratic machine because, "only one . . . [was] born and bred a racist." After calling the white aldermen who selected Sawyer as acting mayor racists, Savage unleashed his biggest broadside: "They (the white aldermen) are all on the other side with Dumb Dumb Daley," the congressman charged, "and when they are on that side there is no question I am on this side."[23]

Savage's remarks affected the campaign in two ways. First, they demonstrated that Evans loyalists' support for Sawyer was, to say the least, very weak. Many even suggested that Savage intentionally sabotaged Sawyer at PUSH because Evans's people knew that a Sawyer primary victory would end any mayoral hopes for their candidate. Second, Savage's remarks, which were played over and over on Chicago television and radio news programs, reinforced prevailing attitudes among media and opinion influentials that only a Daley victory could bring racial peace to the city. (Sawyer's only major newspaper endorsement was from the Chicago *Defender*, the city's leading black paper.) In perhaps the strangest twist to a very racially tangled election campaign, a white ethnic candidate, Daley, was viewed as the best governmental peacemaker because the intraracial civil war raging in the city's once-united black community might flame totally out of control if Sawyer won.

THE DALEY CAMPAIGN: RUNNING LIKE AN INCUMBENT

Rich Daley's stretch run for mayor resembled a motor club travel plan. It was well marked, contained only minor detours, produced few surprises, and got him to his destination by the easiest and safest route. Seldom has a Chicago primary campaign run as smoothly as the '89 Daley effort.

Keying Daley's journey was a remarkable fund-raising apparatus. According to one Chicago investment banker, "Daley's money raisers were smart, cool, and persistent. They were professionals with Washington, D.C., experience . . . they pursued both Democratic and Republican contributors in the business community."[24]

Daley's fund-raising figures were indeed staggering. By early February, he passed $2 million, and two weeks later his campaign hit the $4 million mark. Moreover, Daley was not afraid to go after the "big hitters," the heavy givers. Ten days before the primary election, the Chicago Sun-Times printed a list of Daley's leading contributors, known as the "Daley Dozen." Combined, these twelve individuals, mainly developers and Loop business leaders, had already contributed over $650,000 to Daley. Many of the dozen were Jewish, reflecting a growing distrust between this community and city blacks since Washington's death; others were Republicans who, for business and personal reasons (they liked Daley), wanted to see this Democrat in city hall; still others saw Daley as responsive to their concerns. Whatever the reason, they and many other contributors gave Daley an enormous financial advantage over his incumbent rival, Gene Sawyer.

Daley's grand strategy was to isolate Sawyer and Evans within the black community. Though he would campaign in African-American neighborhoods and genuinely seek black support, realistically he recognized two important political facts: (1) no matter how hard he campaigned in black wards, he would be lucky to receive 10 percent of their vote; and (2) by capturing a big majority of the city's other voting blocs, he could piece together comfortable primary and general election victories without significant African-American support.

His base vote would come from his fellow white ethnics. Though a diminishing voter group in the city, these mainly Northwest and Southwest Side residents could make up as much as 40 percent of the voter turnout. Daley appealed to these voters' social values. He stressed his belief in family, neighborhood, and religion and appealed to their desire for sound fiscal management of city finances. Clearly the race factor worked in Daley's behalf among these voters, but to the state's attorney's credit, he attempted to avoid any racial overtures in his campaign.

The next piece in the Daley electoral puzzle was the city's Hispanic voters. Although they made up about only 7 percent of Chicago's registered voters, they had become one of the swing constituencies in the racially charged politics of the 1980s. Previously Daley had done fairly well with Hispanics, but in 1989 he would run like a whirlwind. In early January, Daley pulled a coup by getting 26th Ward Alderman Luis Gutierrez to endorse his candidacy. Gutierrez, an outspoken Washington loyalist and articulate advocate of liberal politics, shocked his friends in the Evans camp by stating, "I know there are risks but . . . I think that it is important for somebody to be there in the Daley campaign who understands the progressive agenda."[25]

A clever and resourceful politician, Gutierrez's endorsement of Daley was hardly a risk; rather, it was a calculated and timely move by the alderman to join a seemingly unstoppable mayoral campaign. It also reflected a growing belief among Chicago's two main Hispanic groups (Mexicans and Puerto Ricans) that their real social and economic needs (better schools, greater job opportunities, and the like) would be better served by allying themselves with Daley and his establishment associates. Already many upwardly mobile Hispanics were no longer calling themselves minorities; rather, they referred to themselves as ethnics. And by supporting Daley, Chicago's Hispanics demonstrated this new citywide status and political outlook. It was not coincidence that Daley would hold his last campaign rally in Gutierrez's 26th Ward. It not only proved the alderman's new political clout, but it also consolidated a small but vital voting bloc in the new, winning Daley coalition.

The last major piece of the Daley victory puzzle was the lakefront, consisting mainly of six wards known as the East 40s (wards 42, 43, 44, 46, 48, and 49). Residents in this area saw in Daley socioeconomic stability and managerial competence.

A generation earlier, political party reformers filled many of these fashionable neighborhoods. Although such words as "hack" and "machine" still generated pejorative responses among lakefront voters, gentrification and its economic impact had replaced party reform as the vibrant issue in the area. Large chunks of these wards had been invaded by an expanding base of socially liberal but economically conservative white voters. Many of these individuals were investing thousands and thousands of dollars in converted townhouses and lofts, rehabbed two-flats, new condominiums, or even rental units. They wanted governmental stability and economic security—for them the word "movement" meant property values shooting upward. Incredibly, Rich Daley, the bungalow boy from Bridgeport, had become the urban champion of the city's yuppie condo owners along the lakefront.

With all the primary polls showing him enjoying a big lead, Daley packaged his campaign with care. He took few chances in his day-to-day campaign trail activities, refused to take unnecessary risks, limited his appearances, and relied on his competent staff to guide him around potential political land mines.

Unlike his primary opponents, Sawyer and Bloom, Daley avoided many of the seemingly endless neighborhood candidate forums. Given his financial war chest, Daley did not need to rely on free TV exposure. At all costs he wanted to avoid being baited into a misstatement or campaign blunder. Admittedly not a good public speaker or a clever debater, Daley recognized the dangers in frequent free-for-all verbal slugfests. Although his opponents derided Daley for a solo "rose garden" campaign strategy, the state's attorney stuck to his guns, picking his shots for joint campaign debates. Fortunately for Daley, his foes underestimated his verbal abilities while they overstated their own debate competence. Thus, in the publicized confrontations, Daley's performance expectations were so low and his opponents' so high that in almost every case Daley held his own or actually won the joint debate on points.

For example, in late January, Daley and his opponents squared off at a forum sponsored by the Chicago *Sun-Times*. Clearly comfortable with issues such as law enforcement and drugs, the state's attorney showed surprising knowledge in the areas of education, economic development, and affirmative action. Although few in the crowd would have called Daley the new Disraeli (none of Daley's foes would have been mistaken for Gladstone, either), Daley's performance was solid, if not spectacular. By selecting these confrontations judiciously, Daley squelched the concerns of his more lukewarm supporters, especially along the lakefront, that he was too timid or incapable of matching wits with his opponents. Moreover, it reduced Sawyer's and Bloom's charges that Daley was ducking them to campaign rhetoric.

In the 1983 Democratic mayoral primary, Daley received the endorsements of both major Chicago newspapers. In fact, it has been argued that in 1983 the *Sun-Times* and *Tribune* gave Daley's sagging campaign the needed adrenaline to keep him competitive with the frontrunner, incumbent Jane Byrne, until election day, thereby denying her critical support in her close race with the eventual primary winner, Harold Washington.[26]

In 1989 both newspapers (as well as most of the other print and electronic opinion makers throughout the city) again gave Rich Daley their editorial support. The *Sun-Times* claimed Daley had the "potential for bringing about dramatic changes essential for strengthening Chicago's viability . . . and for developing opportunities to improve the quality of urban life."[27] It also argued that Daley was the best mayoral hopeful to handle Chicago's bewildering and desperate educational system because he alone had the legislative experience in Springfield to work with a Republican governor (Jim Thompson) to hammer out a bipartisan solution to this most critical of the city's problems. As for the *Tribune*, they put it simply in their effusive endorsement of Daley by stating, ". . . Daley [was] the only one capable of solving the one consuming, debilitating problem of city government created by the death of Harold Washington—an absence of effective leadership."[28]

OTHER DEMOCRATIC PRIMARY CAMPAIGN FACTORS: BLOOM; WHITE OR WHAT; AND THE GOP

Lawrence Bloom was a third-term alderman from the liberal Hyde Park/University of Chicago community. His South Side 5th Ward was predominantly black (75 percent) and over the years Bloom had mastered the art of playing balance-of-power racial politics at the local level. An early and outspoken supporter of Washington's 1983 mayoral candidacy, Bloom used his widely recognized governmental expertise to push traditional "good government" issues and the black progressive agenda to satisfy his multiracial constituency. However, few elected officials have ever served "at the pleasure of the mayor" more than Larry Bloom. Harold Washington with a mere finger snap could have prevented Bloom's 1987 aldermanic reelection by endorsing a black challenger. Instead, Washington supported Bloom for sound personal as well as political reasons (Washington genuinely liked Bloom, no black potential 5th Ward challenger was a Washington favorite, and by supporting Bloom, the mayor could publicize the rainbow composition of his ruling city council coalition). Washington's death in late 1987 left Bloom vulnerable, if not defenseless, against a black challenge in 1991. Thus, with little to lose and with a belief that he could expand his multiracial 5th Ward–style politics to reach citywide, Bloom became a candidate for the 1989 Democratic mayoral nomination.

From the outset, Bloom's problems were money, name recognition, and winnability. Unless he could get his name and message on television, Bloom's long-shot candidacy was doomed. With Daley tying up most of the lakefront dollars, Bloom's fund-raising efforts were feeble and scattershot. Still, Bloom's campaign had its moments. In late November 1988, Bloom attacked African-American politicians who were attempting to monopolize the selection process of a single progressive mayoral candidate. Appearing with several mayoral hopefuls on a WLS-TV Sunday morning talk show, Bloom said, "Unfortunately they [local black pols] are using the word 'progressive' to mean a black candidate." However, the high-water mark of the Bloom campaign occurred the day after New Year's 1989, when a Chicago *Tribune* editorial heaped lavish praise on the candidate's campaign platform, "Blueprint for Putting Chicagoans to Work." Calling Bloom's positions intelligent and courageous, the *Tribune* told its readers, "If Chicago's mayoral candidates got voter reaction and campaign contributions based on the wisdom of their ideas . . . Bloom would be so far ahead of the pack that this race would be a bore."[29]

Yet behind Bloom's sincere campaign effort there was a partially concealed arrogance towards the other candidates, especially Daley.

Perhaps because he could not match the state's attorney's war chest or carefully planned campaign strategy, Bloom began to sound shrill and unpleasantly egotistical. He carried around a silly "Daley Duck" doll to symbolize his opponent's "ducking" debates; his out-of-town media advisor more than once was heard to say that Bloom would be the best candidate if this were a better city; and during the only formal three-way television debate among Sawyer, Daley, and Bloom, Bloom appeared "smart alecky" and pompous with his repetitive derision of Daley's intellectual ability. Less than two weeks before primary day, Bloom dropped from the race, endorsed Sawyer, and became a nonfactor in the electoral process. It was Bloom's only remaining political option; his campaign simply had no solid voter base. Chicagoans admired Bloom's intellect, but as a campaigner and fund raiser the 5th Ward alderman failed to expand his appeal citywide.

Entering the primary campaign's closing days, Daley had only two fears: that he would make some silly mistake and energize and unify the divided black community against his candidacy; and that unexpected developments in the Republican mayoral primary might cost him vital ethnic support.

The dreaded "tongue slip" surfaced the weekend before election day. According to the campaign watchdog group CONDUCT (Committee on Decent, Unbiased Campaign Tactics), Daley in a speech delivered the previous weekend at a Southwest Side campaign rally said, "You want a *white* mayor to sit down with everybody." In a measured statement, CONDUCT's chairman, John McDermott, a respected civic leader, announced the committee's censure of Daley for the racially inflammatory comment. "We are aware," McDermott said, "that he [Daley] has gone out of his way to distance himself from these kinds of appeals. But it seems to us the facts are the facts— whether deliberate or accidental. . . ."[30]

Daley and his campaign advisors were livid. The candidate angrily denied using the word "white," while his chief strategist and brother, Bill Daley, condemned the censure as "outrageous." Two other key Daley aides, Forrest Claypool and Marj Halperin, suggested that Daley had merely mangled a line from his standard stump speech. The pair argued their candidate's often-spoken words, "What you want is a mayor who can sit down with everybody," inadvertently came out, "You want a *what* mayor who can sit down with everybody."

In some cities, elocution and syntax might not be a very big deal. Candidates delivering countless speeches a day often garble their words or simply misspeak. But in 1989 Chicago mayoral politics, Daley's alleged gaffe was the opening that Sawyer and black pols needed to drive home the point that Daley's kinder and gentler campaign was nothing more than a mask to cover his true racial views.

Unfortunately for Sawyer, the misstatement could not be parlayed into a late anti-Daley surge. First, following some severe internal debate (a Daley fund raiser at the downtown Fairmont Hotel the night of the censure resembled a series of mini-caucuses as the candidate's aides huddled around the room talking about a rebuttal) Daley's outstanding campaign staff challenged effectively the accuracy and purpose of CONDUCT's decision. Second, the black community's split was so large that Daley's blunder could not be viewed as enough of an issue to ignite a Sawyer movement. Third, and most important, Daley's admitted lack of speaking ability worked in his favor. Many Chicagoans accepted Daley's misstatement defense. As was true of his father, young Daley's battles with the English language were legendary. This time Daley would lose the battle, but not the war.

As for the city Republicans, they were experiencing a typical "winter of discontent" mayoral campaign. Their endorsed candidate, Dr. Herbert Sohn, was quietly and politely making the rounds offering the usual GOP political complaints to sparse audiences. His able campaign manager, Chris Robling (a clever and experienced organizer), against all odds, was on the local radio and TV talk show circuit predicting that Sohn had a legitimate shot in a three-way race against the eventual Democratic primary winner and Evans. In reality, local Republicans were disheartened and in disarray as their party seemed destined for another unnoticed burial on election day.

Enter Ed Vrdolyak. The former Democratic party chairman and 10th Ward alderman who had run and lost as a Solidarity party candidate for mayor in 1987 and as the Republican candidate for clerk of the circuit court in 1988 threw his well-worn hat into the mayoral ring. Claiming a groundswell of neighborhood support for their candidate, Vrdolyak allies John "Buddy" Ruel, an iron workers union official, and A. A. Sammy Rayner, a former alderman and a well-known black funeral director, announced a Vrdolyak write-in campaign for the Republican nomination.

Speculation lingers as to why Vrdolyak entered the campaign. In early December he could have had the GOP mayoral endorsement for the asking but turned it down because he believed three key Republican leaders—Governor Jim Thompson, Cook County Sheriff Jim O'Grady, and Cook County party chairman Jim Dvorak—actually were pro-Daley. If his accusation was true in December, little had changed in the subsequent two months to give him much hope that these three key players would unite behind his candidacy in February. Some argued that Sohn was so weak and easily beatable that Vrdolyak believed that he could win the nomination as a write-in, and in the process take enough ethnic votes away from Daley to allow Sawyer to win the Democratic primary. In this scenario Vrdolyak would end up in the enviable position of being the "Oreo cookie creme" sandwiched between two black candidates, Sawyer and Evans, in the April general election. Others simply labeled Vrdolyak's move as the politics of vindictiveness. The former alderman saw his bitter enemy, Daley, on the verge of winning it all and thus was forced to do something dramatic to prevent another Bridgeport takeover of city hall. One Democratic ward leader, commenting on all the Machiavellian scenarios, chortled that, "Eddie's motives aren't complicated . . . he is like a compulsive gambler—he can't stay on the sidelines while there is hot action."[31]

Whatever his reasons, Vrdolyak received heavy, if somewhat dubious, media coverage during his short write-in campaign. In particular, the Chicago Sun-Times reacted negatively to the Vrdolyak effort (some insiders suggested the Sun-Times was still smarting from a publicized 1987 campaign story in which it *accused* but could not *prove* that Vrdolyak met privately with a well-known Chicago mobster). The Sun-Times called Vrdolyak "an over-the-hill Galahad" as it derided his suggestion that he was responding to a genuine people's draft. It labeled his constant candidacies as Chicago's version of a "one-man bum-of-the-month club" and dismissed his political possibilities by arguing that "a Vrdolyak write-in ballot should read 'so what.'"[32]

Still, given the weakness of the Chicago Republican party and its endorsed candidate (Sohn's main response to his new challenger was to go into the latter's ward and hand out literature to shoppers at a Dominick's food store) pros inside Daley's camp did not laugh off Vrdolyak's write-in campaign. Frightened of a Vrdolyak-inspired ethnic voter drop-off in April, many loyal Daley ward leaders suggested that it made sense for them to ask a small percentage of their solid Democratic voters to take a Republican ballot and vote for Sohn on primary day. This strategic "Chicago-style" move was hotly debated by key Daley confidants, but such an action was discounted because of two late-breaking political events: (1) Daley's "white or what" statement, and (2) a slight Sawyer surge as a result of greater coalescing of blacks around his candidacy.

PRIMARY DAY AND THE WINNER

Given the emotions and expectations of the two previous Democratic mayoral primaries, voter turnout on primary day 1989 was relatively disappointing.[33] The energy was not there. The streets, precinct polling places, and ward headquarters were quiet. The wildness and chaos that surrounded the city council's selection of Mayor Washington's successor on December 1, 1987, had given way to a routine and tame mayoral primary election day on February 28, 1989.

A political observer traveling south to north in the city would have been amazed at the election day inactivity. In Vrdolyak's Far Southeast Side 10th Ward, evidence of his late-starting write-in campaign was nearly invisible. Only Daley had yard and window signs and precinct workers passing out literature in front of polling places. In the predominantly black north end of the ward there was absolutely no Sawyer activity or political presence. This latter fact was duplicated in the neighboring middle-class black wards, where the acting mayor needed to register heavy turnout and support to upset the front-running Daley.

It was not until one drove to Daley's legendary home 11th Ward (his family has run the ward since the late 1940s) in the Near Southwest Side, working-class Bridgeport area that one saw traditional election day Chicago-style political spirit. Daley posters and signs were taped, stapled, or tied to almost every window, lamppost, or tree in the ward. For example, on Wallace Avenue between 43rd Street and 41st Street, every single bungalow on both sides of the avenue displayed at least one Daley campaign sign. (On one house Daley's name was advertised with flashing neon lights.) For many Bridgeporters, this primary was the first major step of a two-part political resurrection: (1) to put a Daley back in city hall; and (2) to bring clout (political power) back to their neighborhood.

Near South Side and West Side black wards were almost void of Sawyer workers or political activity. Neither candidate produced much visible firepower in the city's growing Hispanic communities, except for Daley in Alderman Gutierrez's Near West Side 26th Ward. Gutierrez went all out for his new ally with workers and posters. (At Leavitt Avenue and North Avenue, a Daley sign was attached to a tree limb that arched over the entryway to the polling place).

The North Side and Northwest Side of Chicago were Daley country. From the predominantly ethnic and conservative areas near O'Hare Airport, through the gentrifying communities around Wrigley Field, to the high-price lakefront wards, one would have thought that Daley was running unopposed.

As for the actual results, it was a Daley landslide in the Democratic mayoral primary. The state's attorney defeated Sawyer by over 100,000 votes. He won thirty-one of fifty city wards as he garnered 56 percent of the Democratic primary vote (see tables 1 and 2).

As expected, Daley's strongest areas were in ethnic Chicago—four Northwest Side wards (41, 45, 38, and 36) and two Southwest Side wards (13 and 23)—as they gave Daley victory margins of over 20,000 votes. Combined, these six wards alone gave Daley 155,320 votes, or nearly one-third of his citywide vote total.

Not far behind the "Big Daley Six" were his home 11th Ward and the Far Southwest Side 19th Ward (the bailiwick of one of Daley's

TABLE 1   Chicago 1989 Democratic Mayoral Primary Election Results by Votes, Margins and Percentages (presented in ward rank order for Daley by margin)

Ward Number	Daley's Vote	Sawyer's Vote	Daley's Margin	Daley's Percentage
13	29,801	932	28,869 D	97
23	27,815	739	27,076 D	97
41	25,990	1,780	24,210 D	94
45	24,541	1,432	23,109 D	95
38	23,980	1,146	22,834 D	95
36	23,193	1,724	21,469 D	93
19	23,993	4,895	19,098 D	83
11	18,496	2,311	16,185 D	89
39	16,659	1,680	14,979 D	91
50	16,342	2,229	14,113 D	88
12	15,843	1,956	13,887 D	89
14	15,444	2,269	13,175 D	87
43	17,050	3,909	13,141 D	81
35	14,348	1,310	13,038 D	92
47	14,841	2,404	12,437 D	86
33	13,425	1,995	11,430 D	87
40	12,715	1,678	11,037 D	88
30	13,099	2,971	10,128 D	82
44	13,960	4,253	9,707 D	77
32	10,650	2,308	8,345 D	82
42	12,136	6,354	5,782 D	66
26	6,976	2,609	4,367 D	73
46	9,200	4,924	4,276 D	65
48	9,094	4,915	4,179 D	65
49	8,428	4,894	3,534 D	63
18	14,456	11,330	3,126 D	56
31	6,103	3,317	2,786 D	65
10	9,364	6,586	2,778 D	59
25	4,561	2,481	2,080 D	65
22	3,532	1,631	1,901 D	68
1	8,321	7,854	467 D	51
27	1,653	9,078	(7,425) S	15
15	3,844	11,691	(7,847) S	25
7	2,389	10,690	(8,301) S	18
4	2,005	12,938	(10,933) S	13
29	1,050	12,621	(11,571) S	8
28	328	11,902	(11,574) S	3
37	783	12,696	(11,913) S	6
3	408	12,379	(11,971) S	3
2	650	12,903	(12,253) S	3
16	413	13,251	(12,838) S	3
20	457	13,709	(13,252) S	3
5	2,341	15,345	(13,304) S	13
9	1,075	14,848	(13,773) S	7
24	426	14,897	(14,471) S	3
17	466	16,881	(16,415) S	3
34	520	19,225	(18,705) S	3
8	724	21,508	(20,784) S	3
21	598	21,700	(21,102) S	3
6	696	24,460	(23,764) S	3
Absentee	1,404	260		
TOTAL	486,586	383,795	102,791 D	56%
Wards Won	31	19		

D = Daley; S = Sawyer.

closest allies, County Assessor Tom Hynes). The only surprise big-margin Daley ward was the fashionable 43rd along the lakefront, where Democratic committeeman Ann Stepan, another Daley confidant, proved that the state's attorney's appeal was no longer limited to the bungalow belt. The 43rd Ward's 13,141 Daley margin was his thirteenth-best in the city.

Sawyer's ward victories were limited to African-American Chicago. The acting mayor was unable to win a single lakefront or Hispanic ward, the swing voting districts of 1980s Chicago mayoral politics. The leading Sawyer-margin wards were the expected five Far South Side middle-class black wards (6, 21, 8, 34, and 17) that have become major vote producers in the city. In none of the nineteen wards that Sawyer carried was his margin under 7,000 votes, reflecting the contest's strong racial voting patterns.

Percentage-wise, the ward numbers reveal that this contest, like the four mayoral battles involving Harold Washington, was a duel of landslides. Eight wards gave Daley over 90 percent of their vote; in eleven others his totals were over 80 percent. Of all thirty-one winning Daley wards, only the racially diverse 1st Ward gave him a victory percentage of under 55 percent. Most important to Daley was that in not one of the six lakefront wards (42, 43, 44, 46, 48, and 49) and four mainly Hispanic Wards (22, 25, 26, and 31) was his winning percentage under 60 percent.

Sawyer's ward percentages reflected his strong, monolithic black support. In fourteen of his nineteen winning wards, the acting mayor received over 90 percent of the vote. Of his other five winning wards, only in the racially changing Southwest Side 15th Ward (significant white population remains on the west end of this ward) did Sawyer receive less than 80 percent of the vote (75 percent).

A precinct-by-precinct breakdown of the Daley-Sawyer primary battle further clarifies the contest's intense racial voting patterns. Overall, Daley carried 1,667 (57 percent) of the city's 2,911 precincts. In 557 of Daley's winning precincts he received over 95 percent of the vote; in 354 other precincts he won over 90 percent of the vote. Thus, in 911 city precincts (31 percent of the citywide total) Daley received at least nine out of every ten votes cast in the Democratic primary. In almost every case these precincts were located in ethnic Chicago neighborhoods on the Northwest and Southwest Sides.

Similar racial landslide voting results were reflected in Sawyer's numbers from the city's black precincts. In 984 precincts (34 percent of the citywide total), Sawyer received over 95 percent of the vote; in 106 other precincts, he garnered over 90 percent of the vote. In sum, Sawyer won 90 percent of the vote in 1,090 precincts (37 percent of the citywide total).

TABLE 2   Regional and Racial Breakdown of Chicago's 50 Wards

South and West Side Black Wards: 19
  2, 3, 4, 5, 6, 7, 8, 9, 15, 16, 17, 20, 21, 24, 27, 28, 29, 34, 37
Southwest Side Ethnic: 6
  11, 12, 13, 14, 19, 23
South Side Ethnic and Black: 2
  10, 18
Center City Racially Mixed and Hispanic Wards: 5
  1, 22, 25, 26, 31
North Side Lakefront Independent Wards: 6
  42, 43, 44, 46, 48, 49
North and Northwest Side Ethnic Wards: 12
  30, 32, 33, 35, 36, 38, 39, 40, 41, 45, 47, 50

Combined Daley and Sawyer precinct victories of over 90 percent occurred in over two-thirds of Chicago's 2,911 precincts.

Whereas all of Sawyer's landslide precinct victories occurred in the African-American community, Daley was able to produce *eight* precinct wins along the lakefront, where he captured over 90 percent of the vote.[34] The state's attorney also had *three* other precincts that gave him 90 percent of the vote. Precinct 37, Ward 9 (the predominantly white area of Pullman on the city's Far South Side); Precinct 18, Ward 25 (a mainly Italian community located in a growing Hispanic area on the Near Southwest Side); and Precinct 24, Ward 26 (a long standing Ukrainian area in Alderman Gutierrez's heavily Hispanic West Side ward) all gave Daley victory percentages equal to some of his best Northwest and Southwest Side precincts.

An obvious key to the 1989 Democratic mayoral primary was the decreased voter turnout compared to the 1987 Washington-Byrne contest. In the 1989 primary, Sawyer ran over 200,000 votes behind Washington's 1987 total, whereas Daley's numbers were nearly 23,000 votes less than Byrne's losing primary effort.

Broken down by voting blocs, Daley's raw numbers show him running slightly ahead of Byrne in the black wards, behind her in most of the ethnic wards (the only exception to this ethnic trend were wards 11, 19, and 50), behind her in the mixed wards (1, 7, 10, 15, 18, and 27), behind her in three of the four Hispanic wards (the 26th Ward being the exception) and ahead of her in all six lakefront wards. As for Sawyer, he ran behind Washington in every ward in the city.

The candidates accepted victory and defeat with dignity and without rancor, no small feat in itself for 1980s Chicago-style politics.

Daley claimed victory by telling a youthful crowd of supporters packed into Fairmont Hotel ballroom, "We made it . . . and we are not finished yet." Upstairs in a hotel suite Daley's family, friends, and staff were low-keying their victory over Sawyer, as they predicted a tough fight in the general against Evans. Although some old timers tried to compare this primary win over a sitting mayor with the elder Daley's primary victory over Mayor Martin Kennelly thirty-four years earlier, most of the young campaign aides were not interested. "This is not the rebirth of the old machine," said one Daley insider, "this is Rich's personal organization . . . he will call the shots . . . not the party."[35]

To be sure, Richard J. Daley would have been somewhat surprised to see among his son's closest advisors a cadre of lakefronters whose predecessors two decades earlier were fighting the old boss for control of the local Democratic party (in some cases they were the same people).

In 1955, party chairman Daley's victorious campaign was an overt effort to intertwine government and politics into an organizational structure to run the city. In 1989, Rich Daley's primary victory reflected the decline of party organization as a critical factor in gaining mayoral power.

Eugene Sawyer was calm and gracious in conceding defeat. Low turnout in the black wards and rejection of his candidacy by Hispanics and lakefronters had doomed his election-night hopes early in the evening. Some diehard Sawyer supporters blamed Evans for the loss; others suggested that their candidate simply did not project the fire of a Washington or Jackson; still others pointed to the disorganized and unfocused campaign effort Sawyer and his advisors had presented to the voters (although he raised plenty of money, Sawyer was broke at the end and was unable to fund any meaningful precinct organization).

As for the candidate himself, Sawyer congratulated Daley, and told his followers that he would continue to work to eliminate racial disharmony and make Chicago "one city, one people, working together." Sawyer blamed no one for his defeat, told the crowd he loved everybody, and then left the limelight almost with a sigh of relief.

Tim Evans, sounding like Ed Vrdolyak and Tom Hynes two years earlier (they also bypassed the Democratic mayoral primary to run as independents), claimed the primary results put him, "in a good position" for the April 4 general election. Evans argued that the low voter turnout was due to citizen dislike for both Daley and Sawyer and that the winner's diminished total vote made him vulnerable to a "progressive coalition." Unfortunately for Evans, his yeoman efforts to turn Daley's win into a positive spin for himself were tarnished when he admitted his campaign was low on funds and that the prospects of matching Daley's fund-raising efforts were slim.

As for the Republicans, it was resurrection time for Ed Vrdolyak. The former-Democratic-party-chairman-turned-Republican made good on his gamble to win the low-turnout GOP mayoral primary as a write-in. By a little over 1,100 votes, Vrdolyak defeated the endorsed candidate, Herb Sohn, even though he won only seven wards. Fortunately for Vrdolyak, one of those wards—his home 10th Ward—gave him 5,000 votes (43 percent of his citywide total), which was almost seven times greater than Sohn's best ward.

Some Daley strategists expressed concern that Vrdolyak's surprise victory would cause a repeat of the two-whites-one-black 1983 mayoral primary. They were wrong. Evans was no Washington, Vrdolyak did not have the firepower or finances of Byrne, and Daley '89 was a far better candidate than Daley '83. History would not repeat itself.

NOTES

1. Mayor Harold Washington's budget message, October 15, 1987.
2. Personal interview.
3. Chicago Sun-Times, July 14, 1988.
4. Chicago Sun-Times, November 27, 1988.
5. Chicago Sun-Times, October 31, 1988.
6. Evans never referred to Sawyer as "mayor"; it was always "acting mayor."
7. Chicago Sun-Times, October 31, 1988.
8. Chicago Tribune, December 30, 1988.
9. The contests were: (1) Nov. 1988, Cook County state's attorney—general; (2) Feb. 1989, Chicago mayor—Democratic primary; (3) April 1989, Chicago mayor—general.
10. Chicago Sun-Times, December 6, 1989.
11. Ibid.
12. Personal interview.
13. Chicago Tribune, December 20, 1988.
14. Chicago Sun-Times, December 21, 1988.
15. Crain's Chicago Business, December 12–18, 1988.
16. Personal interview.
17. Chicago Defender, December 12, 1988.
18. Chicago Defender, January 5, 1989.
19. Chicago Defender, February 18, 1989.
20. Ibid.
21. Personal interview.
22. Personal interview.
23. Chicago Tribune, February 19, 1989.
24. Personal interview.
25. Chicago Sun-Times, January 6, 1989.
26. See Melvin Holli and Paul Green, eds., The Making of the Mayor: Chicago 1983 (Grand Rapids, 1984).
27. Chicago Sun-Times, February 12, 1989.

28. Chicago *Tribune*, February 12, 1989.
29. Chicago *Tribune*, January 2, 1989.
30. Chicago *Tribune*, February 25, 1989.
31. Personal interview.
32. Chicago *Sun-Times*, February 24, 1989.
33. Vote totals for the major Democratic mayoral candidates:

Year	Votes	Difference fall-off
1983	1,156,707	
1987	1,097,030	–59,677
1989	870,381	–226,649

34. The Lakefront 8—Daley 90% + precincts

	Ward	Precinct
1.	42	8
2.	42	59
3.	43	4
4.	43	18
5.	43	42
6.	44	3
7.	44	22
8.	44	48

35. Personal interview.

CHAPTER 2

The 1989 General Election

Paul M. Green

Almost lost in the excitement and glory of Chicago's mayoral primary were the difficult and unresolved issues facing the city and its residents. The primary made one fact very clear: Chicago's politics could not solve Chicago's problems. The ward-based party power politics that had dominated the city for so long was out of touch with the laundry list of ills facing Chicago.

A century ago Chicago was the growth capital of America. Its population gained a million people every two decades; it was the job center of the Midwest, with its stockyards, factories, and mills providing employment for newly arrived unskilled and semiskilled workers; and although slums and hardship affected a good chunk of its residents, most clung to the belief that the city with the "I will" spirit would provide the urban setting for a better future.

Whatever one's individual status, Chicago was the action center— it was the location where the game would be played. City schools would educate, housing would be found in city neighborhoods, and the dual goals of good jobs and upward economic mobility could all be accomplished within city boundaries.

Although they claimed vast differences in their public policy solutions and political approach, all three remaining 1989 mayoral candidates (Rich Daley, Tim Evans, and Ed Vrdolyak) actually shared one overriding common view: that Chicago no longer was the undisputed action center. Expanding suburbanization, surrounding interstate competition, and the sunbelt phenomenon had battered Chicago's once ironclad hold on the region. For many, Chicago no longer met their social, economic, and lifestyle needs. The unbridled urban boosterism of the late nineteenth century had given way in the late twentieth century to discussions of the underclass, inadequate schools, and personal safety.

The issues of race and class had become joined, and the identification of African-Americans with the socioeconomic ills of poverty had reinforced racial segregation throughout the city. Even the surging developments emanating from the old downtown Loop (dubbed the "Super Loop" by Northwestern University urbanologist Louis Masotti) had an economic/racial twist. Not all gentrifiers, returning suburbanites, yuppies, and housing rehabbers moving into these remodeled areas were white—some were upwardly mobile African-Americans who, with gusto equal to that of their white counterparts, bought into the surging economic revitalization of these limited Near Loop neighborhoods. Income segregation far more than racial segregation was changing city life and its politics, and, like everything else in 1989, this fact played right into Rich Daley's hands.

THE DALEY STRATEGY

Since 1931, the Chicago Democratic mayoral primary has selected the city's next mayor. Even the racially divisive 1983 race between Democrat Harold Washington and Republican Bernard Epton found a percentage of white voters unable and unwilling to vote GOP (a fact that Washington never forgot). Thus, Daley's game plan was relatively simple: convince his opponents and the city's voters that his final victory was inevitable. In fact, many Daley insiders viewed the period between the February 28th primary and the April 4th general election as more of a governmental interim than a political campaign. Obviously Daley had to avoid appearing too self-assured of victory and his organization had to guard against overconfidence, but there seemed little either of Daley's two new rivals could do to stop him.

Besides the enormous boost from his primary win, Daley saw the political playing field remain tilted his way. The African-American community was still split. In an almost surrealistic reversal of roles, third-party candidate Evans was now preaching black unity while the recently vanquished Sawyer was playing the role of the reluctant political warrior. Though at first frightened by Vrdolyak's surprise write-in GOP primary victory, Daley's people recognized quickly that "Fast" Eddie had lost several steps as a political force in Chicago. According to one Daley aide, "From the start we wanted voters—especially ethnics—to recognize the futility of supporting Vrdolyak . . . a vote for Eddie was like throwing your ballot in the garbage . . . a waste."[1]

Like a competent surgical team, Daley's organization dissected the five-week campaign. First, they cut the campaign by 20 percent by having Daley take a week-long postprimary vacation to Arizona. This not only gave their candidate a chance to rest, it also cooled campaign coverage, forced Evans and Vrdolyak to generate their own political excitement, and cut down the possibilities of a Daley campaign gaffe. Second, the wheelmen of Daley's fund-raising machine shifted into overdrive. The avalanche of dollars for Daley gave him almost total control of the paid airwaves and pushed home the theme of his election inevitability. Third, Daley's advisors realized that their primary election coalition of ethnics, lakefronters, and Hispanics was an unbeatable combination, unless there were defections. Thus, voter reinforcement was the main watchword of Daley's short general election campaign. Finally, another reconfirming need was with the press, media, and "good government" types who had adopted Daley as a "born-again reformer" during the primary. With a strong personal desire to eliminate any doubt that he would not be "Boss II," Rich Daley restated his position on several key issues, sounding more and more like a traditional "Goo-Goo" ("good government" reformer).

For example, on the critical issues of schools, Daley advocated the establishment of a deputy mayor for education. This cabinet-level position would be a policy liaison from city hall to the school board and the soon-to-be-elected local school councils. Educational reform was sweeping Chicago, and Daley's views, from increased classroom computer usage to corporate financial involvement in school funding, were in the vanguard of the movement.

In public health, Daley wanted a new cabinet-level officer to coordinate the AIDS fight and was pushing for a health summit meeting with state and county officials to better coordinate health service delivery. On ethics, Daley was out front with his plan to replace the existing Office of Municipal Investigations with an inspector general who would have subpoena power to investigate wrongdoing by city employees.

On management and tax issues, Daley called for (1) reducing city overtime by 25 percent; (2) minimizing the need for the city to hire outside consultants; and (3) having local corporations loan their top executives to the city on a pro bono basis. In short, Daley's positions were consistent philosophically on almost every big and small governmental or political issue that would arise during the campaign. As in the primary, Daley would not allow any opponent to out-reform him.

For some diehard, old-line Illinois reform veterans, Daley's views were exasperating—the boy from Bridgeport's 11th Ward was now preaching their line and in some cases using reform as a weapon against them.

THE EVANS STRATEGY

Tim Evans needed to be the "Back to the Future" candidate in the 1989 general mayoral election. Somehow he had to convince the voters, especially African-Americans, that Eugene Sawyer's just-completed unsuccessful primary campaign was a minor and relatively unimportant skirmish. To have any chance against Daley, candidate

Evans had to demonstrate that the Sawyer interim was an aberration and that he, Tim Evans, was the one and only true political link to the late Harold Washington.

At the same time, Evans was forced into several peculiar and often contradictory political stances. First, although he wanted voters to forget the primary, he also wanted Sawyer and his allies to endorse his (Evans's) candidacy (something that Evans would not do for Sawyer). Second, although Washington had made Vrdolyak the political devil in the black community, Evans would give his old foe a pass, hoping the latter's campaign would gain momentum and thereby take votes away from Daley. Third, in order to minimize the inevitability factor of Daley's primary win, Evans had to demonstrate that the primary's low voter turnout indicated dissatisfaction with both candidates, a fact that would not sit well with diehard Sawyerites. Finally, Evans would have to find the campaign issues and themes that would attract the nonblack members of the Washington coalition while at the same time fostering voter enthusiasm and political frenzy with African-American voters. All of this and more had to be sorted out, organized, and implemented in five weeks.

In retrospect, Tim Evans never had a chance!

THE VRDOLYAK STRATEGY

Ed Vrdolyak's mayoral campaign peaked and died on primary night. Without an organization, a political or fund-raising game plan, and with minimal "fire in his belly" to go all out for the office, Vrdolyak was a shell of his former self. Only his quick-tongued barbed comments concerning his write-in victory and Daley's potential vulnerabilities showed any of the old Vrdolyak spark. However, Daley's win over Sawyer ended any realistic Vrdolyak mayoral hopes.

In real terms Vrdolyak's "long-shot" to "no-shot" mayoral campaign had to convince a large majority of Daley's primary supporters that he and not Daley would not only be the better mayor but also have a better chance to defeat Evans. With little possibility of capturing any meaningful support among African-American, lakefront, or Hispanic voters, Vrdolyak's only hope for an upset depended on ethnic Daley deserters coming over en masse to his banner. The much-discussed backup plan of Vrdolyak's candidacy (prevent a Daley victory by splitting off his ethnic support) was used by Daleyites to further diminish the Republican's stature and effectiveness.

Like a fighter who suddenly grows old in the ring, Vrdolyak often appeared weary and punched-out during the campaign, although at times he did put on a brief dazzling flurry for old times' sake. All in all, there was little Vrdolyak could do to counter Daley's claim that he was a trivial candidate in the race and this fact more than anything else hurt the proud Vrdolyak the most.

THE EVANS CAMPAIGN

In the first week of the campaign, while Daley rested in the West, Evans unleashed all of his pent-up political energy by moving rapidly through the city. Saying, "The real fight is just beginning," Evans appeared on radio talk shows, did the ethnic restaurant circuit, and spoke to almost anyone who would listen. He appealed to Sawyer supporters, many of whom blamed him for the mayor's primary loss, arguing, "there will be some confusion and some fingerpointing but most [of them] are ready to put fingerpointing behind us."[2] He welcomed Jesse Jackson's expected endorsement and played up the endorsements from such outspoken black pols as Alderman William Henry (24), Alderman Marlene Carter (15), and Robert Lucas, head of the Kenwood-Oakland Community Organization and formerly an outspoken Evans foe. Nevertheless, Evans's torrid pace could not outrun the nagging questions of whether real black unity behind his candidacy was possible, whether he could raise the necessary campaign dollars, and where he was going to find the votes (black or nonblack) needed to overcome Daley's 100,000-vote primary margin over Sawyer.

At a March 4th Operation PUSH mass meeting, Jackson laid the unity issue squarely on the political table. "Division," said Jackson, "is our problem, unity and coalition is our solution. There is a civil war going on in our community and within the Harold Washington coalition. Our challenge is to preserve the union."[3] Although Evans, Jackson, other political and community leaders, and black radio talk-show hosts, would push "unity in the community" for the next month, it would never all come together. Bitterness and disinterest among black Chicago voters would deny Evans the movement solidarity enjoyed by Washington in 1983 and 1987.

According to one Evans aide, "Money was a problem in our campaign. . . . we simply didn't have any."[4] This was, perhaps, an overstatement, but throughout the five-week campaign, Evans was not able to raise enough money to run meaningful TV and radio commercials. An expected mid-March media blitz was canceled for lack of funds, a $25,000 campaign donation to Evans from black publishing giant John H. Johnson occurred only after black community leaders expressed outrage over allegations that Johnson was hosting a fund raiser for Daley, and published financial reports found Evans relying heavily on loans from family and friends. Though Evans tried to put the best face possible on his campaign's financial situation, comparing it to Washington's in 1983, in reality he was fighting Daley without a movement or money.

Any Evans hope for a miracle upset victory hinged on registering thousands of new black voters, turning them out on election day, and reconnecting as well as possible with nonblack elements of the old Washington coalition. In the brief postprimary registration period before the general election, Evans went all out to put new voters on the rolls. Though registration rallies were publicized throughout the African-American community and a downtown Bismarck Hotel registration gathering received some media exposure, Evans was not very successful in his new-voter recruiting efforts.

Evans had better luck in garnering old-line white Washington progressives to his campaign; 5th Ward Alderman and mayoral primary dropout Larry Bloom gave Evans a warm endorsement. Calling for Sawyer backers not to engage in voter retribution against Evans, Bloom argued that only Evans understands that, "Chicago will pay dearly for ignoring its unemployed, its uneducated, and its unappealing."[5]

Also throwing their political weight behind Evans were such lakefront liberals as Alderman David Orr (49) and community organizer Heather Booth, as well as such old-line Hyde Park activists as Sam Ackerman and Don Rose. Unfortunately for Evans, these individuals represented the politics of nostalgia more than did his archenemy, "young" Daley. Time and demographics had diminished greatly the power base of socioeconomic liberals in Chicago.

Unquestionably the high-water mark of the Evans campaign was his mass rally at the University of Illinois-Chicago Pavilion, held a week before election day. Trying to capture the spirit and power that emanated from a similar event held for Harold Washington in 1983, Evans told a predominantly black audience of 12,000 cheering supporters, "I am in this fight to win." Using some of the fiercest and most racially charged rhetoric of his campaign, Evans blasted the Daleys (father and son) arguing that, ". . . (Rich) Daley is getting ready to reopen his father's plantation and his new machine is going to be just as bad as the old one, if not worse."[6] Evans claimed that Daley's political tradition was making Chicago the most segregated city in the nation and a place where blacks were victims of police brutality.

Other speakers and a "killer" video tape that chronicled the civil rights movement, Chicago political history, and the evil Daleys also added to an exhausting and emotional political rally that had a mean-spirited racial edge overriding the entire proceeding. Observing the night's activities, one Daley insider remarked, "It's strange that Evans and blacks can basically get away with race-baiting political attacks while a similar predominantly white rally for Daley would be viewed as a gathering of the KKK or the neo-Nazis."[7] Subconsciously many nonblack Chicagoans believed that overt racial appeals had run their course and would demonstrate these views on election day.

As the mayoral contest entered its closing days, Evans's hopes for an election day surprise appeared slim. Despite his nonstop campaigning and brave predictions to the media, the Evans forces were in deep trouble. Final polls showed Evans trailing by double digits, little campaign cash meant no television advertising, and the political split in the black community was cooling the Evans forces' efforts to generate "street heat" (a Chicago term for emotionalizing politics in the black community).

In the end the Evans campaign strategy was reduced to a very simple formula: black voter turnout had to match white voter turnout. If all blacks voted for Evans while some whites did not vote for Daley, Evans would win. As a man committed to coalition politics and who understood Chicago political history and its past voting trends, Evans must have shuddered at hearing his followers utter the simplistic and unrealistic political assessments of his victory chances.

To his credit, Evans never whined or whimpered about his campaign dilemma, disappointments, or frustrations as he carried the battle against Daley until the polls closed. The final results may have surprised some Evans supporters; however, they did not surprise the candidate.

THE DALEY CAMPAIGN

Rich Daley's general election campaign, like the primary, was a carefully mapped-out operation. Back on the campaign trail following his Arizona vacation, Daley oozed confidence as he bantered with the media about his less-than-exhausting public appearance schedule. Victory was the campaign watchword as Daley and his chief advisors worked the voters and the press with a slick dual strategy of campaign concern and electoral confidence. First, they argued that, no, they were not "taking the election for granted" and maintained that Daley was working hard bringing his message to all parts of the city. Second, they admitted that, yes, they were instituting certain activities to give Daley a head start on governing the city following the expected victory on April 4th. It was a virtuoso political performance. One night, Chicago voters saw on television candidate Daley pleading with his supporters not to be overconfident; the next night they heard him announce, four weeks before the election, his official mayoral transition team.[8]

Endorsements flowed to Daley's growing political juggernaut. The Chicago Federation of Labor's committee on political education by a count of 185 to 1 voted to back Daley. The CFL, though no longer the powerful force it had been a generation earlier, still possessed significant economic muscle and manpower. A delighted Daley thanked organized labor for its support and welcomed its campaign assistance, but in crass 1989 political terms this endorsement's biggest contribution to the Daley campaign was that it denied Evans another opportunity to build momentum.

As in the primary, both major Chicago daily newspapers were effusive in their praise of Daley and his candidacy. The Chicago Tribune, calling Daley "Clearly the best choice to deliver what Chicago needs," argued that his campaign had presented the best specific proposals to resolve long-standing city ills and that, moreover, he had, "the drive and the motivation to see to it that they [would] get done."[9] Not to be "out-Daleyed" by the competition, the Chicago Sun-Times put it simply: "Richard M. Daley gets our vote for mayor. No ifs, ands, or buts. He is the candidate best qualified to lead Chicago into the next decade."[10]

As expected, most big-time Illinois and national Democratic politicians joined the Daley endorsement parade (although most black Chicago Democratic leaders held back or supported Evans).[11] U.S. Senator Paul Simon led statewide party officials in calling for a Daley victory, claiming that Chicagoans would see, "a mayor of vision and a mayor of compassion." Massachusetts Senator Edward M. Kennedy (whose relations with the Daleys had cooled significantly during the Jane Byrne administration) joined Daley for a day of campaigning and good-natured political give and take. At a West Side rally, Kennedy endorsed Daley by throwing his arm around the candidate and declaring, "Mayor Daley: That has a nice ring to it . . . [but] the only thing that bothers me about a Mayor Daley . . . is somebody trying to get along on the basis of a famous family name."[12]

The most controversial endorsement of Daley came from national Democratic party chairman Ron Brown, a black who had been a 1988 presidential campaign advisor to Jesse Jackson. Immediately following the mayoral primary, Brown called Daley, pledged his complete support, and offered to campaign for this party's nominee. For most of the short general election campaign, Brown's endorsement of Daley and Jackson's refusal to do the same created ongoing headlines and revealed the racial tensions inside both Chicago and the Democratic party.

Alderman Dorothy Tillman (3), a fierce and vocal Evans backer who, following her "Uncle Tom" comments about Mayor Sawyer, had voluntarily placed her mouth under house arrest, reentered the political arena by attacking Brown. "It's a sad day," bellowed Tillman, "that the first test that this black man has is to stop the liberation of our people and try to turn us backwards."[13] Not to be outdone in the outrageous remark department, Congressman Gus Savage (2) continued the "blacklash" assault against Brown by dismissing the national party chairman as an "Oreo" (black on the outside, white on the inside).

Brown responded calmly and dispassionately to the accusations from pro-Evans city black leaders by making two trips to Chicago to reinforce his endorsement. "I am not the chairman of the African-American Democratic party," Brown told a Chicago Hilton and Towers breakfast meeting of black Daley supporters, "I'm the chairman of the Democratic Party of the United States."[14] Brown added that his support was based not only on the fact that Daley was the Democratic nominee, but also on the fact that he was the best candidate running for mayor. One week later, Brown returned to Chicago for a unity dinner. Despite the presence of black pickets, Brown told a packed Hyatt Regency Hotel audience of prominent local and state Democratic leaders, "The party is standing behind Mr. Daley. We expect him to win on Tuesday."[15]

In raw numbers, Brown's endorsement moved few voters to Daley's column in the black community. What it did accomplish was to reinforce Daley as the party's nominee to the other voting blocs in the city, strengthen his appeal among lakefront liberal-independents, and demonstrate convincingly that Daley was the only mayoral candidate running as a unifier and a healer.

In Chicago perhaps more than any other place in America, local politics has never been a "sissy sport" (a gender-neutral term). From Mr. Dooley, who said, "It ain't beanbag," to former Mayor Richard J. Daley, who once responded to academic criticism of his politics by arguing, "I don't care what the intellectuals or the university professors say," Chicago politics has had a well-earned reputation for toughness. Campaigns still are contested on the streets. Buttons, bumper stickers, posters, window signs, and troops in the precincts still count greatly in local elections. In the 1987 mayoral campaign, Ed Vrdolyak's independent candidacy clearly had the street energy and the momentum in the city's ethnic wards (a fact that helped drive Tom Hynes out of the race). Daley's forces in 1989 would not give Vrdolyak, now the GOP nominee, a similar opportunity. Thus, the battle of Heck's Hall.

On the night of March 9, Vrdolyak forces held a rally at Heck's Hall on the city's Far Northwest Side. Little is truly known (or admitted) as to how the "ruckus" started, except for the following facts. Shortly after the meeting began, a group in the audience began heckling Vrdolyak. The trading of insults quickly turned into an exchange of punches between the partisans. Vrdolyak called the instigators "goons" and accused Daley's brother Bill and 45th Ward Democratic committeeman Tom Lyons of planning the brawl. Both Daleys denied all accusations, and the candidate's press secretary, Avis LaVelle, dismissed Vrdolyak's charges as desperation tactics of "a fringe candidate." Whatever the taunts, the perception was clear: unlike in 1987, Vrdolyak was not going to have a free hand in making himself the ethnic candidate. TV and newspaper pictures of a few pot-bellied, over-age Heck Hall pugilists swinging wildly and poorly at one another drove home this important point. Whether Daley was behind the action or not was politically insignificant; in good old Chicago fashion, Vrdolyak was taught the political facts of life.

Daley's mayoral stretch run to election day seemed wide open and clear. The split in the African-American community continued unabated, Vrdolyak's candidacy was being pushed further off to the sidelines, and the candidate's fund-raising machine was breaking all records for speed and efficiency. Moreover, only Daley had meaningful paid media, his top-notch staff was turning out first-rate issue statements, and his own political transformation bridging the socioeconomic gap from the bungalow to the condo was going well. Not surprisingly, Daley's opponents, especially Evans, desperate for something to slow Daley's momentum, turned to an issue beyond the leading candidate's control: his father's Chicago legacy.

In the 1983 mayoral primary, Rich Daley was surprised that images of his dad and his mother in one of his TV advertisements were viewed more negatively than positively by the voters. Post-1983 conventional wisdom now suggested that many Chicagoans were either new to the city and did not personally remember the elder Daley (knowing of him only by a reputation that had been somewhat tainted by the 1968 Democratic national convention and general citywide race relations) or old-time Chicagoans who did not always have fond memories of "hizzoner." Unlike in 1983, Daley in 1989 did not dwell on his father's mayoral record or political history. He simply responded to accusations that he was going to reinstate the "machine" or "plantation politics" by defending his dad's memory as a son and not a politician.

Ironically, a Chicago *Sun-Times* poll late in the campaign concerning the political impact of the Daley father and son issue revealed that 70 percent of the city's voters claimed it made no difference to them.[16] Like Carter Harrison II before him, Rich Daley was not going to be hindered from winning city hall because his father had held the job.

THE VRDOLYAK CAMPAIGN

Ed Vrdolyak's mayoral campaign never got started, despite the fact that his upset write-in victory had propelled him back to center stage of Chicago politics. However, defeating the well-intentioned but unknown Herb Sohn in a low-turnout Republican mayoral primary was hardly the political spring training that Vrdolyak needed to prepare himself for a general election battle against a powerful major leaguer such as Rich Daley.

Without funds, a campaign organization, or a political battle plan, Vrdolyak's first goal was to gain quickly respectability and acceptance as a candidate. Like Evans, he never had a chance. Following the primary, both Chicago newspapers pilloried him mercilessly. The *Tribune*, commenting on Vrdolyak's victory, said, "It looks as if ol' Rasputin has slithered into the campaign as the Republican nominee."[17] So angered was the newspaper at Vrdolyak's campaign return that they called for the abolition of partisan primaries in Chicago, claiming that the weakness of the local GOP made it "vulnerable to takeover by kooks, charlatans, bush league Machiavellis and failures hungry for a grudge match."[18] *Sun-Times* political editor Steve Neal simply dismissed the once politically potent "Fast Eddie" Vrdolyak as "Past Eddie." The local Republican political hierarchy gave Vrdolyak immediate notice following the primary that he was in for a lonely campaign. County chairman Jim Dvorak said, "I promised that the party organization will avail (Vrdolyak) of its fund-raising abilities . . . but we have no money to give *candidates*."[19] (Vrdolyak was the only Republican running.) Illinois Governor Jim Thompson, the state's leading Republican and a Chicagoan, when asked if Vrdolyak would make the best mayor, retorted, "I think I'll leave that to the judgment of the citizens of the city of Chicago."[20] Thompson then blasted Vrdolyak for blaming the governor for Vrdolyak's crushing defeat in the 1988 election for clerk of the circuit court. Most candidates running for office seek party unity. In Vrdolyak's case, however, most big-time Republicans were unified against him.

Vrdolyak's shoestring mayoral campaign did have its moments. First, a few black politicians and community activists, such as Alderman Anna Langford (16) and Marian Stamps (West Side) endorsed Vrdolyak. Both were Sawyer backers who were seeking retribution against Evans and his allies. Defending her action, Langford came up with the single best political line of the mayoral campaign. "My support for Vrdolyak," said Langford, "is based on the fact [that] his treatment of Harold [Washington] at its worst was better than Tim's [Evans's] treatment of Gene [Sawyer] at its best."[21] Vrdolyak tried to convince Chicago that this trickle of minority support was actually the top of a grand Vrdolyak wave that would spread across the entire African-American community. Few analysts or voters bought his rhetoric or reasoning, and Vrdolyak's black totals on election night proved them right.

A second memorable event in the Vrdolyak campaign was the American flag controversy. An obscure Art Institute of Chicago student named "Dread" Scott Tyler gained national attention by his exhibit, "What Is the Proper Way to Display the American Flag?" Tyler's concept of art was to place an American flag on the floor in front of a ledger in which viewers, while standing on the flag, could write their comments. Picasso he was not. Despite the obvious absurdity of the entire situation, Vrdolyak led a group of American Legion protesters, Vietnam veterans, and pro-flag advocates who demanded that the Art Institute take down the exhibit. Amid the discussions of constitutional rights, patriotism, and free speech, Vrdolyak called for a boycott of all companies that contributed to the Art Institute. Vrdolyak, said one long-time ward pol, was trying to use this issue to become "the city's white Jesse Jackson."[22]

The third and probably most enjoyable event for Vrdolyak was his mayoral debate against Tim Evans. Daley had ducked the debate by using a loophole provided by the debate's sponsor, The League of Women Voters. Originally the league had stipulated that the debate would be open to only those candidates with at least a 10 percent rating in the polls. Vrdolyak had less then half that figure. Daleyites demanded that the debate be limited to their candidate and Evans. The league said no and so did Daley, thus creating the Vrdolyak-Evans two-thirds mayoral debate.

For Vrdolyak it was a momentary political Lourdes. Once again he was "Fast Eddie" slashing at Daley, chiding the media, and then, with a barrage reminiscent of the second Joe Louis/Max Schmelling fight, burying Evans with a series of political haymakers.[23] Evans, a first-rate debater in his own right, was simply overwhelmed by a Vrdolyak who unleashed on him all his pent-up political frustrations. Unfortunately for Vrdolyak, his main opponent was not Evans; rather, it was the absent Daley. Vrdolyak's dazzling performance thus had only minimal political impact.

Vrdolyak closed out his quixotic mayoral campaign quietly. Ignored by most of the media, dismissed by most of the pundits, and unable to raise the dollars for TV, Vrdolyak resorted to brief campaign speeches and news releases on key issues. A few years earlier, his call to eliminate busing as a means of desegregating schools or his promise not to raise taxes for two years while cutting the city budget by $300 million would have been major news stories. In 1989, the response to these proposals was indifference. Only his election eve address to his 10th Ward neighbors made any real news as Vrdolyak lashed out at his former Democratic ethnic allies for making him the fall guy for their own political agendas. "I fought the hard fights," said Vrdolyak (referring to his leadership of the Council 29 that had stymied the Washington administration for three years), "because they had to be fought."[24]

Sympathy and guilt are two feelings that, historically, have had little impact on Chicago politics, a fact that Ed Vrdolyak once knew and would relearn on election night.

MAYOR EUGENE SAWYER—THE MISSING MAN

The moment Mayor Gene Sawyer conceded defeat on primary night, the courtship of his general election endorsement began. His chief suitors were Tim Evans and pro-Evans black community leaders. For almost two weeks, Sawyer was praised and flattered by a whole host of Evans allies, some of whom previously had vilified him for almost sixteen months. In the end, Sawyer, without fanfare or anger, would reject all unity appeals, leaving Evans to fight Daley (as Sawyer had been forced to do in the primary) with a splintered black political base.

The entire courtship process revealed the bitterness between Evans and Sawyer and the personal and philosophical differences between each man's followers. It also brought home the reality of black politics in a post–Harold Washington Chicago. The mayor was gone and he could not be re-created in any of his aspiring apostles.

Evans, on the first day of his general election campaign, announced that he would "love to have Sawyer's backing." Sawyer remained noncommittal. A few days later, Jesse Jackson, playing the same high-profile campaign role for Evans that he had for Sawyer, announced a three-day fast "to bring an end to this war and strife in the Harold Washington coalition."[25] Sawyer again refused to make his intentions known. Finally, Sun-Times columnist Vernon Jarrett, a widely read black journalist and Sawyer basher, attempted to refute claims that Evans forces had held down black turnout in the Daley-Sawyer primary by writing, "Do the Sawyer people really believe that the persuasive power of Aldermen Evans (4), [Bobby] Rush (2) and [Dorothy] Tillman (3) is stronger than Sawyer's endorsement by the Rev. Jesse Jackson, all black newspapers, most black civic leaders, ministers and elected officials, plus day-to-day pep talks by black radio talk show hosts? . . ."[26] Sawyer ignored Jarrett's argument.

Evans and his allies recognized that their courting was not going well when, one week into the process, a group of Sawyer backers announced the possibility of a write-in campaign for their leader. Led by former alderman Clifford Kelley, these diehard Sawyerites argued that a multiracial group of Chicago voters could elect Sawyer (as a write-in) in a four-way general election. Though never a serious political possibility, the write-in scenario reflected the extent of the tensions and hard feelings lingering in the black community.

Seeing the situation getting out of hand and realizing that further delay of a final endorsement would not serve any further purpose,[27] Sawyer ended all speculation three weeks before election day. At a city hall news conference, the mayor announced, "My days of running for mayor are over. Also, I have decided not to endorse any candidate."[28] Sawyer also firmly rejected any further calls for a write-in campaign on his behalf. Although Evans claimed that Sawyer's action did not hurt him at all, clearly Daley was the big winner. There would be no rally or summit uniting the Evans and Sawyer forces and, though Daley would not pick off many pro-Sawyer blacks, he also would not have to worry about the possibility of a huge black turnout for Evans.

Sawyer appeared in the news only twice more during the entire rest of the campaign. The first occasion was when he was given a hero's send-off as he chaired his last city council meeting. Even his bitterest foes showered Sawyer with kind words and political encouragement. His loyal ally, Alderman Anna Langford (16), commenting on the tribute, reminisced "you never got applause before the election, thank God you are getting it now."[29] The other Sawyer headline occurred on election eve when the mayor, responding to the question of whether his 6th Ward would turn out for Evans, said "I am not doing what they did to me when I ran. I'm asking everyone to get out and vote." And with a special irony in his voice, Sawyer answered a final question on Evans's chances of victory by saying "if he loses, they can't blame me for it."[30]

THE CAMPAIGN ENDS

The last week of the 1989 Chicago mayoral election was one of the most boring conclusions of any major campaign in the city's history. Little happened. No new issues were introduced, no damaging charges were raised, as candidates and voters alike grew tired of the repetitive rhetoric and political analysis. It was as if the city that has thrived all its life on politics had simply "overdosed" and was now willing to simply sleep it off. And, as almost everything else in the mayoral primary and general election campaigns, it all worked to the benefit of Richard M. Daley.

As was the case in the primary, there was little election day energy in the black community. Evans's stronghold on the Near South Side appeared only marginally more active than it had been for Sawyer on primary day. Standing on the corner of 47th Street and Cottage Grove Avenue (once a thriving commercial neighborhood), an Evans worker lamented, "It's depressing . . . the people in the community just aren't excited. . . . You know, a few years ago we had hope . . .

now Harold's gone and all of these businesses like Drexel Chevrolet and the Sutherland Hotel are gone also."[31]

Daley signs dominated the Northwest and Southwest Side ethnic neighborhoods. In the Far North Side Rogers Park community, a strange urban/political metamorphosis was taking place along its main thoroughfare, Devon Avenue. In recent years, this predominantly Jewish area had seen a huge influx of Indians and Pakistanis, who opened up a variety of stores and shops catering to the neighborhood's growing Asian population. The Daley name had always been popular among Jewish voters in this ward, but candidate Daley had little to fear from this new ethnic mix. Now, Asian businesses, as had their Jewish counterparts, displayed Daley signs in their windows along Devon Avenue.

DALEY WINS

"We wanted to win," said a beaming and triumphant Richard M. Daley, "but more than that, we wanted to win in a way that would make us proud and set a positive tone for our city."[32] Like his father before him, Rich Daley appeared "humble in victory" as he reacted to his landslide victory over his two mayoral foes. For some old-timers listening to the mayor-elect in the jam-packed Hyatt Regency Hotel, this night was a combination of political restoration and personal redemption. Once again, all was well in their city for once again it had a Mayor Daley. However, dominating the outer and inner circles of Daley's victorious supporters were not the veteran allies of his dad; rather, they were young, well-dressed men and women whose loyalty was solely dedicated to Rich Daley.

Walking through the crowd, one heard a familiar battle cry, "from the bungalow to the condo,"[33] as Daleyites congratulated themselves for uniting two socioeconomic city lifestyles into a solid political juggernaut. Daley's own political consultant and media wizard, David Axelrod, expressed genuine surprise at the size of the victory when he said, "Our hope was to get a clear majority. We never anticipated that it would be this large."[34] Perhaps the best recognition of the city's new, emerging political climate came in a postelection editorial from the very pro-Daley Chicago *Sun-Times*. It said, "Daley has earned goodwill and support . . . there came from him no name calling, no low blows, no temperature raising rhetoric. . . . The old 'machine,' as his rivals relentlessly referred to it, is gone and there is no reviving it or its autocratic ways."[35]

Tim Evans took his landslide loss with pride and dignity. In conceding defeat, Evans told his downcast crowd of well-wishers, "I want you to know that the struggle continues. . . . I don't want you to be discouraged. We will be there."[36] Earlier in the day, Evans reflected on the impact of the schism in the black community on his campaign, stating, "I have no regrets. In this business, one must play with the cards one is dealt."[37] Commenting on the second disaster for the once mighty and unified Harold Washington coalition, West Side alderman and mayoral candidate dropout Danny Davis put the Evans loss in perspective. "Many black voters," said Davis, "were still fighting the December 1 battle of 1987." Indeed, the old turn-of-the-century "rule or ruin" political maxim of Chicago politics had returned with a vengeance. In blunt terms, enough diehard black followers of both Sawyer and Evans saw Mayor Richard M. Daley as less of a threat than having their rival within the African-American community occupying the chair on the fifth floor of city hall.

Ed Vrdolyak was destroyed at the polls. He could not carry a single ward (25 percent vote in his home 10th Ward was his best showing), and out of a total 2,911 city precincts, the once proud and powerful Vrdolyak was able to win a grand total of 2 precincts (19 and 41 in the 10th Ward). No major party candidate in Chicago mayoral history had ever gone down to such an overwhelming defeat at the polls as Vrdolyak in 1989. Still, in the tradition of past landslide losers, Vrdolyak claimed that well-known hollow prize, "a moral victory." The former alderman told a handful of friends and supporters that even in defeat, "we're building a base in the Republican party in this town based on fundamental moral issues." Given his minuscule numbers, Vrdolyak's electoral base was unlikely to be the foundation of any political movement. He and his candidacy were ignored, rejected, and finally decimated.

The numbers tell the magnitude of Daley's victory. He carried the same thirty-one of fifty city wards that he had won in the primary. His victory margin was nearly 150,000 votes over Evans and his overall general election vote percentage against two rivals almost matched his primary vote percentage against Sawyer. In short, it was a Daley landslide (see table 1).

The increased major party voter turnout from the primary to the general election (170,863 votes) made little difference to the outcome. As in the primary, Daley ran like a whirlwind in the Northwest and Southwest Side ethnic wards. Margin-wise, the same top seven margin wards in the primary came through for Daley in the general (all seven, in fact, were in the same margin order). Leading the way were his Southwest Side neighbors; in the 13th and 23th Wards, Daley's victory margins were over 30,000 votes.[38]

The biggest ward-margin jump or increase for Daley between the primary and the general election occurred in the lakefront's 43rd Ward. Under the leadership of ward committeeman and ardent Daley

TABLE 1   Chicago 1989 Democratic Mayoral Election Results by Votes, Margins, and Percentages (Presented in ward rank order for Daley, by margin)

Ward Number	Republican Party Vrdolyak's Vote	H. Washington Party Evans's Vote	Democratic Party Daley's Vote	Daley's Margin	Daley's Percentage
13	1,187	206	32,976	32,770 D	96%
23	1,356	163	30,431	30,268 D	95
41	2,054	367	29,795	29,428 D	92
45	1,490	332	27,727	27,395 D	94
38	1,316	278	27,372	27,094 D	94
36	1,179	1,030	26,566	25,536 D	92
19	1,276	4,871	26,527	21,656 D	81
39	969	766	19,793	19,027 D	92
43	1,027	2,570	21,026	18,456 D	85
50	789	1,620	20,064	18,444 D	89
11	351	2,372	20,101	17,729 D	88
35	961	611	16,945	16,334 D	92
12	903	1,829	17,976	16,147 D	87
47	871	1,627	17,340	15,713 D	87
14	705	2,369	17,363	14,994 D	85
33	605	1,587	16,209	14,622 D	88
40	835	1,064	15,530	14,466 D	89
44	805	3,203	16,990	13,787 D	81
30	702	3,203	15,593	12,390 D	80
32	523	2,103	12,670	10,567 D	83
42	1,028	5,338	15,454	10,116 D	71
48	814	5,119	11,504	6,385 D	66
46	665	5,250	11,546	6,296 D	66
26	325	3,135	8,887	5,752 D	72
49	655	5,218	10,560	5,342 D	64
25	289	1,774	6,453	4,679 D	76
10	6,289	6,987	11,580	4,593 D	47
31	280	4,270	7,853	3,583 D	63
22	209	1,728	4,849	3,121 D	71
18	772	13,211	15,910	2,699 D	53
1	617	8,233	10,651	2,418 D	55
27	187	11,021	2,535	(8,486) E	18
7	455	12,626	3,249	(9,377) E	20
15	250	15,259	4,595	(10,664) E	23
4	295	15,459	2,685	(12,774) E	15
2	276	14,710	1,405	(13,305) E	9
5	362	17,096	3,212	(13,884) E	16
29	179	15,587	1,563	(14,024) E	9
3	137	15,165	833	(14,332) E	5
28	123	15,000	634	(14,366) E	4
20	173	15,991	1,170	(14,821) E	7
37	123	16,239	1,245	(14,994) E	7
16	125	16,690	894	(15,796) E	5
24	149	17,062	793	(16,269) E	4
9	202	17,927	1,573	(16,354) E	8
17	159	20,338	851	(19,487) E	4
34	161	22,674	1,019	(21,655) E	4
8	269	24,324	1,410	(22,914) E	5
6	343	26,425	1,634	(24,791) E	6
21	149	25,927	1,079	(24,848) E	4
Absentee	34	151	521		
TOTAL	35,998	428,105	577,141	149,036 D	55%
Wards Won		19	31		

D = Daley; E = Evans

supporter Ann Stepan, this home to traditional lakefront reform values upped Daley's margin of victory by over 5,300 votes. Other huge primary-to-general margin increases took place in Northwest Side wards 41, 50, and 45, as well as another lakefront ward, 42.

As was to be expected, Evans's best margins came from the South Side, middle-class, black wards. However, as was the case for Sawyer, these areas could not match the ethnic Northwest and Southwest Sides' intensity and cohesiveness for Daley.

The only relatively competitive ward battles (winning margin under 5,000 votes and winning percentage under 60 percent) took place in the city's most racially heterogeneous wards, 1 and 18, as well as in the Southeast Side 10th Ward, where Vrdolyak's vote prevented Daley from racking up another landslide ward victory.

Percentage-wise, the ward returns reveal a replay of the primary. Evans, like Sawyer, received massive support from African-American voters. In fourteen of his nineteen winning wards, Evans won over 90 percent of the vote. His lowest winning percentage was in the 15th Ward, where a small remaining ethnic portion of this racially changing white-to-black Southwest Side ward kept Evans's victory percentage at a mere 77 percent. The problem for Evans was simple: not enough blacks voted. However, it is doubtful that even a united Sawyer-Evans alliance could have energized, motivated, or manufactured another 150,000 black votes to beat Daley.

Daley's general election ward percentages also were similar to his primary total. In the city's eighteen predominantly white Northwest and Southwest Side wards and in the two highest-income lakefront wards (43 and 44), Daley received over 80 percent of the vote. Equally impressive were his vote percentage increases in the city's two heavily Hispanic (Mexican) Southwest Side wards, 25 (11 percent) and 22 (7 percent) and in the Near South Side, predominantly black 2nd Ward (6 percent). This last ward is the home of Alderman Bobby Rush, an ardent Evans backer who was unable to stop a slight movement to Daley among a core of middle-class whites and blacks living in the northeast end of his bailiwick.[39]

As for Vrdolyak, except for his home 10th Ward (25 percent), his ward percentages were all in low-to-middle single digits.

A precinct-by-precinct analysis reveals the scope of Daley's victory. Daley won 1,672 (57.4 percent) of the city's 2,911 precincts. Evans carried 1,237 precincts, and Vrdolyak won the previously mentioned lowly total of two precincts.

Of Daley's 1,672 precinct victories in the general election (he won 1,667 in the primary), Precinct 7 in the Far Northwest Side 38th Ward provided him with his biggest margin of victory, 613 votes. In forty-nine other precincts, Daley beat either Vrdolyak or Evans by over

500 votes. These 500-plus-margin precincts were scattered among fifteen city wards. Though most of these wards were situated on the Northwest and Southwest Sides, the lakefront 46th Ward and the downtown 1st Ward also had 500-plus precincts for Daley. However, the winner's home 11th Ward voters once again led the way in proving their affection for their favorite son by providing him with the most 500-plus-margin precincts (seven) and the only three perfect shutout precincts in the city. In the 11th Ward precincts 6, 37, and 43, Evans and Vrdolyak combined received 0 votes.

Evans was unable to match Daley's precinct landslides. Only five precincts gave Evans 500-plus victory margins. His best precinct was in Ward 8, Precinct 32. This Far South Side, middle-class area gave Evans a 595-vote victory margin. However, two years earlier, this same massive, nearly all-black precinct gave Harold Washington a 793-vote margin. Moreover, in the 1987 general election, Washington's two opponents, Vrdolyak and Haider, received a grand total of 3 votes, whereas in 1989 Daley alone received 32 votes. Clearly, Evans did extremely well in this precinct, but it was not the monster landslide of Washington proportions that he so desperately needed to compete with Daley. Unfortunately for Evans, some Washington voters stayed home, and a contingent of the former mayor's supporters switched to Daley.

Postmortems on Daley's victory and low black turnout were quick to come and varied. Some speculated that black voter dropoff and switching resulted from the feud between Sawyer and Evans; others claimed that it was a plot by money-rich Daleyites, who lured black voters into a state of complacency and apathy; still others blamed the lackluster turnout on the city's black political leadership in post-Washington Chicago. For Rich Daley it mattered little—he had the electoral coalition and the votes.

An incredibly accurate *New York Times* exit poll (it came within a few tenths of a percent of predicting the exact final vote totals) revealed perhaps the most important fact of Daley's victory. All issues of race, campaign war chests, feuds, and campaign strategies aside, the *New York Times* poll showed that 30 percent of Daley voters in 1989 had voted for Harold Washington in 1987. The Daley switchovers were largely lakefronters and Hispanics, with a smattering of pro-Washington ethnics and some blacks. The new mayor's illustrious father had been fond of saying "politics is a game of addition." In 1989, his eldest son followed this advice by reaching out to add new voters and voting blocs to his campaign while his opponents ignored the old rule and engaged in the politics of subtraction by circling their wagons around their existing committed bedrock supporters. Daley won— they lost.

NOTES

1. Personal interview.
2. Chicago *Defender*, March 2, 1989.
3. Chicago *Tribune*, March 5, 1989.
4. Personal interview.
5. Chicago *Defender*, March 15, 1989.
6. Chicago *Defender*, March 28, 1989. ˘
7. Personal interview.
8. Chicago *Sun-Times*, March 10, 1989. Daley's three-person transition team was like almost everything else in his campaign— governmentally and politically astute. The members were:
   1. Clark Burrus—a noted black businessman, chairman of the Chicago Transit Authority, and transition chairman for former mayors Harold Washington and Eugene Sawyer.
   2. John Schmidt, a prominent Chicago lawyer with close ties to lakefront reformers. A Daley friend, Schmidt was active in issues development and fund-raising for the campaign.
   3. Miriam Santos, a young Hispanic lawyer employed by Illinois Bell. Santos would be named city treasurer soon after Daley became mayor. She replaced Cecil Partee, who resigned to take Daley's old spot as Cook County state's attorney.
9. Chicago *Tribune*, March 19, 1989.
10. Chicago *Sun-Times*, March 26, 1989.
11. Three black Democratic committeemen who did endorse Daley, their party's nominee, were County Board Commissioner John Stroger (8), City Treasurer Cecil Partee (20), and Board of Tax Appeals member Wilson Frost (34).
12. Chicago *Sun-Times*, March 11, 1989.
13. Chicago *Defender*, March 16, 1989.
14. Chicago *Sun-Times*, March 21, 1989.
15. Chicago *Tribune*, March 31, 1989.
16. Chicago *Sun-Times*, March 28, 1989.
17. Chicago *Tribune*, March 2, 1989.
18. Ibid. The *Tribune* claimed Vrdolyak fit at least three of the four categories.
19. Chicago *Sun-Times*, March 3, 1989.
20. Chicago *Defender*, March 7, 1989.
21. Chicago *Sun-Times*, March 28, 1989.
22. Personal interview.
23. Vrdolyak's one-minute debate summation will go down as a classic in Chicago political history. Among other things, he accused Evans of dividing the black community by "embarking on a cruel crusade to cripple Mayor Sawyer. . . ." Chicago *Sun-Times*, March 22, 1989.

24. Chicago *Tribune*, April 4, 1989.
25. Chicago *Sun-Times*, March 5, 1989.
26. Ibid.
27. Some insiders have speculated that Sawyer enjoyed watching his one-time adversaries come hat in hand seeking his endorsements for Evans. According to one black committeeman, who insisted on anonymity, "even a class act like Gene is not above seeking a little revenge against his enemies."
28. Chicago *Sun-Times*, March 14, 1989.
29. Chicago *Sun-Times*, March 30, 1989.
30. Chicago *Sun-Times*, April 4, 1989.
31. Personal interview.
32. Chicago *Tribune*, April 5, 1989.
33. I am the author of the line, and many Daley supporters enjoyed yelling it back at me as I observed their celebration.
34. Chicago *Sun-Times*, April 5, 1989.
35. Ibid.
36. Ibid.
37. Chicago *Tribune*, April 5, 1989.
38. Six wards, 13, 23, 41, 45, 38, and 36, gave Daley a larger vote margin than Evans received in his best ward, 21.
39. In the 2nd Ward, Daley received 30 percent of the increased voter turnout between the primary and general election, when his numbers are compared against those of Sawyer and Evans.

Young Richard M. Daley (*top*), son of Richard J. Daley, politicking with his family in his father's first mayoral campaign in 1955. (*Holime*)

A 1974 photo of Chicago Mayor Richard J. Daley and his son, State Senator Richard M. Daley. Old pro Daley took great pride in his son's fledging political career. *(Office of the Mayor)*

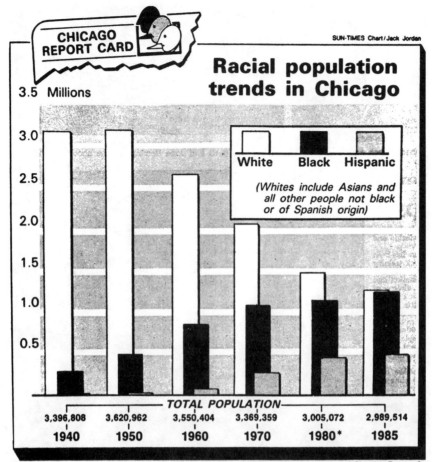

SUN-TIMES Chart / Jack Jordan

CHICAGO REPORT CARD

Racial population trends in Chicago

3.5 Millions

3.0

2.5

2.0

1.5

1.0

0.5

☐ White ■ Black ☐ Hispanic

(Whites include Asians and all other people not black or of Spanish origin)

──── TOTAL POPULATION ────

| 3,396,808 | 3,620,962 | 3,550,404 | 3,369,359 | 3,005,072 | 2,989,514 |
| 1940 | 1950 | 1960 | 1970 | 1980* | 1985 |

SOURCES: Sun-Times analysis of U.S. Census tracts for 1940-1960 figures. City of Chicago Dept. of Planning analysis of U.S. Census figures for 1970-1985 figures. *Asians represent 66,673 of the white population.

Demography is destiny in Chicago politics. The close racial balance requires multi-ethnic coalition building for any mayoral aspirant. *(Chicago Sun-Times)*

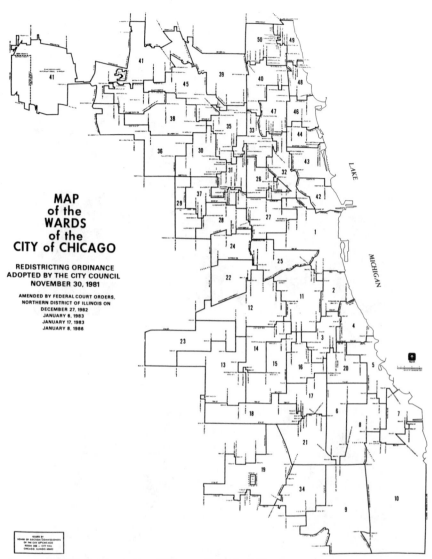

MAP
of the
WARDS
of the
CITY of CHICAGO

REDISTRICTING ORDINANCE
ADOPTED BY THE CITY COUNCIL
NOVEMBER 30, 1981

AMENDED BY FEDERAL COURT ORDERS,
NORTHERN DISTRICT OF ILLINOIS ON
DECEMBER 27, 1982
JANUARY 6, 1983
JANUARY 17, 1983
JANUARY 8, 1986

A map of Chicago's wards. *(Chicago Board of Elections)*

In 1986, Luis Gutierrez's election as alderman (26) gave Mayor Harold Washington control of the city council for the first time. Gutierrez, a loyal supporter of Washington's programs, in 1989 would split with many of his former allies and endorse Rich Daley. *(Holime)*

Harold Washington displaying the *Chicago Sun-Times* following his renomination victory over Jane Byrne in 1987. It is doubtful that any black politician in Chicago will ever match the intensity of support that Washington received from the African-American community. Washington (to use one of his favorite lines) was *sui generis* to black voters. *(Chicago Sun-Times)*

A host of mourners gathered at Harold Washington's bier, including the major actors in Chicago's continuing mayoral drama. From left to right are: Ald. Bobby Rush (2), Ald. Anna Langford (16), Ald. Eugene Sawyer (6), Ald. Jesus Garcia (22), Rev. Jesse Jackson, Ald. Tim Evans (4), Ald. Danny Davis (29), and Cong. Gus Savage (2). *(Chicago Sun-Times)*

Cook County Board President and Democratic Party Chairman George Dunne *(right)* and Ald. Eugene Sawyer (6). Dunne told Chicago's white aldermen that Washington's successor had to be black. *(Monroe Anderson)*

Chicago's second African-American mayor, Eugene Sawyer. A gentle and gracious man, Sawyer never was able to overcome the furor that surrounded his selection by the city council to succeed the late Mayor Washington, who died in November of 1987. (*Monroe Anderson*)

Acting Mayor Eugene Sawyer (*left*) and his press secretary, Monroe Anderson. Sawyer, in a brief sixteen-month term and under much pressure, turned in a creditable record of pushing through a needed tax increase, breaking a taxi monopoly, and getting the ball rolling for development at O'Hare International Airport. (*Monroe Anderson*)

PART TWO

Voting Blocs in the 1989 Mayoral Election

The white community is now united for the first time in a decade.

Alderman Edward M. Burke (1990)

. . . older and more conservative constituents—who were regular voters—often resented their portrayal of Hispanics as an underprivileged minority group that shared common interests with blacks. Instead, these older constituents viewed themselves as part of an immigrant American tradition that believed in working hard within the system. . . . These Hispanics shunned the liberal view that blamed the system for society's failures. And they viewed with suspicion the Hispanic leaders' alliance with the black community.

Jorge Casuso (1990)

What Richard Daley offered to the lakefront was a combination of what the lakefront . . . always wanted. It wanted an efficient, honest operation that works well and is reasonably progressive on social issues.

David Axelrod, media advisor, Daley campaign (1990)

CHAPTER 3

White Ethnics

Alderman Edward M. Burke

The mayoral race of 1989 was a triumph for the regular Democratic organization. It should not in any way be viewed as a return to "machine" politics, but instead as an affirmation of traditional politics. By that I mean legwork politics on behalf of the regular organization candidate—the kind of effort that used to elect mayors, and even presidents, before the advent of television.

This is not to say that television did not play a major role in the campaign, but rather to point out that Richard M. Daley succeeded in reaching the people through tried-and-true methods, not sound bites and photo opportunities. Solid advance work and an unrelenting campaign schedule took him to every ward in the city— white, black, and Hispanic. Of course, the TV cameras were there, but candidate Daley—who opened his campaign with the confession that he was not "the best talker"—did a good job of playing to the crowd, not the cameras.

Daley's opening tack struck an empathetic chord amongst the so-called white ethnics—Irish, Italian, Polish, and Eastern European—who happily elected his father six times in a row despite the senior Daley's convoluted syntax. Great oratorical skill is not a high priority among this segment of the electorate, many of whom still cherish the fractured language of their immigrant ancestors. In contrast, the colorful, fiery speaking styles of black leaders such as Harold Washington and the Reverend Jesse Jackson appeal to their constituents, and it could probably be argued that Eugene Sawyer's soft-spoken style may have contributed to his limited appeal among black voters this year.

It is no secret that white ethnics were not viewed as members of the much-touted Harold Washington coalition, and 1989 was the first election in ten years that offered these voters a regular Democratic candidate from their own ranks in the general election. Recall that Jane Byrne ran against the organization, even though she was a product of it—just as, most insiders would agree, Harold Washington was.

Needless to say, the fact that Rich Daley happened to be the son of Chicago's most popular, most enduring, and, in many ways, most effective mayor—not to mention his namesake—provided white ethnic voters with an easy choice, and provided committeemen in white ethnic wards with an easy task in getting out the vote.

The formula for Rich Daley's victory was simple: play it straight and stay above the fray. The strategy obviously appealed to white ethnics, who were tired of confrontation politics, infighting in the black community, and reform politicians attacking "the machine," when it was not so long ago that the machine—far from being a dirty word—was credited with making Chicago "the city that works."

Nevertheless, his victory will not be a return to the days of patronage politics, as some have suggested. Those days are gone forever and even the most cynical revisionists do not believe that the mayor's office can ever be the patronage cornucopia it was before Shakman. And Rich Daley would not want it to be.

At the least, the Daley administration can be a respite from the confusion of the past decade—four different mayors in ten years, council wars, Greylord, budget deficits, upheavals in the executive suite, and elections that turn on such factors as the weather. Voters of every ethnic stripe view this election as a chance for the politicians to stop fighting and start taking care of the problems in the city, such as crime, education, and transportation needs.

White ethnics tend to regard the death of Richard J. Daley in 1976 as the end of an era that has given way to divisions in the white community—divisions that gave the city its first woman mayor and its first black mayor. Although these developments may have met with resistance from old-line party regulars, ultimately they can and should take pride in them. It is, nevertheless, the case that the city government has undergone dramatic fluctuations with each new administration since 1976; but, given the duration of the elder Daley's reign, such fluctuations were inevitable.

It is somewhat ironic that the man now positioned to rescue Chicago from the confusion that followed the death of Richard J. Daley should be his son. Back in 1983, Richard M. was viewed as a spoiler in challenging incumbent Jane Byrne for the nomination, a move that paved the way for Washington.

Although there was no question then, as now, of Richard M. Daley's qualifications to run the city, there may have been some resentment of him for bucking tradition by challenging the incumbent and, as a result, splitting the white vote. Traditions die hard in the City of the Big Shoulders, and there has been an unspoken tradition among party regulars that you go further by waiting your turn than by challenging the incumbent.

Rich Daley's advantage in '89 was that there were no veterans from the white ethnic ranks to contend with. Jane Byrne's loss to the lesser known Aurelia Pucinski in the Democratic primary for clerk of the circuit court reinforced the perception that she was no longer mayoral material, and the only other ex-mayor, Michael Bilandic, was happily ensconced as an appellate court judge.

None of the likely contenders for the fifth-floor office was from the eldest ranks of the party, and quite a few, myself included, are only in their midforties. That is just a reflection of the changing makeup of the city council.

Formerly known as "The Gray Wolves" because of their age and, I suppose, their less-than-laudable images, Chicago's city council today includes twelve members under the age of forty, one under thirty, and only nine over sixty. The average age is forty-eight, two years older than the mayor, who is seven years younger than his father was when sworn in.

The past few elections have wrought many changes amongst the white ethnic segment of the electorate. People who were accustomed to voting the straight Democratic ticket for generations freely crossed party lines to support Ed Vrdolyak in '87 over Washington. But, despite Vrdolyak's undeniable popularity in Chicago, virtually none of the regular Democratic voters would cross party lines for Vrdolyak with Daley at the head of the ticket—and a man who almost won the mayoralty two years earlier as an independent could not even carry his own 10th Ward as a Republican.

This says that white ethnics, as a voting bloc, remain committed to the ideals of the Democratic party as it exists and has existed in Chicago. It also says that, despite the changes of the past decade, racial politics still runs deep here and our candidates can exploit these prejudices if they so choose.

Hopefully this kind of divisiveness will come to an end. It should be remembered that the black community in Chicago has been a cornerstone of the regular Democratic organization since the 1930s. Under the late Congressman William Dawson, five black wards consistently delivered overwhelming pluralities for the party in local as well as national elections.

White ethnics remain a majority bloc in the city, but the past ten years have shown that they are nowhere near as dominant as they once were. They must cooperate with minority voting blocs or they will compromise their political goals. Chicago is a different city today than it was even ten years ago. Hispanics, Asians, and nonethnic white voters, who are generally characterized as "lakefront" voters, represent growing segments of the electorate. The Hispanic population in particular is young and not very politically active yet, but in time it could represent anywhere from 20 to 30 percent of the electorate.

Nobody understood the changing makeup of the electorate more than Harold Washington, but the lesson was far from lost on Richard M. Daley, and it showed in his campaign as well as in his appointments following his election.

He is poised to take the city into the last decade of the century. He is of an age that he can hold on to his job for a while if he can keep enough people happy. He knows that means that his appointees and his programs must reflect the city's rich cultural diversity.

Acting Mayor Eugene Sawyer and Alderman Tim Evans also know this, but forgot that a divided black community is no strength at all. Just as Daley and Byrne opened the door for Washington, so did Evans and Sawyer open the door for Daley. The swing voters—Hispanics, lakefront whites—certainly lived up to their name by coming out solidly for Daley, despite claims by the Evans camp that he was the rightful heir to their support.

The white community is now united for the first time in a decade and, with Sawyer's political future on the shelf for the time being, perhaps the black community will rally fully behind Evans, who is promising a mayoral run in 1991. However, he will not even be a contender if he fails to reunite the Washington coalition, and that starts in his own backyard. If he cannot pull together the blacks, he will stand little chance of drawing Hispanic and white support.

Chicago will likely continue to draw on the black and ethnic white segments of the electorate for its leaders in the immediate future, but neither segment will ever be successful if they underestimate the rest of the voters. As we have seen, Washington's coalition was just that—Washington's. It did not hold together for Evans, it did not line up for Alderman Lawrence Bloom's abortive candidacy, and it will not reemerge by itself without a good reason and a charismatic candidate to resurrect it.

Rich Daley will have to do something fatal for that to happen and, given the fact that the next election is just around the corner, it is unlikely that he will. More likely, he will take the wind out of his opponents' sails by playing his first term just like his campaign—clean, safe, and straight. White ethnics will love it, blacks will have little cause to complain, and the swing voters will remain content.

Furthermore, if the perceived differences between whites and blacks can be mended, as perhaps they will be under Mayor Daley, the Chicago Democratic political organization will once again become a potent unit of the national Democratic Party—even one that can rival its heyday in 1960, when it was considered the John Kennedy king maker.

I might add that Chicago's racial divisions reflect the divisions that plague the party on a national level—divisions that have yielded just one Democratic president in two decades. Party unity gave us

Roosevelt and Kennedy in the White House; disunity gave us Nixon, Reagan, and Bush. The once solidly Democratic South has gone Republican as liberals such as McGovern, Mondale, and Dukakis have reached out for the support of the growing black political community. Again, no Democratic candidate has emerged on the national level with the persuasive powers to keep old-line Catholics, Jews, blacks, southern whites, northern liberals, and union members under one umbrella.

As a lifelong Democrat, the son of an alderman, and an alderman myself for two decades, I know the importance of maintaining unity. Ethnic identifications mean less today than when I was first elected in 1969, and the significance of whether someone is white, Hispanic, Asian, black, Catholic, Jewish, Muslim, Baptist, or atheist will continue to decline.

We all want better schools, safer streets, steady jobs, and unlimited opportunity. Rich Daley did a good job in Campaign '89 of avoiding the issues that divide and focusing on the issues that unite. The politician who keeps that in mind in forging his agenda will enjoy the broadest support and create the strongest organization. Self-evident as that statement may seem, it is all too often forgotten in the heat of the campaign.

CHAPTER 4

Hispanics

Jorge Casuso

With the special 1989 mayoral election just weeks away, 26th Ward Alderman Luis Gutierrez was faced with a political decision he knew would change the course of his ambitious career: Should he endorse the candidacy of Alderman Timothy Evans, who had been anointed as Harold Washington's legitimate successor by all of the allies who had helped Gutierrez rise to the top? Or should he back State's Attorney Richard M. Daley, whose candidacy was viewed by Gutierrez's camp as the return of the dreaded "machine" their alderman had run for office to crush?

The choice seemed obvious, Gutierrez's long-time supporters thought. After all, it was the high-strung alderman's fire-and-brimstone speech after Washington's death that had urged them to march on city hall in support of Evans.

But now, on a sleet-swept January night, the diehard Gutierrez workers who had gathered for the slate-making vote watched in angry disbelief as the alderman they had helped elect threw the support of his ward organization behind the son of Richard J. Daley, the late "boss" of "the machine."

Overnight, Gutierrez's cleverly orchestrated slating earned him the code names "the tyrant," "the renegade," "the defector," "the traitor." But the rancor he had incurred among his most loyal supporters was a small price to pay for what he could gain. For Gutierrez's decision to endorse Daley was not based on a whim, nor on a sudden change of heart. It was a carefully calculated move that, if it paid off, would pay off big.

* * *

A Chicago *Tribune* poll conducted in early December had helped reinforce Gutierrez's hunch. The telephone poll of 201 registered Hispanic voters showed that in a one-on-one showdown with Evans, Daley would win with 81 percent of the vote. Many Hispanic voters felt that Daley could continue the calmer, more stable reign of his father, whom they recalled fondly. They remembered the mayor who, years ago, had cut ribbons and handed out plaques and favors.

In addition, the fractious political wars that for five years had divided the city made them only more willing to forget the stranglehold of Daley's political machine on Chicago's Hispanic communities.

Forgotten were the reigns of Vito Marzullo and Thomas Keane, long-time Daley ward bosses who ran the city's Mexican and Puerto Rican communities like fiefdoms. For years these aldermen ignored the changes that had transformed the once Polish, Irish, Italian, and East European enclaves. These men became powerful, and, in Keane's case, wealthy, politicians, and they handed out patronage jobs to their loyal white ethnic constituents and cleaned and repaired their streets, while Hispanic sections decayed in neglect.

But that legacy was forgotten on February 18, when Daley and Mayor Eugene Sawyer faced off in the Democratic primary. According to an exit poll by the Midwest Voter Registration Education Project, 68 percent of Hispanic voters pulled the lever for Daley, whose backers and allies had been the lifeblood of the old machine. Daley was more qualified, the voters told the pollsters. And besides, it was time for a change.

On April 4, Hispanic voters reiterated their solid support, giving Daley 71 percent of the vote to Evans's 20 percent and Republican candidate Edward Vrydolyak's 9 percent in the general election, according to the exit poll. It seemed that in just two weeks, Hispanic voters had veered away from the "progressive" course charted by liberal Hispanic politicians under Washington's four and a half years in office.

* * *

Until Harold Washington's 1983 mayoral election, only one Hispanic alderman, Joseph "Jose" Martinez, had sat on the city council in recent memory. (A long-forgotten Mexican alderman, William Emilio Rodriguez, who considered himself a German socialist, had served on the council from 1915 to 1918, and had run for mayor in 1911.) Martinez, an unknown lawyer with ties to former alderman Keane's brother, had been appointed in 1981 by Mayor Jane Byrne as a way of courting the city Puerto Rican vote. The appointment was a favor to Keane, who had been convicted of mail fraud and stripped of his seat, but who had found the time to deftly draw new ward boundaries that kept the mayor's allies in power. It was that very map that Mexican and Puerto Rican activists had challenged in court, a challenge that forced the creation of four majority Hispanic wards.

By Washington's 1987 reelection, four Hispanic aldermen had joined the fifty-member council. Three of them, Aldermen Jesus Garcia (22), Raymond Figueroa (31), and Gutierrez, had been swept to victory by the rock-solid support of black voters. The fourth, Alderman Juan Soliz (25), had won his first election to the state house in 1984 on the strength of Washington's black followers.

But although Hispanic activists chalked up their victory to the triumph of the much-touted "black-Hispanic coalition," the results were not so clear cut. Faced with "machine" and "independent" Hispanic candidates, Hispanic voters—contrary to popular belief—did not vote overwhelmingly for the "independent" candidate. For although Hispanics had been empowered by the Washington movement, they had not completely shed their traditional alliance to white politicians. It was an alliance that for years saw Hispanic voters oppose the scrappy, under-funded Hispanic challengers who periodically surfaced and fell during the pre-Washington era.

* * *

The liberal, second-generation Hispanic activists who rallied behind Washington's candidacy were only the most vocal political faction within Chicago's diverse Hispanic communities. The products of the civil rights movement, they deftly courted the media, which appreciated their flair for rhetoric. Some of them, such as Garcia, were lifelong residents of Chicago. Others, such as Soliz, had moved here to launch their careers. Gutierrez, on the other hand, had moved back and forth between Chicago and Puerto Rico. Wherever they were raised, they had few ties to the mainstream social clubs and mainstream community groups in Chicago's Hispanic neighborhoods. They launched their careers as outsiders, rallying attacks against the established political organization.

But their older and more conservative constituents—who were regular voters—often resented their portrayal of Hispanics as an underprivileged minority group that shared common interests with blacks. Instead, these older constituents viewed themselves as part of an immigrant American tradition that believed in working hard within the system. Many had joined labor unions, lodges and, most American of all, the Democratic party. These Hispanics shunned the liberal view that blamed the system for society's failures. And they viewed with suspicion the Hispanic leaders' alliance with the black community. Faced with the choice between Democratic candidate Harold Washington and unknown Republican candidate Bernard Epton, many Mexican voters, who are staunch Democrats, voted against the black candidate in the 1983 general election.

During Washington's first term in office, some of these older Hispanics warmed up to the congenial mayor, and more of them joined younger, more liberal Hispanic voters, who gave Washington a larger mandate in 1987. But after Washington's death, it became apparent that the tenuous black-Hispanic coalition that had been held together by a charismatic personality was broken. Only Washington had the capacity to build bridges across the city's two segregated communities. Without Washington or an ideological ally such as Evans as mayor, the new breed of Hispanic leaders stood to lose much of their power.

And so, Gutierrez's choice paid off. While the other three Hispanic aldermen watch Daley's administration from the sidelines, Gutierrez has become its Hispanic spokesman, his face constantly grinning from the pages of Spanish-language newspapers, his words beamed across the airwaves. He has become a Hispanic power broker of sorts, approving high-level Hispanic hires, chairing the housing committee, and dining with real estate moguls.

But Gutierrez's dilemma, and the controversy his decision provoked, is not over. It will be replayed by Hispanic politicians as they face the same predicament in the new decade. As a political operator with ties to the Washington coalition put it, "The train was already pulling out from the station, and Luis jumped on board."

With little chance that Daley will be unseated any time soon, Gutierrez's colleagues must now decide whether to chase the train or wait by the tracks for one that may not come.

CHAPTER 5

Lakefronters

Greg Hinz

In the mythology of Chicago politics, the North Side lakefront is the great bastion of those "L"-folks whose name Michael Dukakis could not bear to name. It is the home of trendy quiche-eating-and-chardonnay-quaffing liberals, do-gooders who, if not quite as far to the left as in antiwar days, still will labor to save whales, the disenfranchised, and political reformers.

As with all good myths, this one is part fact and part fantasy.

For certain, the six wards that stretch north from the Loop to suburban Evanston do respond to a mix of social liberalism, prudent fiscal policy, and antiestablishment calls to throw out the grafters. The lakefront sired just about the only opposition Richard J. Daley faced in the latter years of his reign, sending reformer Bill Singer and later Dick Simpson and David Orr to the city council. It gave its votes to blue-ribbon Republican candidates such as Governor James Thompson and former State's Attorney Bernard Carey, but has not voted in decades for a Republican for president. Ronald Reagan, for all his extraordinary popularity, never carried a lakefront ward. Instead, the lakefront wards are the kind of place where one state representative, Ellis Levin, regularly reports 90-plus percent margins for legal abortion on his constituent surveys.

Simultaneously, that same lakefront gave Edward Vrdolyak—the ultimate dark, conservative, race-rattling figure of Chicago politics—a plurality over Harold Washington in Chicago's 1987 general mayoral election. In fact Mr. Washington, although garnering crucial votes on the lakefront, never could top 44.5 percent of its vote, his figure against Jane Byrne in the 1987 Democratic primary. Washington actually got a smaller share of the general-election lakefront vote in 1987 (40.2 percent) than he did in 1983 (40.8 percent). Even though Chicagoans had had four years to observe that he had not turned city hall over to Jesse Jackson and Louis Farrakhan. Even though the city's media in this media-conscious area unanimously backed Washington. Even though Washington advisors crafted his message that he had returned power to the neighborhoods with a particular eye toward quality-of-life-conscious lakefronters.

The lakefront is actually "an integrated microcosm of the city as a whole," in the words of long-time Vrdolyak political advisor Joe Novak. "It reflects all parts of the city." White lakefronters may be twice as willing to back a black mayoral contender as their ethnic peers in the Northwest and Southwest Side bungalow belt, conceded Washington and later Richard M. Daley consultant David Axelrod. But three to four times as many consistently voted for white mayoral candidates in the '80s, he adds.

In some ways, the lakefront is, to borrow a New York City term, Chicago's Upper East Side. Its southern- and eastern-most reaches glitter with soaring high-rises and restored Victorian homes filled with lawyers, bankers, journalists and other power brokers, many of them Jewish. But to the north, the lakefront is a bit of the South Bronx. Each of its northern three wards, the 46th, 48th, and 49th, is about 40 percent black and Hispanic, according to the latest population estimates from the Chicago Department of Planning. And all six wards, on their west ends, retain a Catholic parish-oriented, single-family-home character quite in keeping with that of white ethnic neighborhoods well to the west. Call them Queens.

What all that meant, in terms of the 1989 mayoral election, is that the lakefront, along with Hispanic neighborhoods, was the only area of the city with an even somewhat substantial swing vote. The Northwest and Southwest Sides could be counted on to vote overwhelmingly white, the South and West Sides overwhelmingly black. Perhaps a third of lakefront votes were legitimately up for grabs. The question for the candidates was how to snatch them.

* * *

Although he entered the campaign season as the clear favorite on the lakefront, State's Attorney Richard M. Daley had reason to be cautious. Acting Mayor Eugene Sawyer, after a creaky start, had begun to reap at least the financial rewards of incumbency. A second primary foe, Hyde Park Alderman Lawrence Bloom (5), was a North Side lakefronter in spirit if not in geographic fact, a sharp-speaking political reformer known for blasting patronage waste and Vrdolyak the Evil. Most significantly, though, the often self-conscious, ill-at-ease Daley had suffered a very painful belly flop in the six lakefront wards in his 1983 race for mayor, drawing not even a third of the vote despite worshipful press coverage and ringing endorsements from such lakefront leaders as former Alderman Marty Oberman (43) and State Senator Dawn Clark Netsch. Moreover, advisors such as Axelrod were telling him that merely "winning" the lakefront would not be enough. To insure against the possibility that Sawyer could somehow work out things with his foe and fellow black, Alderman Timothy Evans (4), Daley would have to run somewhere around 60 percent of the vote, nearly twice his 1983 vote.

But if Daley faced hills, Sawyer and Bloom had to climb mountains.

Sawyer was bedeviled from the beginning by a soft personality that ran counter to a Chicago-wide tradition of selecting a tough chief executive to keep "gray wolf" aldermen in check. The first taste most Chicagoans got of Sawyer was on the night the city council selected him to be acting mayor; he literally fainted and then changed his mind three times before finally accepting the job. Then he appeared indecisive at best in deciding how to discipline aide Steve Cokely, who delivered a series of politically devastating speeches suggesting that Jews were deliberately infecting black babies with AIDS and was otherwise guilty of serious offenses.

Sawyer was the kind of guy who, almost unbelievably for a mayor, would order a limo carrying him and a traveling reporter to pull over in a parking lot for forty-five minutes because he was running ahead of schedule. Nice, but not tough. When the fact that Evans North Side allies such as Alderman Helen Shiller (46) and organizer Don Rose were sitting out the Democratic primary was added, Sawyer's task was monumental.

Bloom's obstacle course was, if anything, harder. He had to convince voters and financiers that he was in the race, that money and votes pledged to him would not be wasted.

Bloom did score some favorable ratings in the early polls. One *Tribune* survey showed him with a quite respectable 19 percent of the vote in what turned out to be the eventual three-way contest among him, Daley, and Sawyer. But what got the big coverage in the *Tribune* that day was its second finding, that Bloom would get only 5 percent in a much larger field. The higher 19 percent number "was in the last paragraph of the story, on page 23 or something like that," a bitter Bloom recalls. "I had a chance with lakefront voters if I could have shown a possibility of winning." The *Tribune's* story—"either an error or a deliberate mistake"—was devastating.

Whatever remaining chance Bloom had vanished after his grating, miserable performance in the sole televised TV debate. "Like chalk on a blackboard," Axelrod summarized. City hall reporters put it a little more bluntly on a mockingly libelous bulletin board they run in the city hall press room. Bloom is "the only Jew in Chicago without money" the board declared.

The Sawyer/Bloom foibles left the well-funded Daley in position to stick to a careful, cautious high road, big on bland, carefully calibrated paid-media pitches, and light on dangerous TV and radio talk shows.

"It was clear from the beginning that the lakefront was ready for change. There was a general sense of drift," Axelrod puts it. "It was clear that constituency above all would respond to the message that we needed strong leadership to get beyond the politics of race and controversy" of the council wars era. "The Cokely episode underscored the weakness issue. . . . Bloom played a Socratic role. He was viewed as a good critic, but not as someone who could run the city." Ergo, Daley's seemingly unending TV spots plugged the message, "It takes a strong leader to move a great city forward."

Says former Alderman Singer, a major Daley backer who eventually became vice chairman of the Interim Board of Education, "What Richard Daley offered to the lakefront was a combination of what the lakefront, in my opinion, always wanted. It wanted an efficient, honest operation that works well and is reasonably progressive on social issues." The strategy was to tell the lakefront just that.

A somewhat riskier part of the strategy was Daley's decision to make an all-out effort to capture what became the political darling of Election '89, the North Side's sizable if disorganized gay voting bloc.

No one knows the size of Chicago's gay community, centered on the lakefront, or how many of its members carry a gay identity into the polling booth. Bob Adams, executive director of the Impact gay political action fund, estimates "a minimum of 20,000 gays" among 180,000 or so registered lakefront voters. The Illinois Gay and Lesbian Task Force's Tim Drake cites a higher figure, 35,000 to 40,000, but concedes that perhaps half will vote along other lines without a good reason to oppose one or another candidate. The best independent figures can be drawn from the 1987 election, when gay physician Ron Sable came within a couple of thousand votes of upsetting Regular Democratic incumbent Bernard Hansen. The Sable race, combined with a hugely successful gay voter-registration drive, helped the pro-gay Mr. Washington pick up 4,800 votes in the 44th Ward between the 1983 and 1987 Democratic primaries, about 1,000 above his gains in other lakefront wards.

All of that convinced the political establishment that the gay vote was the fulcrum that levered the key lakefront that could swing the citywide total. And thus every major mayoral candidate except Vrdolyak lobbied hard on behalf of a gay civil rights law that ended up passing the city council around the time candidate petitions were filed in December 1988. The suddenly pro-gay field of candidates ended up mostly nullifying each other's gay credentials. But the gamble was worth it because it came at little risk. In the Chicago political environment, "voters on the Northwest and Southwest Sides aren't affected by special pitches to the lakefront," Novak says. "The Northwest Side grumbled some about Daley's gay rights pitch. But, in the crassest terms, people on the Northwest and Southwest Sides only wanted to vote for a winning white mayoral candidate."

In the end, Daley ended up surpassing his handlers' fondest hopes in the primary. He got 68 percent of the vote, compared to 28 percent for Sawyer and 1 percent for the by then dropped-out Bloom. "The mood of the lakefront matched the message of our campaign, and the message of our campaign matched the mood of the lakefront," said Axelrod. "Lakefront voters are socially liberal because they see social liberalism as necessary for a positive quality of life. . . . Daley comes across as someone focused on local [quality-of-life] issues." Bloom sees it a lot differently. Echoing Washington's crucial by mediocre lakefront showings, he concludes that, in 1989, lakefront votes "went for the white candidate who could win."

* * *

If the lakefront shares anything with the rest of Chicago, it is a fundamental, almost instinctive loyalty to Democratic mayoral candidates in the April general election. The only partial modern-day exception was the Harold Washington/Bernard Epton clash in 1983. The 1989 race was not to be another.

Vrdolyak, with one foot already in the political grave, was a joke from the beginning. He was never popular on the lakefront, and was seen only as a rough-edged alternative to black control at city hall. With Daley nominated, there was no reason to even give Vrdolyak a hearing. "You know how ex-boxing champions, in their declining years, sometimes turn professional wrestler to make few bucks?" asks an operative for another candidate who asked not to be named. "It was kind of like that with Eddie. 'Come see the once-great Ed Vrdolyak wrestle an alligator.' "

The Evans camp had somewhat brighter hopes. After all its candidate was fundamentally a nonthreatening political insider, a well-to-do, pinstriped Kenwood attorney (Kenwood is an attractive, affluent neighborhood north of Hyde Park) and long-term Democratic committeeman who needed Washington's help to defeat independent Toni Preckwinkle in the 4th Ward's 1987 aldermanic election. Evans also had the services of crack organizer Don Rose, who played a crucial role in Jane Byrne's 1979 upset of Michael Bilandic.

But the split with Sawyer left Evans's black base split. It forced him to appear to cater to the some of the city's most controversial figures, such as Uptown organizer Slim Coleman and the outspoken

Alderman Dorothy Tillman (3). Neither would help on the lakefront, or with the black businessmen that Evans desperately needed to fund TV ads.

"Race was less important on the lakefront than in other areas. I just wasn't able to get enough of them to hear my issues," Evans says today. "We needed at least another $500,000. We didn't have it."

Axelrod argues that Evans was miscast from the beginning, a Mc-Luhanesque "cool" figure playing a "hot" leader of a movement. "Evans has the soul of an accountant. . . . He basically is a middle-class guy, a devoted family man. But, in order to beat Sawyer, he needed to be way out on the fringe. He was trying to be something he wasn't: Harold Washington, a super black leader."

Evans smiles at that, because there were two men Axelrod approached for work early in the campaign: Richard M. Daley, and Timothy Evans. "If I was not what I appeared to be, why would he [Axelrod] come to me?" Evans asks. "I believe in what I said. I discussed issues the press just didn't cover. I was, and am, the progressive candidate."

The final general election vote in the six lakefront wards: Daley 72 percent, Evans 22 percent, Vrdolyak 4 percent.

* * *

Where do the 1989 mayoral election totals leave a lakefront that, slowly but surely, continues to gentrify from south to north, with the current dividing line somewhere just north of Irving Park Boulevard? Will it become more like Arlington Heights, solidly mainstream Republican, or the lakeshore suburb of Evanston, pricey and tony but still mostly Democratic and mostly liberal?

The answer is as varied as the election totals.

Singer, who in some ways can be credited with launching the lakefront's independent era in his 1969 election as alderman, agrees the lakefront has changed as baby boomers have aged. But he draws a line: "Lakefronters also may not be as liberal as everyone thought, but they are significantly more socially progressive than other Chicagoans." Singer further argues that his former allies, black progressives, have changed as much or more than their white counterparts. "Social progressives of all backgrounds reject the Lu Palmers of the world," he says, referring to the head of the Black Independent Political Organization. "There are many blacks who have moved well beyond where blacks and whites united previously."

Bloom snaps a retort: "Blacks have lived through twenty years of seeing whites [such as Singer] fail to respond to black candidates like Harold Washington." In his view, the lakefront change has been significant but incremental. "What's significant? Five or seven or ten points?"

Axelrod, whose office wall bears the framed newspaper headlines "Harold Again!" and "Daley elected," sticks by his quality-of-life view. The key to the lakefront is immediate, inward issues, such as good schools, reasonable taxes, safe streets and, yes, a certain concern with racial equity, he says.

And Evans? "There never is a guarantee of winning in politics," he answers. "Race was less important there than elsewhere. . . . I don't think that they'll stick with Daley. They'll see him for what he is."

Ald. Edward Burke, from the Southwest Side 14th Ward, has been a major force in Chicago politics for two decades. Controversial, smart, and tough, Burke played a key role in the city council's selection of Eugene Sawyer to succeed Harold Washington. *(Holime)*

According to Eugene Sawyer's press secretary, Monroe Anderson, Rev. Jesse Jackson (right) was "bamboozled" by supporters of Ald. Tim Evans (4) into supporting Sawyer after Washington's death. During the 1989 campaign, Jackson became Sawyer's number one supporter, as this photo indicates. (Monroe Anderson)

Mayor Eugene Sawyer (right) and Police Superintendent Leroy Martin outside Wrigley Field (home of the Chicago Cubs) prior to the first night game held at the field. Sawyer was instrumental in pushing through an ordinance that allowed the Cubs' management to put lights in the ballpark. (Monroe Anderson)

Mayor Sawyer with Aaron Freeman (right), Chicago's leading political satirist, following a Say No to Drugs rally. Although he was criticized for his lack of political toughness, Sawyer, during his brief term, impressed many Chicagoans with his sincere commitment to the city. *(Monroe Anderson)*

Mayoral candidate Ald. Tim Evans (4) telling members of the City Club of Chicago why he would be a better mayor than his rivals. Evans never was able to capture the magic of the late Harold Washington. *(Don Neltnor—City Club)*

Tim Evans attending a Far North Side health fair sponsored by twenty Jewish organizations. During the campaign Evans tried hard to ease tensions between the city's African-American and Jewish populations. (*Chicago Sun-Times*)

Tim Evans (*with arm raised*) at the Ida B. Wells public housing project on the South Side, trying to rally black voters behind his candidacy. (*Chicago Sun-Times*)

Flamboyant and controversial Cong. Gus Savage (2) shoving local CBS-TV political reporter Mike Flannery following a heated discussion of Savage's alleged sexual misconduct toward a Peace Corp volunteer in Africa. Savage's belligerent attitude hurt both the Sawyer and the Evans campaigns. *(Chicago Sun-Times)*

The only televised debate among the Democratic mayoral primary candidates found Richard M. Daley performing better than expected. The participants were *(left to right)* moderator John Callaway of WTTW-TV *(back to camera)* and candidates Eugene Sawyer, Richard M. Daley, and Lawrence Bloom. *(Office of the Mayor)*

Long-shot Democratic mayoral candidate Ald. Lawrence Bloom (5) stressing his reform credentials at the City Club of Chicago. *(Don Neltnor—City Club)*

Dr. Herbert Sohn, the endorsed Republican candidate for mayor, who fell before the sudden write-in campaign of Edward Vrydolyak. *(Chris Robling)*

A picture for the archives: 1989 GOP mayoral candidate Edward Vrydolyak *(standing)*, the late Harold Washington's major nemesis during "council wars," shaking hands with Jesse Jackson during a radio show. Shown with the pair are *(left to right)* Bruce DuMont of WBEZ *(with headphones)*, Sam Panayotovich, 10th Ward GOP committeeman, and *(backs to camera)* Ald. Danny Davis (24) and political advisor Phil Krone. *(Don Neltnor)*

Candidate Edward Vrydolyak stopping for lunch at a Maxwell Street hotdog stand. Most of the time Vrdolyak's low-key campaign generated very little media or voter interest. *(Chicago Sun-Times)*

PART THREE

African-American Mayoral Politics in Chicago—After Washington

No one did anything to us, but us. We fell on the sword. . . . [Jesse] Jackson had been suckered into believing that Evans truly was the heir apparent. . . . [A] full year later . . . Jackson concluded that he was bamboozled.

Monroe Anderson, Mayor Sawyer's press secretary (1990)

A virtual model of middle-class integrationist rectitude, Evans came to be viewed . . . as a raging radical and black nationalist. At the same time . . . he had a difficult time shaking the stigma of his early career as a member of the old machine. . . . as a wolf in sheep's clothing, an old-line machine politician who held his community in poverty-pimp bondage to get votes.

Don Rose and Jim Andrews (1990)

CHAPTER 6

The Sawyer Saga:
A Journalist, Who Just
Happened to Be the Mayor's
Press Secretary, Speaks

Monroe Anderson

So there will be no doubt about where I am coming from or where I am going, let me say this first: Eugene Sawyer got a bum rap and a blunt shaft.

This is not the voice of Acting Mayor Sawyer's press secretary speaking, mind you, although there is the distinct possibility that you will hear it from time to time later on. But rather, this is the opinion of a veteran Chicago journalist who studied and covered Chicago politics for sixteen years before curiously crossing over to the other side. By the time the particular but peculiar political process of selecting Mayor Harold Washington's successor began on Thanksgiving Eve of 1987, I knew, either professionally or by reputation, quite a few of those cast in the background, many of those waiting in the wings, and most of the central players.

As a matter of record, I was the first reporter to predict publicly that the next mayor of Chicago could—contrary to the prevailing political wisdom—be black. I made that prediction in an op-ed page opinion piece I wrote in late September of 1982. The op-ed article ran in the Chicago *Tribune* on November 8th. On the same day, on the front page of the same issue of the *Tribune*, coincidentally, I also scooped every other reporter in town by breaking the story that Harold Washington was in the mayoral race.

I mention this only as a matter of background before attempting to sort out the Sawyer administration dilemma and the black political debacle that followed. Let me begin at the beginning, which, as everyone knows by now, actually was the end of the Washington era and African-American political power in Chicago. Oh, one last thing first.

As an African-American in Chicago, attempting to speak to African-Americans in Chicago, I am compelled to state the obvious: No one did anything to us, but us. We fell on the sword—and, as I write this—continue to complete our self-inflicted political disembowelment.

* * *

On December 2, 1987, I was a Midwest bureau correspondent for *Newsweek* magazine. Somewhere around 1:30 A.M., I turned off my television set and called it a night. That was some time after the Evans faction began playing parliamentary procedure. I covered city hall for the *Tribune* for a short stint right after Washington became mayor and, for nearly a year and a half, wrote a weekly political column on the *Tribune's* op-ed page. Therefore I knew those kinds of parliamentary maneuvers for what they were—stalling tactics. It was all over except for the speech making, the name calling, and the final roll call. "Sawyer," I thought to myself as I began drifting off into a fitful, too-short night's sleep. "I can't believe it's Sawyer. Mayor Sawyer."

As was the case for an overwhelming majority of African-Americans in Chicago, Mayor Washington had taken on a larger-than-life persona for me. Early on, as the first black member of the *Tribune's* city hall bureau, I closely followed and duly reported Mayor Washington's trials and tribulations during what political satirist Aaron Freeman dubbed "council wars." It was during that period that I first met Eugene Sawyer. Washington was on one of his many super-celebrity-mayor excursions. This time it was to Oakland, California. For reasons that were not explained, and did not seem to matter to any of Chicago's traveling press corps, 6th Ward Alderman Sawyer was part of the mayor's entourage. During a reception there, Sawyer introduced himself to me. We had cocktail conversation for about three or four minutes. I do not recall what we discussed. However, I do remember my initial impression at that time: Eugene Sawyer was a nice man. A little quiet, but very nice. And somewhat boring.

Maybe it was because I found Sawyer so nice, so quiet, and so subdued that he did not immediately come to my mind as the natural successor to the wily warrior, the man with the quick tongue and the disarming shrug, Harold Washington. But, in retrospect, I realize that I too fell victim to the images, lies, and propaganda born out of Mayor Washington's untimely death. When Washington died at his desk the day before Thanksgiving, I, like most Chicagoans, was startled and stunned. I was also captivated by news accounts of the political maneuvers to replace him. Like so many thousands of Chicagoans who had listened carefully to those media reports and the word on the street, I thought the next mayor of Chicago would be none other than 4th Ward Alderman Timothy Evans.

As I would later learn, the impression that Evans was the gate keeper of the Washington legacy was no more than a notion—and a misleading one at that. In politics, public perception and what is really going on are twains that seldom meet. So while Evans enjoyed the public persona of being Harold's right-hand man, in reality the inside story featured someone else. It was Eugene Sawyer who functioned as Washington's key alderman. "Gene was the invisible senior statesman among the Washington 21," recalls Grayson Mitchell, the mayor's first press secretary.

Sawyer, a dependable, knowledgeable, nuts-and-bolts legislator, was the linchpin in Washington's council machinery. The 6th Ward alderman was the first committeeman to bolt from the Regular Democratic Ward bloc to support Washington's candidacy for mayor, risking considerable political retaliation from Jane Byrne. Sawyer, who was president pro tem of the city council at the time of the mayor's death, was the one who usually forged a consensus among the black and progressive aldermen so that the mayor enjoyed a united front on the council floor. And Sawyer was a valued consultant to Washington, whose political experience was rooted in the Illinois state legislature and the U.S. Congress, not in municipal government. It was Sawyer who tutored the newly inaugurated mayor on how the council floor worked, giving him a practical rundown on the players while telling him the score. And it was Sawyer who, from the floor, signaled Washington on the podium to indicate how many more votes the mayor needed to pass a motion. "Harold had a lot of respect for Gene's judgement," Mitchell said. "It was always solid."

Eugene Sawyer had two glaring weaknesses, however. He was media shy and too soft-spoken for his own good.

Tim Evans was something else. Tim Evans was an illusion. Shortly after the council wars erupted, Mayor Washington needed a point man to carry on the fight from the floor. Evans was articulate, photogenic, and eager to bask in the glow of the television cameras. He became the designated face and voice of the new Washington administration but never the brains nor the heart and soul. Evans served as a public prop but seldom as a behind-the-scenes support. Although Evans was bright and capable, he lacked one crucial ingredient: follow-through. Tim Evans, Washington administration insiders sighed, was not reliable. Not dependable. Evans had a reputation for not being on time. Politically, Evans was thought to be too cautious and conservative by many of the Washington progressives. And Evans was not known for doing his homework. On a number of occasions, according to Washington administration insiders, Evans's floor speeches had to be written for him because he had not prepared himself well enough to discuss the issues without prompting.

It was because of Sawyer's strengths and Evans's weaknesses that

Jacky Grimshaw, Ernest Barefield, and their aldermanic allies, Bobby Rush and Dorothy Tillman, sought to exploit the public perception rather than the political reality. "Tim was controllable," says a former Washington administration insider. "He was a complete captive of their 'movement.' "

To be fair, I would like to mention one tangential factor that obviously played a part in the Washington coalition schism. For the first three and a half years of its existence, the Washington administration was under siege. Naturally, a bunker mentality took hold. A talented, all-pro politician, Washington understood that after his reelection the prudent thing to do was to make peace with the loyal opposition. Operating on the theory that, in politics, "there are no permanent friends. No permanent enemies. Only permanent interests," he buried the hatchet in the same resting place where patronage lay dead and danced upon. After Washington's death, many of his supporters experienced post–council wars traumatic flashbacks. An automatic reflex of theirs returned. If those of the 29 mentality went left, then those with the 21 philosophy had better look to the right. The 29 whispered Sawyer, so some of the 21 got the irresistible urge to shout Evans.

Before Washington's death, few voters beyond the boundaries of their respective wards, knew—or cared—much about either Evans or Sawyer. Within hours after Washington's burial, that was no longer true. Thanks to an instant burst of revisionist history coupled with a not-so-spontaneous combustion of modern myth, the twin creations of the Washington legacy and the Sawyer sellout were conceived. Or, to be more accurate, ill-conceived. Tim Evans became "the heir apparent," a designation that a week earlier was neither in the air nor apparent. Gene Sawyer became, in Alderman Tillman's disingenuous words, Monty Hall, out to make a closed-door deal at his people's expense. The Evans transformation gave credence to the old axiom about possession being nine-tenths of the law. Motivated by fear and selfishness, those in power—the Washington administration without Washington—decided that an Evans succession to the mayor's seat was in their best interest. Once that self-serving decision was made, making fiction look like fact hinged on their skills in telling the big lie, staging the big event, and organizing the big demonstration.

But before those relatively easy pieces could be put into place in this political chess game, the king had to be put in check.

If there was anyone big enough to fill Washington's shoes and assume the Washington legacy, it was the Reverend Jesse Jackson and only the Reverend Jesse Jackson. The civil rights leader was drum major and chief cheerleader in the black political movement that led to Washington's election as mayor of Chicago. The night of the primary victory, a sharp split developed between Washington and Jackson after the latter commandeered the mike and shouted the battle cry, "It's our turn." Washington, who wisely waited in his hotel suite for definite election results before making a victory speech, was furious with Jackson for a couple of reasons. The first one had to do with Jackson's bad habit of stealing the spotlight any time and every time he got the chance. The second and more substantive one was based on Jackson's action alienating almost every white voter in the City of Chicago. Washington put Jackson at arm's length after that. Once he won (narrowly) the general election, his star eclipsed Jackson's as the king of the black leadership hill in Chicago—and challenged it on a national level. Overnight, the nation's third-largest city became too small to nurture the substantial political egos of both men. For about a decade, Jackson had been the 800-pound gorilla among Chicago's black politicians and the big, bad wolf to the city's white power structure. Suddenly, Jackson found himself playing Tonto to Mayor Washington's Lone Ranger. It didn't take long before Jackson acted on an urge to move up and out—shooting for the American presidency as a consolation prize. To nearly no one's surprise, Jackson's quest for the presidency failed. But the African-American preacher did so much better than anyone—with the possible exception of his most fervent followers—expected that he became the undisputed champion and spokesman for black America. An uneasy accommodation between the newly elected black mayor of Chicago and the newly crowned leader of black America followed.

Jackson, who chronically was a prophet without honor in his own city, even managed to take on the aura of national black statesman at home. So much so that Washington, who was late and reluctant in endorsing Jackson during his first presidential run, was quick and emphatic in endorsing the civil rights leader the second time around, describing Jackson as "a force for good."

Had Jackson been around when Washington died, it is unthinkable that he would have let the division occur, let alone unwittingly precipitate it. But, as fate would have it, Jackson was out of the country and therefore out of the loop on November 25, 1987. When he learned of the mayor's death, Jackson was nearly halfway around the world at the Kuwait Hilton, where he was attempting to shore up his presidential timber. He immediately headed back home. All of Jackson's information on the political wheelings and dealings in selecting Washington's successor was spoon-fed to him by Grimshaw and Barefield, who warned the civil rights leader that the African-American community was about to lose city hall in his absence. By the time Jackson returned to O'Hare Airport, he was a one-man disinformation campaign waiting to happen.

With Washington dead, Jackson once again was unquestionably

the best and the brightest black politico in town. But this was one time
that the best man could not win: Illinois state law decreed that the fifty
members of the Chicago City Council must select a mayoral successor
from among their own. Jackson was not a member of the city council
and therefore not eligible for consideration. Unable to assume the
mayoralty, Jackson opted for the post of king maker. Proclaiming himself a peacemaker, Jackson obviously had heard the big lie and took it
to heart. Although his public posture was that of the neutral negotiator
attempting to forge a consensus candidate for the Washington coalition, he clearly favored Evans. During the regular PUSH meeting the
Saturday following the mayor's death, Jackson stood at the podium,
flanked by Evans and Sawyer. Although Jackson thrust both men's
extended arms upwards, he thrust Evans's hand upwards with much
more enthusiasm. Jackson's body English spoke volumes to volumes.
Jackson had been suckered into believing that Evans truly was the heir
apparent who had the tacit support of the black community at large.
Using the full force of his overt popularity and implied authority in
subtle ways, Jackson's misinformed understanding became the
African-American community-at-large's misled conviction. It was a
full year later, when he returned to Chicago after taking another stab at
winning the Democratic party presidential nomination, that Jackson
concluded that he was bamboozled. He tried to right the wrongs. But
by then it was much too late. The African-American community's ni-
hilistic political course was set and not about to be altered.

In the days following the mayor's death, Chicago's African-
American community was so thoroughly in the throes of shock and
disbelief that anything but the truth seemed feasible to a large portion
of it. Rumors, lies, and conspiracy theories, anything that gave com-
fort while placing blame, were desperately embraced. I visited city
hall the last day that Washington's body lay in state. As I viewed the
open casket, a weeping African-American woman in her early fifties
stood beside me. She shook her head and moaned, ''It's a shame the
way they murdered that man.'' On WVON, the black talk radio station,
where conversation stopped making sense the day the mayor died, all
sorts of conspiracy theories were voiced about how he was killed.
More than one member of the mayor's security force—almost all of
whom came from the ranks of the black nationalistic Afro-American
Police League—were admonished by an anguished black for allowing
''them'' to murder Mayor Washington. One theory had him poisoned.
Another had him dead from a cocaine hotshot (there has never been
any report or evidence of drug use by the mayor). Perhaps the most
bizarre theory attributed the suspected ''murder'' to the mayor's press
secretary and confidant, Alton Miller, who happened to be the only
person in the inner office with Washington when he suffered the heart
attack on November 25. And who happens to be white.

In that perversely paranoid atmosphere, lies stood on their own, developing legs and racing forward as "the word on the street." The next logical move in this topsy-turvy tall tale was to stage the big event. Hours after Washington's remains were laid to rest on Monday afternoon, a "memorial" for the late mayor was held at the Pavilion of the University of Illinois' Chicago campus. In the wake of a legitimate memorial for the late mayor, an Evans-for-Mayor rally was grafted. As a journalist with more than a passing interest in the Chicago political scene, I planned to attend the gathering. However, when I discovered it would be broadcast live on WBEZ, the local public radio station, I opted to listen instead. What I heard, I found disquieting. Conspiracy theories hung in the air like so many funeral buntings. The principal conspiracy, warned speaker after speaker, was to disenfranchise the black-Hispanic-progressive coalition that had fought so hard to reform city hall. These maleficent conspirators planned to deny Tim Evans, Harold's right-hand man, his rightful role as heir to the fifth floor of city hall. Harold had to be spinning in his grave.

And so spiel after spiel was spun. Then Vernon Jarrett took hold of the mike. If anyone could be classified as a one-man black journalist conglomerate, it was Vernon Jarrett. He was a columnist for the Chicago *Sun-Times* and a member of that newspaper's editorial board; a commentator on WLS-TV, the Capital Cities/ABC-owned and -operated station in Chicago, as well as the talk show host for "Vernon Jarrett: Face to Face," a public service program there; and a major stockholder at WVON-AM radio. Jarrett also had served as a sort of professional mentor and role model to me. It was his name I used, when I was an assistant editor at *Ebony* magazine, to get a job interview at the Chicago *Tribune*. And it was his Friday slot on the *Tribune's* op-ed page that I inherited when Jarrett quit as a columnist at the *Tribune* to go across the street to the *Sun-Times*. Although the "memorial" had taken a decidedly pro-Evans political tack, I expected a different direction from Jarrett, who had been a close friend of Harold Washington. I thought an honest-to-goodness eulogy would come at last. I expected that although Vernon would pepper his remembrance with politics, any such observations would not be buried hip-deep in unfounded conspiracy theories and fabricated fables.

My expectations went unmet. Ten minutes into a diatribe that was so hysterical that I feared that Jarrett was experiencing a nervous breakdown, I needed a reality check. I left the radio to find my wife. "Joyce," I shouted in amazement, "come here. You've got to hear this. Vernon has gone over the edge."

Just how far Jarrett had gone became increasingly clear as time went by. Jarrett's strident town crier role the night of the Pavilion rally became his public persona, replacing his well-respected identity as a crusading advocacy journalist. Paul King, an African-American contractor who is president of the Chicago Business Council, likens Jarrett's transformation to that of the Howard Beale character in the 1976 movie *Network*. Shouting, "I'm mad as hell and I'm not going to take it anymore," the Beale character, a television news anchor, went from giving the news to being the news. Eventually the Beale character, who was played by actor Peter Finch, went so far off the deep end that he ended up encouraging viewers to throw their TV sets out the window.

Columnist Jarrett played the Pied Piper in a real-life political drama, ushering six years of African-American progress in Chicago politics out the window. It was Jarrett, more than anyone else, who managed to keep the invention of the Washington legacy and Evans as the heir apparent in the public domain. It was Jarrett, as much as anybody else, who created the impression in Chicago's African-American community that the mayoral competition was exclusively between Sawyer and Evans—no white candidate need apply. It was and remains a mystery to me just how Jarrett became so mired in his own fiction. The only sense I can make of it is that Jarrett is a staunch traditionalist. His columns frequently start with historical references or quotes from earlier decades and slowly work their way to current events. Keeping that in mind, perhaps Jarrett was set on the traditional line of succession, where the second in command follows a fallen leader. It was this sort of thinking that called for Ralph David Abernathy, rather than the younger, more energetic, and talented Jesse Jackson, to succeed the slain Dr. Martin Luther King, Jr. Because Evans was Washington's floor leader, Jarrett must have persuaded himself that this was the only proper progression.

Whatever thought process Jarrett may have gone through, once his mind was made up, it got stuck on that one note. Jarrett served as the unofficial minister of misinformation for the Evans faction. His radio station, WVON, day in and day out played a key role in allowing unquestioned assertions and half-truths to mold community opinion, fostering the effigy of Acting Mayor Sawyer and ministering to the phantasm of should-be mayor Evans. Column after column, Jarrett praised Evans while damning Sawyer. The acting mayor did nothing right, while the 4th Ward alderman could do no wrong. There were no shades of gray applied to either man. There is no doubt in my mind that if Jarrett had not constantly and consistently beat the anti-Sawyer drum, the rift in the African-American community would have stood a remote possibility of healing.

A lot of young African-American journalists looked up to Jarrett because he was a pioneer who not only succeeded against all odds but exacted the best revenge by living well. So many, such as the *Chicago Defender's* Chinta Strausberg, WVON's Ty Wansley, and WVAZ's Debra Scott, followed his lead down that slippery slope into partisan journalism. They played the same politics he played and contributed to the loss for the African-American community. There was no pretense of the journalistic staples of objectivity or fairness with Jarrett and little from them. There is a lesson to be learned from this. Had these journalists played it straight rather than choosing sides and toeing a party line, the one thing they thought they were trying to prevent—the loss of Harold Washington's seat to his white political adversaries—could have been prevented. It was their good intentions that paved the road to the eventual outcome. It was Jarrett's fiery, misguided speech that set the stage during the Monday, November 30, rally for much of what was to follow.

By the time the roll was called for the special council meeting on Tuesday, the memorial rally had inflamed passions to a flashpoint. The city's Department of Human Services, at taxpayers' expense, generously provided transportation for busloads of demonstrators destined to clog city hall. Before the council could get around to doing its business, there was barely any room in which to do it. The big protest was raging according to the blueprint. Concerned citizens, mostly black, were here, there, and everywhere. The crowd of thousands, packed inside and out, had no understanding of the required procedure in selecting a mayoral successor. But, thanks to the disinformation campaign that had been waged the day before, it "knew" a deal had been made to cut the Washington coalition out.

As early as Thanksgiving Day, Sawyer had enough council votes to become the next mayor of the City of Chicago. Although the bloc of white ethnic aldermen who had staunchly opposed Washington for three and a half years sought vainly to select one of their own, mainly 32nd Ward Alderman Terry Gabinski, for the post, Cook County Democratic Party Chairman George Dunne would have none of that. Dunne was politically astute enough to know that choosing anyone but an African-American to fill Washington's seat would mean political suicide for the local party and possibly rioting in the streets. Once the white ethnic aldermanic bloc came to accept that political reality, Sawyer was their obvious choice. Besides being well liked by his aldermanic colleagues and well schooled in council affairs, Sawyer had two other attractive attributes as far as the white ethnic members were concerned: He was not particularly ambitious and even less articulate. Sawyer suited the likes of the old anti-Washington 29 well because they believed he could either be controlled or, if not controlled, then defeated in a special election.

In the thick of the fight over the succession, Sawyer offered Evans his personal council vote, if the 4th Ward alderman could muster the other twenty-five. That was not about to happen. Evans was not especially loved or respected by most of his colleagues in the council.

The greatest irony, I believe, is that the system worked. The best man was, in fact, chosen. Washington, without a doubt, was what the African-American community needed as its first mayor, a razzle-dazzle warrior with a clear vision of the big picture. Sawyer was the perfect person to succeed Washington. He was a bridge for a city that was attempting to heal itself racially. A peacemaker. A doer. Someone who knew what it took to get the garbage picked up, to keep the streets cleaned, and to get the potholes filled.

By Thanksgiving Day, Sawyer knew he had enough votes to lock up the post. But in the days that followed, the 6th Ward alderman watched in dismay as the propaganda machine transformed him from the guy who was liked by everybody who knew him to the man who was hated by everybody who did not know him. He watched as his support among African-American aldermen was stripped away. At one point he had the signatures of fourteen of the council's sixteen African-American aldermen on a resolution calling for him to be elected as Washington's successor. That number shrank to six as an organized terror campaign ripped its way through the black community. African-American aldermen who supported Sawyer started receiving profane calls laced with death threats. The threats, the calls, those targeted, followed a pattern so plain that there could be little doubt that it was all orchestrated.

Dismayed by the crowd of 3,000 inside the council chambers and the crowd of nearly that many out on LaSalle Street, Sawyer, who is by nature reticent, easygoing, and noncommittal, wanted to postpone the vote for a couple of days. The delay, he hoped, would give the crowd—and the community it came to represent—time to get some understanding of the legislated process that was destined to take place.

No one doubts that Sawyer felt the heat from the passionate protesters. There is some question, however, about how he reacted. Wendell Peete, a six-foot-three-inch 320-pounder who was chief of police for Cook County Hospital and a member of Sawyer's ward organization, acted as a bodyguard to the man who would be mayor that night. Peete, who has since parted ways with the former acting mayor, says Sawyer may have fainted or his knees may have buckled. Peete says that although the mayoralty was Sawyer's for the taking, the alderman was badly affected by the intense hostility of the crowd. "He kept saying he needed some time," Peete recalls. "He kept saying, the perspective is wrong. The community's perspective is wrong." Sawyer readily admits that he believed that the African-American community misunderstood what was happening. However, he is adamant in insisting neither of two things happened: He did not faint; his knees did not buckle. As he was maneuvered through the throng back to his council seat, Sawyer says the crush of the crowd literally lifted him off his feet; he was physically carried through the swarm. At the point where the crowd thinned out, Sawyer came crashing to the ground. In other words, his knees did not give out; his people let him down. Assuming it happened as Sawyer says it did, it was a prophetic occurrence.

From that decisive moment forward, whether he drooped or was dropped really did not matter. The image of Eugene Sawyer as a weak-kneed, tenderfooted stumbler was fixed permanently in too many minds. The 10 P.M. nightly news on December 1 turned into expanded live coverage of the city council proceedings, and by then television reporters already were making references to and quips about Sawyer's knee-buckling episode. Later in the live coverage, 14th Ward Alderman Ed Burke, a seasoned electronic media performer who surely must have known the cameras were rolling, ostentatiously pointed his finger in Sawyer's face as the two men met behind glass walls. If the walls had ears, they would have heard Burke warning Sawyer that his opportunity for succeeding to the mayor's seat was now or never; that the existing voting bloc would not hold during a two- or three-day waiting period. That, in essence, Sawyer was the not-so-great black hope. It did not, of course, play that way on the tube. It was Boss Burke telling Tom Sawyer, in articulate body English, what to do. That silent image, broadcast to scores of thousands of television viewers, was the coup de grace. Eugene Sawyer was Humpty-Dumpty. Millions of dollars in television campaign ads, iron-jock political ploys, and staunch human decency aside, Sawyer could not overcome the image of the meek, weak, plantation-raised pol being ordered around by Burke, the zealous, vitriolic lieutenant of the anti-Washington council war.

Sawyer's mayoral race was over, long before it started. (My 20/20 vision on this, I must admit, is greatly enhanced by hindsight.)

There was other bad symbolism. Sawyer was sworn in as mayor at 4 o'clock in the morning, "like a thief in the night," to borrow a phrase from Washington. Unfortunately for Sawyer, hundreds of thousands of viewer-voters were still watching the live broadcasts, and many were turned off by what they saw.

As the newly sworn-in acting mayor, Sawyer found himself being shuttled from a bad situation to a worse one. The government, and its department heads, were not his. They were Harold Washington's. Many of them believed the images and propaganda being spread, and therefore operated openly as Evans sympathizers and Sawyer saboteurs. Worst of all, there was nothing the acting mayor could do about it. Those classical clichés, "caught between a rock and a hard place," and "damned if you do, damned if you don't," became Sawyer's watchwords. There could be no house cleaning during his watch. To fire the saboteurs, malcontents, and misfits would have given some credence to the Evans-Tillman-Grimshaw-Rush combine's smear that he was a puppet of Burke and the boys. Not to fire them left him open to sabotage, with even high-ranking officials in his employ working furiously against him. It also played into the public perception that Sawyer was too weak-willed to take charge. To say it was a no-win situation is to speak in understatement.

The end result cannot be emphasized enough: Sawyer wore the mantle of loser, long before he lost.

Knowing that Sawyer's support was soft, if not nearly nonexistent, among his natural constituency, the white ethnic aldermen applied pressure from the other side. The recurrent pitch went like this: Gene didn't frighten Chicago's white ethnics the way Harold had. Gene was somebody they could sell to the voters in their wards. All Gene had to do was to stop listening to the Tillmans and Rushes of the city and do the right thing. Fire the gaggles of city workers who were working against him. They named names. Hire a gaggle of their people to work for him. They had names. If he cooperated, he would be mayor for as long as he wished. But if he did not play ball, they were going to run one of their guys against him. And that would be that.

Being caught in that Catch-22 position was the bane of the Sawyer mayoralty. Sawyer was savvy enough to know he could not and should not trust the siren song that the white ethnic aldermen sang. Yet there was another irony here. Washington, whose base was in the integrated 5th Ward, was a semi-strange bedfellow to the so-called lakefront liberals. Sawyer, whose base was in the solidly black middle-class 6th Ward, was firmly rooted in African-American political philosophy. Had Sawyer survived the Evans-Daley double-team, the 6th Ward could have become to African-Americans what the 11th Ward had been (and currently is) for Irish-Americans. Unfortunately for Sawyer, he did not have the luxury of contemplating political dynasties. Instead, he had to focus on political survival. If he was to continue as Chicago's second black mayor, he had to shore up and broaden his base. That was no simple task with the Evans faction working overtime at undermining his efforts, his accomplishments, and his good intentions.

The most serious crisis of the Sawyer administration sprang from the trick bag in which the acting mayor found himself. The day before a Chicago *Tribune* story broke reporting that a member of the Sawyer administration, Steve Cokely, had made anti-Semitic statements, I was warned by a friend at the newspaper. I called the mayor to explain to him what was going into the May 1st Sunday *Tribune* and what sort of media hounding and pounding would follow. Before I completed my rundown, the mayor stopped me. Jumping to the logical conclusion I was leading to, Sawyer blurted: "I'm not firing Stevie." Steve Cokely had been a special charity case of Alderman Sawyer's for the better part of two and a half years. Cokely, who was one of those people who never seemed able to connect all the dots when going through an extended thought process, had attracted bad press nearly three years earlier when, while serving as an aide to 8th Ward Alderman Marion Humes, he attacked Columbus Day as a racist holiday that did not deserve celebrating in America. Humes dropped Cokely like the hot potato he was. Good Samaritan Sawyer picked him up and set out to try to rehabilitate him. When Alderman Sawyer became acting mayor, he gave Cokely the low-level administrative post of community liaison. Cokely's new job called for him to be Mayor Sawyer's eyes and ears in the more radical grass-roots segments of the African-American community. Media reports, predictably, made Cokely sound as if he were an integral cog in the policy-making machinery. By implication, one of Sawyer's top administrative aides was a wild-eyed, hare-brained, anti-Semitic bigot.

The Cokely story broke early Saturday afternoon. By late Saturday night, Sharon Gist Gilliam, the mayor's chief operating officer, Erwin France, his most reliable advisor, and I all had talked to Mayor Sawyer at home, attempting to persuade him to get rid of Cokely. He either did not listen or did not hear. Those who had his ear on the Cokely issue whispered wrong-headed advice. Several key members of his security detail and some of the black aldermen in his camp did not see the issue as the anti-Semitic, hateful episode it was. To them it was simply a black-and-white issue. If Sawyer was seen as siding with whites against a black, once again it would seem to his natural constituency that he was a tool of the anti-Washington whites. Meanwhile, Sawyer's traveling aide, Derek Shelton, was telling the mayor that the brouhaha would blow over. It was obvious to me that it was only going to blow us away if we did not hurry up and get it behind us.

That weekend was long and punishing. Monday was just as bad. Chief Counsel Judson Miner, Commissioners Joan Harris and Liz Hollander, and other Jewish members of the Sawyer administration were on the verge of open revolt. Chicago *Sun-Times* columnist Irv Kupcinet mysteriously and uncharacteristically canceled a private, one-on-one lunch appointment with the mayor. By noon, I had had one of my staff writers prepare a short, to-the-point press release announcing Cokely's resignation. Cokely was summoned to the mayor's office. My understanding was that the mayor would ask Cokely to tender his resignation. Should he refuse, he would be fired. After a twenty-minute closed-door private meeting with the mayor, Cokely emerged wearing a smug smirk. When I entered the mayor's office, I was told that Cokely would issue an apology. I shuddered and handed Sawyer the "Cokely resigns" press release. "Okay, Your Honor. But sooner or later, we're going to have to release this."

Politics aside, there were personal reasons for Sawyer's aversion to canning Cokely. Rather than viewing Cokely strictly as the political liability he was, Sawyer saw him as his charge and as the father of two small children who had to be clothed, housed, and fed. There was also a cultural element at work here. From childhood on, African-Americans are lectured constantly on the importance of having a job. In a community where unemployment is discriminantly disproportionate, having a job takes on iconic preeminence. Therefore, firing people does not come easily to an African-American in a position to do so. Harold Washington had a hard time doing it. So did Eugene Sawyer.

There was one other striking similarity between the two African-American mayors. Both men were legislators, not executives. They were in the practice of seeking consensus rather than bossing people around. By the time he died, Washington understood that as mayor, as the city's chief executive, he sometimes had to utilize the surgeon's scalpel and wield the butcher's axe. That was a lesson Sawyer was waiting to learn. "Sawyer's style of hearing everybody but not stopping anybody worked to his detriment," observes Erwin France, Sawyer's brilliant, city-contract-laden advisor.

Cokely's Monday apology failed to ameliorate anything. By Tuesday, it was becoming increasingly clear that government was screeching to a standstill. The media became an angry mob on a self-righteous mission, intent on tarring and feathering Mayor Sawyer. Cokely had to go. Arrangements were made for Sawyer to meet with Cokely at the McCormick Hotel. That meeting turned into a meeting with the Mau-Maus, a bittersweet nickname given to the most vocal, most aggressive, and most doctrinaire of the African-American grass-roots leadership. After a long, stormy session with them, it was agreed that Cokely would be allowed to resign. The next morning, Cokely met with the mayor again. Cokely was in tears as he told Sawyer that he could not resign because his manhood was on the line. His nationalist brothers would think he had punked out. That he was not black enough. Later that day, a press release came out of my office announcing the firing of Steve Cokely. But by then irreparable damage had been done. The Jewish community and a healthy portion of the liberal white community was lost. However, the equation in the black community changed very little—if any at all.

Except for taking it on the chin in the Cokely fiasco, Mayor Sawyer was weathering relatively well. Considering how things started out and how things were going, the first six months were much better for the Sawyer administration than anyone would have predicted. A newspaper story about a $30,000 finder's fee paid to Sawyer proved to be too dense, too complicated, too far in the past, and too void of sex appeal and visuals to stimulate much television coverage and therefore much public outrage.

With no executive experience and little popular support, Sawyer managed to keep the government not only going, but going smoothly. That is particularly significant, I think, when you stop to consider that Sawyer literally was thrust into the job without any aspiration or preparation, and that he did not get one day of the customary honeymoon accorded newly elected public officials by the news media. An appreciable amount of his early success had to do with the efforts of Erwin France, his much-maligned one-man transition team. France held Sawyer's hand and guided him through troubled waters for the first three months or so of the new administration, until the neophyte mayor had developed his administrative sea legs.

That Sawyer was such a quick study should come as no surprise. His sixteen years of council experience and the relationships he had developed over the years with his fellow aldermen worked to his advantage. And he had served as the chairman of the crucially important rules committee after Washington finally gained numerical advantage in the council. Thus, the 6th Ward alderman knew how to move things through the council. He knew which buttons to push—and when—to get things done. And that is exactly what he did.

Acting Mayor Sawyer had enacted the late Mayor Washington's 1988 budget and a needed $66 million tax increase before he had been in office a month. In January 1988, he got council approval for legislation that broke the taxi monopoly in the city, something that Mayor Washington had not been able to do. In February, Sawyer managed to round up enough aldermanic support to get a bill passed allowing lights in Wrigley Field so that the Chicago Cubs would no longer be the only team in major league baseball unable to play night games at home—a feat his five predecessors were either unwilling or unable to accomplish. Sawyer got the ball rolling for private development of land around O'Hare Airport. During the Sawyer administration, an unprecedented agreement was reached with the fireman's union, guaranteeing labor peace for four-year chunks of time. And, after a number of failed attempts, under Sawyer's leadership the city council finally passed a long-overdue human rights ordinance that protected gay and handicapped citizens from discrimination in employment and housing.

Seeing how well Sawyer performed under the most adverse conditions, I convinced myself that he could become another legendary Chicago mayor if only the shackles were stripped away. In the long run, I believed, an election in 1989 would work to the acting mayor's advantage, because after winning, he would have the necessary mandate to put his imprint on city government. I probably was the only person in the entire administration who felt that way; everyone else seemed to think that Sawyer needed Harold Washington's full term in order to build a toutable record while letting the wounds in the African-American community heal.

I innocently believed that an actual mayoral election—and all there was at stake—would serve as a wake-up call to the African-American community. That this selfish Evans ego trip would be exposed for what it was and that the community would rally to the common cause. That the African-American community would embrace the "bird in the hand" principle and come to understand that holding the mayor's seat was critical in both real and symbolic terms to its economic and political development. But there was one small piece of the puzzle I overlooked: There was not enough time for the benefits of having one of your own running city hall to trickle down.

Michael Scott, who has held positions in the Byrne, Washington, Sawyer, and Daley administrations, points out that the average African-American in Chicago never got a sense of what having power at the top meant. Washington never had the chance to get many of the services down to the little people. For the first three and a half years of his administration, Scott notes, Washington did not have a majority vote in the city council. After the court ruled that key wards had been gerrymandered and called for special aldermanic elections, the balance changed. But by that time, Washington was running for reelection, and all his energies and resources went towards that end. Seven months after his second term got under way, the mayor died. The African-American community did not fully realize the benefits of having one of their own in the fifth-floor seat. That and the protracted family feud took their toll. The 1989 election found many African-Americans apathetic again.

My own political short-sightedness was surpassed by that of those in the Evans camp. They envisioned a crusade clone mirroring the one that swept Congressman Washington into city hall. They failed to realize that a passionate crusade, like the loss of one's virginity, happens only once. That same emotional excitement can never be experienced twice; a copycat crusade was an impossible dream. But in its quixotic folly, the Evans faction went to court, brandishing a lawsuit, forcing an early election and its unavoidable ending. Had it not done that, I would not be writing this. The white ethnic pols were not about to risk a heated political backlash by seeking a 1989 election. Had the Evans camp not forced a legal showdown, an African-American would be sitting in the seat Harold Washington was elected to hold until the term expired in 1991. A singular-minded white Chicago, which never stopped believing that the black mayoral victory in 1983 was a fluke, merely seized the time by taking advantage of an inopportune split in the African-American community.

Even if the December 1 and 2 fiasco and the resulting community cleavage had not been so maledictive from the beginning, the Sawyer mayoralty definitely was doomed in the end because the special election campaign effort turned out to be a tragedy of errors. It had the wrong man with the wrong strategy reporting to the wrong people for the wrong reasons.

There are obvious reasons why things occurred the way they did. First and foremost, the campaign fund-raising arm also was the political think tank. As a general rule, fund raisers know how to raise money but know little about political strategy. If fund raisers and strategists are comingled, the result is bad politics. All during the campaign, for example, Al Johnson, a retired millionaire Cadillac salesman who could best be described as a political dilettante, used his ties to the purse strings to influence or put a stop to ideas, people, or positions.

With the bean counters at the helm, the campaign committee went down South and downscale to select Louisiana accountant Reynard Rochon to manage the effort to make Acting Mayor Sawyer the mayor. Had the Daley and Evans camps conspired together, they could not have found a worse man. Rochon was an outsider who had little interest and less appreciation for the subtleties and nuances of Chicago politics. His philosophy on municipal election campaigns aped former Vice-President Spiro Agnew's viewpoint on ghettoes: if you've seen one, you've seen them all. In a mayoral campaign, according to the Rochon paint-by-the-numbers scenario, all cities had community groups that had to be co-opted, a few key reporters who could be seduced, and commonplace political problems that called for simple political solutions. Thus, any big-city mayor had to be against drugs, for law and order, and against tax increases. Though this obviously was a cookie-cutter approach, Rochon implied that it had a proof-in-the-pudding credibility because he had managed the successful second campaign of Philadelphia Mayor Wilson Goode. As I saw it, it was Frank Rizzo, not Reynard Rochon, who won that race for the incumbent mayor. Had anyone except the overtly racist Rizzo run against Mayor Goode, who allowed the Philadelphia police to bomb an entire block in an African-American neighborhood, the outcome would have been decidedly different.

Larry Horist, the veteran Republican political consultant who became the Sawyer campaign's second political press secretary, notes that Rochon had a penchant for taking press opportunities that should have been executed by the mayor or one of his two media spokesmen—Horist or me. Although Rochon's media forays were sometimes blatantly self-promotional, no one in the Sawyer campaign seemed to notice or care. Further complicating the matter, Rochon was an absentee campaign manager who spent nearly as much time at home in New Orleans as he did on the battlefront in Chicago.

Rochon did, however, have a few workable strategies. The best among them was his push, from the beginning, to seal Evans's political coffin by any means necessary. As long as Evans was perceived as a political factor, Sawyer would not be able to rally all the troops for a victory. At first there was the carrot approach. Sawyer assured Evans that should an accord be reached, Sawyer would use his mayoral clout to ensure that Evans was the second most powerful man in Chicago. It was a no go. Later on, Sawyer offered to pull some behind-the-scene strings that would lead to Alderman Evans becoming Congressman Evans. No good. Finally, Sawyer reminded Evans that he (Sawyer) was not the type who would want to be mayor for twenty years and that he would be willing to step down after a term or two and throw his full support behind Evans. No deal. Unwilling to work it out, Evans and those calling his shots had a fight-to-the-death wish.

Believing its own concocted press clippings, the Evans camp operated under the illusion that Sawyer was the one who could be knocked out of contention. But this time, reality slapped the Evans campaign in the face as it tried futilely to line up some support from the African-American business community while Sawyer racked up one fruitful fund raiser after another.

Because the Evans campaign never had any evidence to support the bill of goods it had sold people about the Sawyer "sell-out," it grasped at the tactics it knew best: dirty deeds. Alderman Tillman turned up the volume on her name-calling tactics, declaring that the mayor was "an Uncle Tom." Borrowing a page from its successful initial strategy of fostering false images, the Evans gang resorted to orchestrating a boo campaign. Everywhere the mayor went, Evans operatives would start booing, giving the impression that Sawyer had gone beyond being unpopular to being reviled. This time the Evans faction was tripped up by its own tired tricks. Tillman's name calling, the constant booing, and the pimping of the late mayor's name fueled a steady climb in the polls for Sawyer.

However, the nastiness took its toll. Sawyer, who by nature is someone who loves to be loved, frequently was immobilized by the virulent hatred he encountered from the Evans faction. Many of Sawyer's supporters began to wonder whether the mayor really wanted to continue as mayor. That impression, naturally, was exploited by the Evans camp, which spread rumors that Sawyer did not want the job but merely was holding it for someone from the anti-Washington side.

Unfortunately, the acting mayor did not do enough to dispel those rumors. Those closest to him recalled how, just months before fate pulled him into the mayoral maelstrom, Sawyer was floating the idea of not running again for his aldermanic seat. Now that he was mayor, they sometimes wondered whether he still harbored a secret desire to get away from the madding crowd and settle comfortably in his easy chair, because he seemed to take little interest in the running of his special election campaign. Although there definitely was an air of indifference, much of it may have resulted from the unending gauntlet of political opposition and the accompanying obstacles that Sawyer had to face day after day.

One situation was constant throughout the Sawyer mayoralty and special election campaign. During all of his lengthy political life, Sawyer was a low-key, low-visibility public servant. Political analyst Bruce DuMont recalls a number of occasions when Sawyer accompanied then Alderman Clifford Kelley to WBEZ studios, where the 20th Ward alderman was scheduled to appear on the radio show "Inside Politics." DuMont says he frequently invited Alderman Sawyer to participate on the program. Each time, Sawyer declined. Not much changed once the alderman became the mayor. Although he saw to it that he was as open and as available to the media as any Chicago mayor, the shy Sawyer did so while heaving a deep sigh. Because Sawyer was not a media creature, and because his maiden media excursion on December 1 had turned him into a boogeyman to his natural constituency, the challenge was to change him from being unknown and unpopular to being as familiar and comfortable as a pair of old shoes.

Rochon's efforts to achieve this impossible mission boiled down to a one-two punch of TV commercial clips and community coffee sips. A slick media consultant was brought in from Boston to film the mayor's campaign commercials. With the exception of the dumb-dumb Daley spots, in which the state's attorney was portrayed as being unable to complete a full sentence without cue cards, these commercials were of the pretty-picture, feel-good genre, giving a rundown of what had been accomplished in a short amount of time. The coffee sips, on the other hand, were off-limits to the media. That was just one of many Rochon mistakes. Sawyer was at his best in small, intimate groups.

But the greatest shortcoming of the campaign was that aside from its media efforts, it had little going for it. The campaign overbought media while failing to put enough financial resources early on in such essentials as placards, buttons, campaign literature, and field offices. As a result, there was little evidence of a field operation. In the end, the Sawyer campaign proved to be top-heavy with generals but lacking crucial foot soldiers. When campaign posters were finally bought, there was no one to distribute them to supporters who would put them in the windows of their homes. Most of the time the campaign head-quarters had two, only two, secretaries answering the telephone, so when those who were interested in volunteering called, it was almost impossible for them to get through. Those who managed to get through seldom were lucky enough to have anyone get back to them.

During the campaign, on more than one occasion Larry Horist and I commiserated about the lack of a cohesive campaign strategy. There was no theme. No vision. No position papers were published. Al-though the campaign was selling Sawyer as the mayor for all the people, too much time was spent securing his base. One critical cam-paign worker grumbled, "We keep sending him back to the same black churches over and over again." The mayor was a victim of his cam-paign's scheduling in other ways as well. So many stops would be jammed into a single day that some had to be dropped along the way. The mayor found himself outrunning the media assigned to cover him. "It was an island of things," says Horist of the campaign, "that never connected."

I am going to make one other related point. The 1983, 1987, and 1989 Chicago mayoral races all were miscast. Although they were not reported that way, those contests were nothing more than a variation on an old American theme: an emerging ethnic group exercising its political muscle to make its way further into the mainstream. Irish-Americans did it a century ago. Other hyphenated American groups have done it in other parts of the nation at other times. Our skin color and our unique history in this nation do not allow African-Americans the luxury of being just another developing ethnic group. We always are dealt the race card. Granted, sometimes we ask for it, but often we do not. It does not matter. We are dealt it whether we want it or not. So, rather than being an American ethnic group, we are a racial group. Rather than being recognized as the largest ethnic group in this na-tion, we are classified as a minority in white America. It follows natu-rally that the mayoral contests, rather than being covered along the lines of an African-American against an Irish-American, were reported and voted along racial lines. White against black. Although it was not articulated that way, I do not believe that African-Americans were vot-ing skin color so much as they were voting ethnicity. However, the lion's share of the European-Americans voted race, regardless of creed or national origin. In Chicago in 1989, a united white racial front pre-vailed over a divided African-American ethnic bloc.

As early as July of 1988, Alderman Burke proved to be clairvoy-ant. After months of anti-Sawyer political games from Evans and his small band of aldermanic allies, the acting mayor reluctantly moved on the long-overdue council reorganization. Evans, Tillman, Rush, and others in their rump group finally were stripped of their council committee chairmanships, their clout, their patronage, and the enormous discretionary funds that accompanied the posts. With the vote over and the Evans contingent out, Burke and 33rd Ward Alderman Richard Mell stood in the men's room off the council chambers, gloating as they washed their hands. A non-African-American television reporter, who was also in the council men's room at the time, alleges that he overheard Burke make this omniscient observation to Mell: "The niggers will never get together after this."

Enough said.

CHAPTER 7

How Evans Lost the Race

Don Rose

James Andrews

The 1989 special Chicago mayoral election was one of those epochal Chicago events, reversing a ten-year trend and leading to long-term redirection and political change. It saw the unraveling of progressive black-white political relationships, the apparent shattering of a small and fragile black-Latino alliance, and at least a temporary end to political unity within the black community itself. It saw, as well, the most racially polarized election in the city's history (as measured by race voting)— despite the least vociferous public rhetoric of the decade. The Timothy Evans campaign, to which the authors served as professional consultants, was both victim of and contributor to these results.

The seeds of Evans's defeat—and of the political movement that had coalesced around Harold Washington during the preceding six years—were sown the moment the late mayor collapsed in his chair on the day before Thanksgiving of 1987. A series of ironic events, many within but many outside the control of Evans and his campaign, became a row of coffin nails, yet it would take more than a year before the coffin was firmly nailed shut and defeat became a certainty.

Most ironic of all, perhaps, was the development of Evans's blurred, contradictory image. A virtual model of middle-class integrationist rectitude, Evans came to be viewed by large segments of the white population, as well as by some blacks, as a raging radical and black nationalist. At the same time, in other sectors of both communities, he had a difficult time shaking the stigma of his early career as a member of the old machine.

In the days immediately following the death of Harold Washington, insiders could see significant operational weaknesses in Evans himself, weaknesses that contributed to his failure to gain the support of his fellow aldermen for the post of acting mayor, although it is questionable whether even a perfect effort would have been successful. Then, as it became clear that Evans was the favorite of the immense crowds that gathered inside and outside of city hall on the decisive days of December 1 and 2, 1987, the image of the crowd, itself the strongest weapon in Evans's arsenal became a limiting factor in his ability to forge a winning coalition.

A further irony was that during what may have been the most tidal event in the recent history of political race relations, the Steve Cokely affair, Evans played what should have been the most healing role of any public official. However, time, events, and his own upside-down image conspired to subvert his role, and he in fact suffered more severely than the true cause of the problem, Acting Mayor Eugene Sawyer.

Another irony was that the very fact that a special mayoral election was held in 1989 can be attributed in large part to Evans and his inner group of supporters, all of whom believed that it would be to his decided advantage. Until relatively late in 1988, the fatal 1989 election was viewed as an Evans victory.

Possibly the greatest irony of all was the nature of the campaign itself, in particular the contrast between the final two contestants, Evans and the eventual winner, Richard M. Daley. Here was a remarkable reversal of roles, with Evans, the insurgent, running a low-tech, labor-intensive campaign, reminiscent of the old machine in pretelevision days, while Daley, scion of the old machine itself, ran the kind of high-tech, media-oriented, computer-directed campaign one normally associates with insurgents who manage to overthrow old-line political organizations.

Of course, the big difference in the conduct of the campaigns was money: Daley's $7 million-plus fund-raising effort made all things possible, while Evans barely brought in $1 million, most of it too late. Compounding the problem was the Evans campaign's decision to use its limited dollars in the least efficient way possible. A decade earlier, when Jane Byrne began the trend toward insurgent mayoral victories, she was outspent by a ratio far greater than that of Daley over Evans, but decided to use her meager funds almost entirely for paid advertising. The lack of funds also hampered Evans's ability to hire top professionals in key campaign positions.

For Evans, paid advertising was needed for more than just cost efficiency. As was true of Byrne in 1979 and Washington in 1983, Evans ran without the editorial support of the major media. But here the similarity ends. Byrne and Washington had the advantage of the kind of friendly coverage that accrues to sentimental favorites fighting plucky, game battles against the odds. But on the strange communications landscape of 1989, it was Daley, the money-laden frontrunner, who emerged as the media darling. Not only did he enjoy the unanimous support of the editorial boards and station managements, he also became the sentimental favorite of the working press and thus gained extra time, space, and what seemed to be an endless stream of favorable "incidental" commentary. Evans, on the other hand, in spite of the efforts of a few commentators and analysts to treat him equitably, was at first treated as a formidable but frightening figure and later as a sure loser, consigned to that special place the mainstream press reserves for politicians on the radical fringe.

In hindsight, these many ironies and twists of fate combined to produce a total defeat. Evans's multiple images—here a machine hack, there a nationalist tool, there again a loser—severely crippled his fund-raising efforts and alienated potential liberal support in the press and the larger community. In the face of these overwhelming barriers, the decision to run the least cost-effective and message-oriented campaign drained Evans's slight financial reserves and did nothing to combat his ever-worsening image problem.

Further, the Evans campaign itself had no coherent strategy—or perhaps it had too many strategies, few of which were executed adequately. Like the Washington campaigns before it, it had several often competing factions with different agendas within the campaign. But unlike Washington, who fostered factionalism while assuring that no faction ever got the upper hand for long, Evans attempted to foster consensus while allowing one segment of his coalition, the so-called movement element, to dominate his campaign. On the political side, this only served to alienate other coalition components essential to victory and kept some important figures out of the campaign.

On the strategic and tactical side, the overwhelming ward-and-precinct bias of the community-based organizers, their inexperience in the dynamics and finance of large campaigns, and their embarrassing lack of media savvy combined to create the campaign's most controversial images as well as its almost prehistoric tactics. In the end, the Evans campaign came more and more to resemble the only kind of campaign the controlling faction knew about—a ward race. Fought on a street level, with posters, literature blitzes, primitive sloganeering, and no media strategy, the campaign devolved into a race for alderman of Chicago.

The campaign failed because it did not generate the needed turnout in the black community. Black turnout ended up being even more important to Evans than to Washington because so much of the white and Latino vote had already been irretrievably lost before the Evans campaign began in earnest. The direction of the campaign, the Evans image, and the campaign's many problems precluded amassing the kind of special interracial, interethnic coalition that Washington had forged.

The turnout problem centered on two issues. First and foremost was a sense of defeatism and futility within the black community, which had in effect been told for months before the election that Evans could not and would not win. This issue was fed—and in some views dominated—by the second issue, the question of a split within the black community based on the relationship between Evans and Acting Mayor Eugene Sawyer. That relationship, or lack thereof, was in turn the result of strategies and tactics emanating from the dominant factions in both the Evans and Sawyer camps and from both men's personal responses to the issue.

Early in his term, it was widely perceived, especially within the Evans camp, that Eugene Sawyer could not win a 1989 election under any circumstances. It was expected that he could be driven out of the primary race, or would eventually drop out, but the Evans forces developed no meaningful effort to make that a reality. The kinds of attacks mounted against Sawyer, such as booing at public events and, especially, Alderman Dorothy Tillman's repeated characterization of him as an "Uncle Tom," ultimately backfired and brought sympathy to the victim.

Meanwhile, the black business establishment, trying desperately to hold on to what it had, hardened its lines in support of Sawyer. Evans could not penetrate their ranks for funds or other support, which deprived him of a major element of Harold Washington's political constellation.

A faction of the Evans campaign apparently preferred a third-party effort from the outset, although the final decision was not made until late in 1988. That faction also was the most hostile to Sawyer, leading the assault against him. Late in the primary election, after first professing to want good relationships with the Sawyer forces for the general election to come, the "movement" faction grew fearful that Sawyer could win the primary, and thus would be unbeatable in the general. It persuaded Evans to make a definitive, door-slamming statement that he would not lend any form of support to Sawyer's primary, despite the fact that Evans's polling showed that 54 percent of all black voters and half of his own supporters wanted him to endorse Sawyer. And the "movement" faction made no secret of its intention to depress the Sawyer primary vote.

The disassociation statement and the impression of an active effort to depress Sawyer's vote sealed the campaign's fate: there would never be enough time for the rift to be healed in the five-week general election period. But rather than vote against Evans, many Sawyer sympathizers in the black community joined those who were generally despondent and sat out the general election, despite a last-minute "healing" drive led by the Reverend Jesse Jackson.

The turnout problem also was related to the issue of voter registration, which in turn was affected by the performance of the Evans campaign as well as by problems that had begun to develop while Washington was alive.

Meanwhile, the Daley forces were assembling one of the most impressive political coalitions to emerge in Chicago since his father refined and broadened the old Democratic machine in the late 1950s. The "new machine," in keeping with the times, would be capital intensive rather than labor intensive. It would utilize advanced political technologies, it would develop an unprecedented level of ideological flexibility that recognized new constituencies and new realities, and it would move its patronage base from traditional political jobs to the pinstriped corridors of law firms, financial organizations, and development companies. In a city whose economy had gradually shifted from manufacturing to service and from the production of capital to the trading of capital, the old blue-collar machine, with its outmoded design and shrinking constituency, was replaced by a new, sleek, white-collar model.

Great battles are won before they are fought. The fighting is a denouement, a final playing out, of a series of maneuvers. This series of maneuvers itself constitutes a strategy, and Evans's strategy was either to become the sole black candidate in the primary election or to make Sawyer into a nonfactor. Obviously this strategy, played out poorly for a year, was a dismal failure. By December of 1988, Evans, who had been the dominant black contender for mayor for an entire year, was forced out of the primary election in the face of Sawyer's superior resources, Evans's lack of organization and significant institutional allies, and the dominant presence of Daley.

There were, in the long run, a number of serious issues underlying the 1989 campaign. They had to do with race and class, with urban development policy, with education, with the reemergence of a united business establishment into the city's political affairs, and with the retrofitting of the machine, which once was thought to be gone for good. It was, as the future shall show us, only dormant, but was metamorphosing in its dormancy into a discernably new entity, without the harsh and jagged edges of the old one.

* * *

The political birth of Tim Evans as a mayoral contender began on the evening of Monday, November 30, 1987. Ever since Harold Washington's death the preceding Wednesday, aldermen and committeemen of all camps had been engaged in furious back-room maneuvering to elect a successor.

Some of the old-line white regulars first favored filling Washington's chair with Alderman Terry Gabinski (32), a white protege of U.S. Representative Dan Rostenkowski. Others had learned from their blind opposition to Harold Washington for five years: the best way to assure a united black community in the coming 1989 election was to instill a white ethnic in Washington's seat. Thus, the focus of many white and black regulars shifted toward the mild-mannered black Eugene Sawyer of the 6th Ward.

The truth about the Sawyer elevation may never be known, but the evidence that the whole process was a masterfully orchestrated Ponzi scheme is compelling. Almost from the moment of Washington's death, Sawyer supporters began to gather signatures on a resolution in support of Sawyer's election. Although there is no question that the eventual resolution contained the names of as many as fourteen black aldermen, there was a certain chain-letter, pyramid-scheme quality to the signature gathering. While Sawyer's black supporters gathered signatures from other black aldermen, some powerful white political figures were engineering a similar signature-gathering operation from white aldermen. Many of the blacks—and, it seems, some of the whites—were being told that Sawyer already had the support of enough whites, plus the commitment of a sufficient number of blacks, to win. Black as well as white aldermen thus were presented with what seemed to them a *fait accompli*, and a tough choice: sign the petition for a man who may *already* have the votes to be mayor and who certainly will see who was with him and, just as importantly, who was not, or don't sign and let the chips fall where they may. Nearly everybody signed.

A game theorist's delight, the deal that installed Sawyer was nevertheless very fragile. By Monday afternoon, forms were filed with the city clerk to call a special council meeting on Tuesday to get the voting out of the way as quickly as possible. Everything was moving on schedule, but the schedule was that of the deal itself and not, to Sawyer's everlasting regret, that demanded by the delicate political sociology of the city. And so two schedules were put on a collision course: the deal, which demanded immediate closure, and the city, which required a decent interval. They collided at the most inopportune place and time: Monday, November 30th, at a public memorial service for the late Mayor Washington attended by over 15,000 people.

Word reached the stage that a city council meeting would be held the next day to elect a new mayor. The place went up for grabs, not so much because of Sawyer—most of the people there did not really know him—but because the sudden calling of a meeting revealed to even the most naive observer the presence of a deal that had to be closed right away. Reacting as people do to a high-pressure salesman who wants you to sign the forms before you've had a test drive, the crowd became indignantly angry. Along with a substantial part of the city, it needed a way to voice its suspicions and vent its frustration.

Enter Tim Evans. Only a little better known than Sawyer, Evans was the perfect symbol through which the conflict between the deal and the city could be played out. Young, handsome, and articulate, Evans had been Washington's political right hand for five years. Needing an alternative, not to Sawyer, but to the timetable of the deal, the crowd at the University of Illinois Pavilion and, if we can believe the December 1987 polls, three-quarters of Chicago's black community chose Evans.

Evans lost the council vote the next day, in a dramatic climax to the events that had started the evening before. Some 10,000 people jammed into the council chambers, the first three floors of city hall, and out onto LaSalle Street, filling an entire city block. Sawyer, who could hear the thousands of chanting demonstrators on the streets outside from his office in city hall, began to buckle. He walked out onto the council floor to the jeers of the crowd and collapsed. While he was wavering, the deal was running out of time. If Sawyer did not accept, the whole scheme of pyramided expectations would collapse. Sawyer spoke with Evans. Burke threatened Sawyer. Mell hollered into the television cameras. Sawyer prayed with his pastor. Evans, the strain showing, announced, foolishly, that Sawyer "didn't have the votes." In the end, at 4:01 A.M. on December 2nd, 1987, Eugene Sawyer, a gentle man placed by fate into a maelstrom where his will would never have taken him, was sworn in as mayor of the City of Chicago.

Now it was Evans who had to act fast, but it seemed to some that the experience of two full decades without a single political setback left him unprepared for the task before him. Like Richard M. Daley before his first mayoral race in 1983, Evans had never suffered a political defeat. Evans began his career in the 4th Ward organization of the late Claude W. B. Holman, one of the wiliest but most obeisant members of the old Daley machine. Holman promoted the young attorney rapidly within his 4th Ward organization, setting the stage for Evans to succeed him both as alderman and as committeeman upon Holman's death in 1973. By the time Harold Washington was elected, Evans, though still a young man, had become a ward powerhouse in his own right, handily defeating all comers, even in 1983, when Washington made no endorsement in the 4th Ward contest. Impressed with his political skills and his willingness to break from the machine, Washington quickly elevated Evans to the position of floor leader, then head of his political organization and chairman of the city council finance committee. By the time Washington died, Evans, at forty-five, had become the second-most powerful politician in Chicago. He had everything going for him. His instinct told him to move, but instead, in the face of conflict among the various factions supporting him, he held back. It was time that never would be made up.

* * *

In the aftermath of the Sawyer succession, candidates in black wards whose aldermen had voted for Sawyer began circulating petitions for ward committeemen. The process was haphazard and lacked central direction from the start. But, in spite of the confusion and disarray, one ward should have been the prime target: Sawyer's Sixth.

Sawyer, after having second thoughts, decided to stand for reelection as ward committeeman. Given what eventually happened in wards considerably less independent than his, it is clear that he would have lost had he been opposed. Yet some serious candidates were talked out of running, and no suitable alternatives were found. The acting mayor, who could not have been elected to *any* office in the black community in the spring of 1988, was left unopposed, while every alderman who had voted for him went down to defeat. Had Sawyer lost, Tim Evans might be mayor of Chicago today.

Still, Evans's strength and Sawyer's profound unpopularity following the March primary were clear. This was the time for Evans to begin to pull together the pieces for a 1989 run for mayor. What happened instead is still among the great mysteries of that year. Following the March debacle, it was Sawyer, not Evans, who held a major fund raiser; it was Sawyer, not Evans, who hired professional staff and consultants to reshape his terrible image; it was Sawyer, not Evans, who began to reach out to the black business community, demanding support as the incumbent black mayor.

Sawyer was caught between his black opponents, who were working openly to knock him out, and his white council allies, whose votes he needed but whom he could not trust. Yet he went on, building an organization and raising substantial sums of money. Coupled with Evans's lack of activity at the height of his power, this would pay many dividends later.

At the time, though, each of Sawyer's steps forward seemed to be followed by at least two steps back. And right after Sawyer's successful April fund raiser, in the early edition of the Sunday, May 1, Chicago *Tribune*, came the worst of these setbacks: a story that not only would erase whatever small gains Sawyer scored after his primary defeats, but also would set back decades of slow, painful progress in the city's race relations, which culminated in the Washington years.

The *Tribune* story told of the vitriolic, anti-Semitic, anti-Christian rantings of Steve Cokely, a top Sawyer aide, including the bizarre allegation that Jewish doctors were injecting black babies with the AIDS virus. This and other equally ludicrous charges were made in "lectures" given by Cokely before audiences of Louis Farrakhan's black Muslim sect and preserved on tape for resale by the group.

Up to that point, Cokely had been a minor figure at the fringes of the nationalist movement, familiar to some listeners of black radio for his Lyndon LaRouche–like conspiracy theories that featured such familiar villains such as the Trilateral Commission. He first came to public notice in October 1985, when, as an aide to then-Alderman Marion Humes (8), he denounced Columbus Day and its traditional parade as a "racist idea."

Humes dropped him quickly, but he was hired immediately by Sawyer, then an alderman, to serve as a liaison to the militant black community. He was retained in the role when Sawyer assumed the mayor's chair, often acting as eyes and ears, bringing back information on who was attending Evans rallies and public meetings.

Sawyer had been given information about Cokely a month earlier, but had taken no action. Even after the story was published, Sawyer failed to move, temporizing with pieties about how he had assumed a paternal role for Cokely and was rehabilitating him. Public outrage, led by Jewish spokespersons, was immediate, calling for the aide's head. Evans, reached by the *Tribune* just before departing for a municipal finance officer's meeting in Atlanta, said there was no room in public life for statements such as Cokely's, but stopped short of asking for his firing, believing that the act was imminent.

But Sawyer did not move for days, during which time he defended Cokely in the media and met with nationalist leaders who urged him to retain Cokely. But while negative editorial reactions continued to stream out and the subject of black anti-Semitism was tarring the front pages, no major black leaders spoke out against Cokely, with the exception of the late civil rights leader Al Raby and, to the surprise of many, Alderman Dorothy Tillman. Even the Reverend B. Herbert Martin, Washington's pastor and the nominee to head the city's human relations commission, made an ambivalent statement about how anti-Semitic comments had a "ring of truth" in the black community. Danny Davis, the alderman of the 29th Ward and a candidate for mayor who had strong links to Chicago's white progressives, at first defended Cokely and then hedged badly.

If the city's Jewish population, long considered the most open and liberal on race relations among white ethnic groups, ever needed a nightmare image of black anti-Semitism, the combination of Cokely's remarks and silence from black political leaders provided it. The episode also gave pro-Daley writers such as Andrew Greeley and Eugene Kennedy the opportunity to run an I-told-you-so routine about the city's black leadership, fanning racial fires from what looked to be the moral high ground.

Jewish voters had given Harold Washington a greater percentage of their votes than had any other white voting bloc—almost twice that of Protestants and three times that of Catholics. But from that week forward there was a continued refrain among many Jews, even from those areas that had given Washington his earliest support, that they would never again support a black for mayor.

Evans returned from his trip on Wednesday, May 5th, and determined immediately to call for Cokely's firing, which he did the following morning on public radio and then in television and newspaper interviews. Within hours, Sawyer was spurred to action and announced that he had fired Cokely. The Evans position, strongly worded and—had it been delivered a day earlier—enough to make him a hero in the Jewish community, was buried in stories about the firing.

Ironically, those who would have most welcomed his statement remained unaware of it throughout the campaign—many of them strangely identifying Evans with Cokely and anti-Semitism in a persistent blurring of events. Yet more than the careers of Tim Evans, Gene Sawyer, and many others were at stake here. The Cokely affair would go on to have a dramatic long-term impact on the realignment of Chicago's liberal and progressive political blocs.

* * *

Meanwhile, the Dunne-Madigan faction of the regular Democrats was preparing a maneuver that, while destined to fail, propped up Sawyer in the short run. The election for mayor, they declared, should be held in 1991. To anyone reading the law, the argument was absurd. But Dunne and Madigan, joined at first by the governor of Illinois, lent force to the argument.

The Chicago Board of Elections, which had been deferring action on the matter, said that it would wait for a ruling from the State Board of Elections. The state board, controlled by Madigan, Thompson, and Attorney General Neil Hartigan, had absolutely no jurisdiction in this area. This forced the Evans contingent into court and into a publicity campaign. The offensive showed Thompson flip-flopping on the issue; at the last minute, he blinked. The state board deadlocked, with the four Republicans voting for 1989 and the four Democrats voting for 1991. This knocked the ball back to the Chicago board. Out of excuses, and under relentless press assault, the Chicago board capitulated and ruled in favor of a 1989 election. In the middle of May, the circuit court agreed, and the election date was set.

In the interim, the Sawyer operation was able to co-opt a huge segment of the black business community, and their April fund raiser, run under the cloud of ambiguity surrounding the election date, was a smashing financial success. The election date controversy opened the door to the black business community for Sawyer. Fearing for jobs, contracts, and general access to the mayor's office for the next three years, black businessmen embraced Sawyer. Once they had made their investment, even the changed date did not change their minds. Evans's money problems, already bad because of his inertia, were nearly insurmountable after this point. Evans had won the March electoral battle, but was outmaneuvered on the financial front in April.

Finally at the end of June, in a hastily prepared press conference with little more support than he had shown earlier, Evans announced an exploratory committee. But for months afterward nothing more was done. Sawyer continued to raise money; Evans raised next to nothing. Sawyer continued to build an organization; Evans's allies could not even agree on an office manager.

By summer's end, the presidential campaign was gearing up. Local operatives for Dukakis, attempting to steer clear of the Evans-Sawyer situation, unwittingly made a decision that would have long-term impact: they launched a pay-as-you-go registration campaign in Chicago's black community. Because the premayoral registration occurs in January, the autumn registration prior to the November election usually produces greater numbers and thus has greater impact on the subsequent mayoral race. Seeking not to show favoritism to Evans, who controlled the bulk of the city's deputy registrars, the Dukakis campaign determined to pay registrars per registration rather than paying organizations to organize volunteer registrars. The results were abominable. Many previously successful organizations now found it impossible to recruit volunteer registrars (who works for free while others are getting paid?) and a set pattern of registration work in black neighborhoods was thus destroyed. A registration drive that could have netted hundreds of thousands of new voters ended up netting hardly any. Not only did the registration fiasco cause Dukakis to lose Illinois, it ultimately caused the loss of a black mayor in Chicago.

The end of the registration period saw a serious decrease in black registration. For six years previously, substantial pressure had been mounted by the Washington operation against unlawful purges of voters. This, coupled with a general inexperience and the out-and-out sloppiness of many black ward committeemen, led to massively padded voter rolls in the black community. Voter registration in the entire city appeared to remain constant between the 1987 and 1989 mayoral elections, in black and white wards alike—despite demographic estimates that more than 20,000 people move per month in the city of Chicago. If only half of these people are voting-age adults, this means that 120,000 people should be registered and purged each year just to maintain *status quo ante* in registration. Because mobility in the black community is much greater than in the white wards, far and away the greatest percentage of new registrations should have been black.

The Dukakis-led debacle was the only major voter registration campaign launched in the two years between Washington's reelection and the 1989 elections. It grossed about 140,000 new voters; about the same number were purged. However, registrations and purges should have totaled nearly twice that number. In 1984, just one year after the massive infusion of more than 250,000 new voters in 1982 and 1983, about 150,000 new voters were added to the rolls during the 1984 presidential contest. This amounted to between 350,000 and 400,000 voters put on and taken off the rolls in two years. The 1989 number, if one includes the pre-1987 registration, could easily have been more than 200,000 short of that. Yet because the voter rolls remained constant at about 1.56 million, this leads to the conclusion that going into the 1989 election there were probably between 100,000 and 200,000 black voters who were unregistered simply because they had moved. And this does not count blacks who came of age in the 1987–89 period or those who migrated to the city.

With no significant premayoral registration drive, the success of any black candidacy may have been doomed from the very start. If this hypothesis is correct, black turnout may have been higher in real terms than initially believed. Indeed, if only 65,000 black voters were listed on the rolls at stale addresses, this would account for a full 10 percent black turnout depression from 1987 levels, and nearly half of Evans's losing margin.

* * *

By mid-fall, with polls showing Sawyer trailing Evans by four and five to one, it looked as though—despite huge campaign coffers and the inactivity of the Evans forces—Sawyer was heading into the tank. In late October, with far more advance planning and better organization than had characterized his earlier forays, Evans announced his candidacy for mayor at the hotel where Washington had announced six years earlier. For the first time in months, Evans was receiving almost universally good press. His campaign finally appeared to be getting off to a solid start. Just after the November election, Evans scored another triumph: the Illinois Supreme Court unanimously rejected the Sawyer forces' appeal in the election date case. There definitely would be a special election for mayor in 1989.

Early November was the bleakest it would ever look for Sawyer, and the best for Evans. While things were looking up on the outside, they were still going nowhere. Nearly a month after his announcement, Evans still had no campaign manager and no staff. A few volunteers and a network of community organizers were all that kept Evans's campaign from foundering completely. And there still was no money: a finance chair had yet to be recruited, which became more difficult every day with mounting pressure from the Sawyer business combine. There were no major fund raisers and no formal field operation, although nominating petitions were due in three weeks.

The campaign was being run collectively through an interminable series of meetings, and with no one making day-to-day tactical or strategic decisions, with no money, with no formal organization of any kind, and with a press corps following the candidate's every move. There was bound to be a point when it all came unglued.

In the last week of November 1988, Evans grass-roots supporters unilaterally launched a series of "memorial services" on the first anniversary of Harold Washington's death. A memorial event or two might have been helpful, but for some reason they scheduled seven of them. At one of the services, Alderman Dorothy Tillman (3) launched an attack on Acting Mayor Sawyer, referring to him as a "mumblin' Uncle Tom, shufflin' around city hall." Sawyer responded in a Nixonian way: he was not, he said, an Uncle Tom. Had things stopped there, it might have been a score for Tillman. But they did not. Tillman held a press conference where she repeated her statement . . . then another press conference . . . followed by another memorial service . . . followed by another press conference. The "Uncle Tom" story was acquiring a life of its own. Sawyer, initially hurt by the reminder of how he assumed office, gained sympathy. Evans, tied to Tillman and publicly silent as the story grew, was losing every day.

The spectacle came to a horrendous end on December 1, at a city council meeting called by Evans's allies to commemorate the anniversary of Sawyer's election. A weak hand was played too soon: the turnout was tiny. Far from demonstrating strength, the small crowd was seen for what it really was: a political campaign in mortal trouble.

* * *

Richard M. Daley, Cook County state's attorney and son of Chicago's longest-serving mayor, was defeated in his first bid for his father's old job in 1983 because he played his hand too soon. For six years he had been waiting for a moment like this one, but probably doubted it would ever come. Now it looked too easy. Two black candidates, each with one hand on the other's throat and one foot in his own mouth. A business community aching to kick the reformers—and the blacks—out of city hall and establish a new kind of machine with themselves as central cogs. A white ethnic community waiting to reclaim the throne. A black community divided. A Latino community, dispirited, wanting a still bigger piece of the pie.

Daley was leading all potential candidates in trial-heat polls, beating both Evans and Sawyer in separate one-on-one contests. Evans, because of his intense core of support, was clearly the strongest challenger, but his campaign was on the rocks. Sawyer, who announced that he was in to stay, was in far too deep a hole to climb out before the February election, no matter what his resources. It was a good electoral bet. Evans might force Sawyer out of the primary race, but his inferior resources not only made this less likely by the day, but also made it less likely that he could pull a winning bid together even if Sawyer left the race. Finally, either Evans or Sawyer could drive the other into an independent run in the general election. This would assure that in a primary Daley would face either an Evans with few resources or a Sawyer with few votes, as the candidate waiting for the general would find it hard to give up his trump card to the other in the primary. If Sawyer waited until the general, his business supporters would strangle Evans financially. If Evans waited until the general, his grass-roots supporters would strangle Sawyer electorally.

About the only situation that did not look like a sure winner for Daley was if either Evans or Sawyer dropped out early, thus allowing time for a united effort to develop. By the first week of December, it was clear that, of all possibilities, this was least likely to happen. And so, with petition filing a week away, with the pretense of his swearing-in to a new term as state's attorney over, and with an ideal political and electoral situation, Richard Daley announced that he was again a candidate for mayor of Chicago.

The heat was on—and increasingly it came to be directed at Tim Evans. The Reverend Jesse Jackson, identified as an Evans partisan in December 1987, now called for Evans to run in the general and Sawyer in the primary. Every day a new story hit the media about Evans's lack of funds and his lack of organization. Only with the announcement that former Washington chief of staff Ernest Barefield would become Evans's campaign manager did the press frenzy die down.

What Barefield found was at least as bad as any media account: the campaign was a wreck. Barefield concluded that Evans had to run in the general election. Campaign insiders turned their attention from winning the primary to leveraging Evans's weak position into as much support as possible in the general. Finally, in the last week of December 1988, standing with his own supporters and some Sawyer boosters who had come aboard in a spirit of compromise, Evans announced that he would be the candidate of the Harold Washington party in the general election. The frontrunning candidate for mayor of Chicago for nearly a full year, Evans had been forcibly driven out of the Democratic primary contest.

By the beginning of 1989, the contestants had taken their positions on the field, and the battle was ready to be joined. Like so many classic contests, this one was over before it started. Daley would be elected mayor in a walk.

* * *

Still, there were some faint rays of hope for the Evans camp as the new year began. The Sawyer problem seemed, for the time being, out of the way. A campaign manager was in place. Some effort at fund raising had begun. And a staff was slowly being assembled.

Even at the time, however, it was clear that a whole year of failed political jockeying had had a deleterious effect on Evans's image. Some of his own supporters, when polled, responded that Evans was somehow dishonest or disingenuous, mentioning Evans's association with the old machine. Others responded that Evans was a bit too "radical," and many of these mentioned his political allies. If there were to be a new and consistent Evans image, it would have to result from heavy television advertising, but this would not come to pass.

Daley began his campaign by acknowledging in his first TV spot the one thing that all polling data showed was his weakest point: the fact that he was not a good speaker. He also hastened to point out that this did not mean that he was either stupid or incapable of being a good mayor, that he "knew how to run a government." The second Daley problem was that half the city's voters still thought that he was an old-time machine politician. His campaign dealt with this problem not so much by what it did, but by what it did not do.

First, the county chairman, George Dunne, refused to call a slating session—a session that Daley would have won, but that might have doomed his campaign from the start. A gathering of white machine Democrats meeting behind closed doors to anoint one of their own as mayor was one of the great symbols of Chicago politics and would only have served to reinforce Daley's image as a somewhat less grand reincarnation of his father. The lack of a slating session allowed him to run as something of an independent while garnering support from the worst machine committeemen—the best of both worlds.

Similarly, Daley did not follow the tradition of appearing before groups of precinct captains at ward meetings. He was presented in picture-perfect "community" settings, addressing "issues" and, most importantly, not presenting the image of a candidate supported by a bunch of machine hacks, even though the "community" audiences were often composed of precinct captains and other machine hangers-on. Finally, Daley rarely appeared in public with any symbols of the old machine, particularly office holders.

The contrast with the Evans campaign is striking. While Daley was assiduously avoiding appearances with white regular Democrats, Evans was almost invariably seen with the symbols of his problems. For more than a year, he was seen at major news conferences, rallies, and other public events with Dorothy Tillman looking over his shoulder. So strong was the public's connection of Evans with Tillman that Evans's own polling showed that Evans's esteem ratings were more strongly related to Tillman's than to anyone else's, including Harold Washington and Jesse Jackson.

Though she had been at the forefront of progressive political causes for years, Dorothy Tillman's strong, outspoken stands had made her among the most unpopular politicians in the City of Chicago. Yet the Evans campaign put no distance between the candidate and his unpopular colleague. Whereas Daley tried his best never to remind the public of his most unpopular allies, Evans flaunted his.

The open association among Evans, Tillman, and other perceived "radicals" allowed the public and the press to make cognitive leaps, associating Evans with every negative and hostile statement emanating from Chicago's black community. So, for example, Evans was more bloodied by the Cokely episode than Sawyer. Jews rated Evans an abysmal 2 on a scale of 0 to 10, while they rated Sawyer nearly 6. So, too, was Evans crowned with the thorns of Gus Savage's racial remarks about Daley—remarks originally made at a rally for Sawyer. At various other points, the press tarred Evans with remarks made by nationalist leaders, many of whom had opposed Evans in the black community for a year.

At the same time, Daley was able not only to distance himself from his problem brethren, but also to substantially shut them up. Unlike the 1983 debacle, there were few racist remarks from white committeemen, no overt racial incidents, and only a few racial missteps. The discipline of the Daley operation, down to controlling the normally out-of-control committeemen, was a definitive element in his victory.

While marginal white and Latino voters were skillfully shielded from the reasons to vote against Daley, long-standing racially motivated proclivities to vote against any black candidate were given an underpinning by the vast array of negative Evans images. Moderate white and Latino voters could fix on the vocal "political friends" of Evans. And thanks in part to a misleading series in the *Tribune* in the summer of 1988, more liberal voters could focus in on Evans's image as a wolf in sheep's clothing, an old-line machine politician who held his community in poverty-pimp bondage to get votes.

* * *

Nations, it often has been remarked, are always fighting the last war. This seems as true for political wars as it is for the real thing. Given Evans's massive image problem, the strategic decision not to run television advertising was without question the campaign's worst. It was based not just on a lack of resources, but also on a view that voter mobilization was all that was needed, a belief based on the Sawyer turnout disaster in the primary. Sawyer's problem was mobilization. Evans's problem was persuasion. Sawyer persuaded, but never mobilized. Evans mobilized, but never persuaded. The result for both men was the same.

The Evans campaign never developed a clear, cohesive strategy to create a positive image for the candidate and garner sufficient votes to win. Indeed, each week there seemed to be a new strategy. The message zigged and zagged. At one moment, the Evans campaign was standing up to Sawyer on principle; at another, it seemed to be begging for his support. The campaign first decided that it had to go up on television before the primary, then the very people who had most severely savaged Sawyer said that preprimary television would offend the Sawyer people. These same people then immediately went out and said openly that they were going to depress the vote for Sawyer.

In the end, the campaign devolved into a kind of strategic feudalism, with each lord having, not tactical, but absolute strategic control over his barony. Thus, the field operation—which, given that there were no paid media, ended up as the functional campaign—exercised total control over the content of all printed material. What this material conveyed was purely at the whim of a small group and was totally disconnected from all other aspects of the campaign. It was not informed by polling, not related to any public relations strategy, hardly connected to the little paid media Evans did have, and—except in the case of CHA—not targeted to any of the groups with which he had problems.

Like all organizations, the Evans campaign took on the shape and personality of those who were really in charge: community organizers and ward politicians with little experience in larger campaign efforts. The difference between a race for mayor of a city the size of Chicago and a race for alderman is not one of degree, but of kind. The successful neighborhood campaigner is a mobilizer; the successful big-city, statewide, and national campaigner is a persuader. Concerned less with absolute numbers than with statistical probabilities, he seeks to increase the probability that more people will be for him on election day than against. He thus is concerned not only with how *many* are for him or against him, but how *strongly* they are for him or against him.

Seen in this light, the Evans campaign was a local contest transferred to a citywide level. Concerns about negative image, relative intensity of support, or voter's attitudes about the probability of victory were replaced by talk about coffees, visibility, and literature blitzes. Run by ward leaders, both elected and nonelected, Evans's campaign concentrated almost totally on getting out the vote.

The lack of television advertising prevented the campaign from selling what was an eminently saleable candidate among marginal constituencies, specifically lakefront whites and Latinos. Significantly, it also contributed massively to a lack of legitimacy of the candidate and the campaign among marginal black voters. While the press was spreading gloom and doom about the campaign to everyone who would listen, the campaign itself, by not engaging the electorate on television, in effect confirmed everything the press had to say. Only in hindsight can we say that Evans's vote, in the main, came out on its own. Evans's problem, which was evident all along, was that he did not have enough votes.

* * *

Weeks before the election, everyone knew that Evans did not have enough votes. Evans's poll, taken in late February, showed two important trends, both of which were ominous. The first was that the strongest Evans supporters were at least 10 percent less likely to vote than the strongest Daley supporters. The second was that an overwhelming majority of probable voters thought that Daley would win the general election, and that, even among black voters, less than a majority thought that Evans would win.

Especially in light of the fact that the campaign was doing no persuading, increasing the vote probability of Evans voters and convincing Chicago's black community that Evans could win became the most important strategic objectives of the campaign—objectives that, if not achieved, would cause Evans to lose. And it was in this area that the Daley campaign beat Evans most soundly.

One week before the primary election, when the Sawyer phenomenon was at its zenith, only 16 percent of Sawyer's voters said they would vote for Daley in the general election. This number reduced itself naturally after the primary as black Sawyer voters reconciled themselves to Evans, and it could have been reduced to nothing at all if there had been a general perception that the Evans candidacy had a chance. The real significance of the Evans-Sawyer "split" was that the more it was discussed, the more it actually fed the perception that Evans could not win the election.

The turnout among blacks in the 1989 general election was 63 percent; among whites, it was 78 percent. This compares to the 1987 general election, when the turnout was 74 percent among blacks and 75 percent among whites. Over the two mayoral elections preceding 1989, the "normal" spread between the black vote and the white vote was three to four percentage points. In the general election of 1989, it was fifteen points.

An increased black vote between the primary and general elections explains the difference between the 383,000 votes received by Sawyer and the 428,000 received by Evans. The increase in the actual spread between the white vote and the black vote, with the white turnout actually approaching the level in the Epton contest (1983 general election), explains the increased Daley winning margin—up from 100,000 in the primary against Sawyer to 150,000 in the general against Evans.

Although the relatively low black turnout can be best explained by the inculcation of an attitude of doom and defeatism in the black community, the rise in the white turnout was due to several factors. The first was that the Daley campaign ran an effective get-out-the-vote operation, using solid precinct work combined with repeated mailings and massive phone-banking operations. The second factor was the presence of Ed Vrdolyak, whose candidacy initially was thought to be a plus for Evans, but which turned out to be an immense plus for Daley.

The more the press portrayed Republican Vrdolyak as a spoiler who would "split the white vote" and elect Evans, the more incentive there was for the more docile and secure Daley voters to act to ensure that what the press was telling them might happen would not happen. Next was the bandwagon effect. The excitement of being with a winner historically has had the consequence of increasing turnout among a candidate's core supporters. In 1987, Harold Washington was perceived as a sure winner in the general election, and the result was a decline in the white vote and an actual *increase* in the black vote over the 1987 primary. The 1989 election was, at least with regard to turnout, the 1987 election in reverse.

Finally, no one should deny the impact of the 1983 primary on white voting patterns. The idea that a divided white vote caused the nomination of Harold Washington was perhaps the single greatest shibboleth to come out of that tumultuous campaign. The "vote split" message was drilled into white voters for years, and when the reality of a repeat performance confronted them in 1989, the white electorate bloc-voted in a way that they had not done since the 1930s. They also turned out in a display of collective rationality on a grand scale. Each voter came out to vote for Daley to make up for their neighbors' imaginary votes for Vrdolyak. Of course, Vrdolyak's vote was a fantasy, but for white turnout—and for Daley—it was an effective one.

In the end, Daley crushed Evans, and with him a progressive coalition that little more than a year earlier had been on the verge of a genuine solidification of political power. What Chicago might have looked like had this process been completed is now beside the point. What Chicago might now come to look like under the new Mayor Daley—and the wholly different coalition that elected him—is the question at hand.

* * *

The urban political machines of the past century were blue collar in their base, labor intensive in their electoral activities, and served as providers of basic social welfare services and patronage employment. Not surprisingly, they grew rapidly in periods of severe economic depression—when the labor they needed to operate effectively was selling at a discount and when the services and the small-time jobs they could offer as rewards were selling at a premium.

In the extended economic expansion following World War II, most of the nation's old machines withered and died. Under Richard J. Daley, Chicago was a notable exception. While the leaders of machines in places as diverse as New York, Philadelphia, and Kansas City saw their power base crumble in the face of rampant suburbanization and rising economic expectations, Daley realigned and thus preserved Chicago's machine by bringing in major elements of the business and finance community—typically, in most places, the leading forces for political reform and, in fact, his major opponents in his first run for mayor in 1955. This alliance, unique to America's big cities, melding big labor and big capital, blue and white collars, and minorities, was key to making Daley, in the words of the late political analyst Sidney Lens, not the last of the old-style bosses, but the first of the new-style bosses.

Politics itself was changing with the economy and with the times, becoming less dependent upon the old-fashioned precinct captain. In his place came television and the modern techniques of persuasion, which were not only new and more powerful, but increasingly more cost effective as well. At the same time, the facts of urban life, such as increasing crime, brought fewer and fewer captains to their neighbors' doors, and had fewer and fewer neighbors responding to their callers. The increasingly atomistic and anomic nature of modern urban life combined with increased economic opportunities and higher labor costs to make the old-time captain into a dinosaur.

In 1972, Dan Walker upset the Daley machine and became the first media-elected governor of Illinois. In 1979, Jane Byrne became the first media-elected mayor of Chicago, aided by a social uprising induced by the machine's response to the great snowstorm of 1978–79. She, in turn, was upset by Harold Washington under similar circumstances—both a social uprising in the black community and a clever media campaign to help capitalize on it.

Washington, despite charges that he was building a new machine, never really organized one, though he had some of the elements in place and an immense personal popularity that permitted him to elect many candidates with his own endorsements, delivered through electronic media and the mail.

He and Byrne raised and spent huge sums of money—nearly $10

million each during their terms—fully understanding that modern electoral techniques and the political organizations of the day would be capital intensive rather than labor intensive.

In the late 1980s, it cost upwards of $4 million to run a rigorous campaign for mayor of Chicago, and double that for governor of Illinois. The massive infusions of cash necessary for such campaigns simply cannot come from golf outings and putting the squeeze on patronage workers. Not even the average municipal contractor can cough up scores of thousands of dollars relative to his financial return.

Such money now must come from institutions where the benefits of government run, not in the hundreds of thousands of dollars, but in the millions: law firms, financial organizations, and developers. Thus, the $50,000 or $100,000 contribution to candidates becomes the ticket to municipal and gubernatorial access for such institutions, who cast their bread upon the waters to see it return many times over. The term that emerged for this process during the tenure of Governor James Thompson was "pinstripe patronage."

This, then, is the next and higher stage of the new urban political machine, which must spend millions upon millions to feed the media monster (rather than the families of precinct captains) and utilize contemporary technologies, such as computerized mailing and phone banking.

The important cogs in the new machine are not the ward bosses and sewer chiefs of old, but developer-businessmen such as Paul Stepan and lawyer-lobbyists such as William Singer. The old political bases in the once legendary "river wards" are now peopled by unreliable, if not hostile, minorities whose antipathy to the new machine, with its capital-intensive, snatch-and-grab world view, is as strong as once was their unrequited loyalty to the old one. The new machine's political bases have indeed shifted to locales such as Lincoln Park's 43rd Ward—home of both Singer and Stepan—and once the home of the political reform and anti-machine sentiment. The yuppie, rather than the welfare recipient, is the target voter of the new machine.

The election of Richard M. Daley provided the first toehold on political power for this new coalition. Under the tutelage of his brother William Daley, who learned much about the new politics during national elections in 1984 and 1988, and with the guidance of David Axelrod, a rising media consultant who is now a trusted insider, a new Mayor Daley is evolving, retooling and rebuilding a new machine that could, as did his father's, dominate the city's politics and economics for many years.

The struggle to control ghetto land was the dominant battle of the 1960s. The battle of the 1990s will be the developer-led crusade to fully gentrify not only Chicago's lakefront, but all areas proximate to the central business district, for political realignment benefiting new machine politicians and financial gain for the businessmen who are their loudest cheerleaders. Who wins and who loses clearly will determine the political makeup of Chicago as it heads into the twenty-first century. The ultimate winner may emerge, not because of the political savvy of the new Daley machine or the relative disorganization of the opposition, but because of a change in the economic conditions that made the rise of the new machine possible in first place.

PART FOUR

The Press and the Polls

We covered the campaign and covered it and covered it. . . . Take Gene Sawyer—he was so nice, we looked like we were beating him up. Larry Bloom came in for a program carrying little blue cards reminding him to do everything, even smile. And then there was Tim Evans, unrelenting, pontificating. [Daley is] the master of the short bite. . . . To put it mildly, Richie just beat the shit out of us.

John Callaway, discussing "Chicago Tonight" TV coverage of the
1989 mayoral campaign

In earlier mayoral races, Harold Washington's formula for victory over a single white candidate was: (1) monolithic support among black voters; (2) high black voter turnout; (3) nearly one-fifth of the white vote; (4) nearly half of the Hispanic vote. . . . Sawyer fell drastically short. . . .

Richard Day, Jeff Andreasen, and John Ross (1990)

CHAPTER 8

Media Coverage: The Chicago Daley News

David Fremon

It was a historic election, that 1989 contest to fill out the vacancy left by the death of Harold Washington. The Daley dynasty reestablished itself, as Richard M. captured the mayoral seat held for twenty-one years by his father, Richard J. A white mayor entered city hall, making Chicago the first major city in which a white defeated an incumbent black. And for once, Chicago's press made no pretense as to its choice in the mayoral election.

Richard M. Daley dominated Chicago's 1989 special mayoral election from the onset. Just as he dominated the political events of the election, so also did the son of the late mayor dominate its media coverage—and the major media were all too willing to be submissive.

One word popped up continually when journalists and political insiders described the election. "The media were disgraceful. They were so slanted and biased in favor of Daley," said *Crain's Chicago Business* columnist Mark Hornung.[1] Greg Hinz, political editor of the Lerner newspapers, added, "The Chicago media did a first-class job of biased reporting in the just-concluded mayoral campaign."[2] "The game in town was to make Daley mayor, from a press standpoint," according to Larry Horist, who served as media spokesman for Eugene Sawyer and later Edward Vrdolyak. "This was the most biased treatment I have ever seen in an election."[3]

It was Daley's election from the beginning, so much so that one could divide the campaign into three parts: the time before December 5, the day he entered the race; the remainder of the primary campaign; and the general election. During all three of these segments, Chicago's two major daily newspapers fit their coverage to be most advantageous to Richard Daley and most detrimental to major challenger Timothy Evans. The other candidates were pawns, to be manipulated in ways that would turn favorable to Daley and unfavorable to Evans.

THE PRE-DALEY CAMPAIGN

Eugene Sawyer never stood a chance. Blacks disliked him because he was selected acting mayor by anti-Washington white and renegade black aldermen. Whites preferred Sawyer only over Timothy Evans, but were prepared to abandon the man they helped put in the mayor's office if an electable white candidate came along. Given this atmosphere, Sawyer presented an easy media target in the months leading up to the mayoral campaign.

And the media took aim and fired. They attacked Sawyer, the man who opposed a 1989 special mayoral election; Sawyer, the man who promoted a budget that offered hefty pay raises to allies and piddling ones to those city officials not in his favor; Sawyer, the man who proposed megabucks consultant Erwin France as school board president because "There's a lot more involved than teaching kids, there's jobs and money."[4]

Most important, there was Sawyer, the man who waffled for nearly a week before firing Steve Cokely, an aide found to have promoted anti-Semitic and anti-Christian beliefs. The acting mayor received much publicity—nearly all of it negative—following the Cokely episode. If he had Jewish support beforehand, he lost it afterwards.

Incidents such as the Cokely affair should have played into the hands of Sawyer's chief black rival, Fourth Ward Alderman Timothy Evans. The self-proclaimed heir to the Washington legacy and the consensus choice of black voters, Evans had the opportunity to capitalize on Sawyer's misfortunes. But he failed to do so.

Evans's coverage in the major media was negative from the onset. He was portrayed as a rabble rouser—or the candidate of the rabble rousers. The Tribune account of the scene outside city hall during the December 1–2, 1987, election described "mobs of angry, mostly black voters crowding the streets and storming the corridors of City Hall," almost comparing the scene to the French Revolution.[5] Those who were at the scene, however, remember a noisy but peaceful group, no more dangerous than, say, the fans at a 1970s White Sox game.

The harshest attack against Evans came as part of an August 1988 Tribune series called "Chicago on Hold: The New Politics of Poverty." An August 30 headline proclaimed "Votes give CHA slums a reason for life" and the article that followed implied that Evans favored renovation of six CHA high-rise buildings in his ward instead of their replacement by a racially and economically integrated community of apartments and townhouses because those high-rises provided votes he needed to win his elections. "In the 1983 primary, Evans outpolled [his opponent] by 1,688 votes to 56 votes—a 30-to-1 margin in the 10 precincts of the 4th Ward located in Oakland. Across the ward he defeated her by only a 2–1 margin."[6] Those numbers may be true. But what the *Trib* failed to mention was that Evans won reelection in 1987 with 77 percent of the vote, carrying every precinct but one. In other words, the paper's theory that the alderman tried to preserve a slum because he needed its votes does not hold water.

Evans rebutted the *Tribune* story, claiming that he opposed developer Ferd Kramer's plan mainly because he opposed displacement of ward residents. Nonetheless the image of Evans as maliciously anti-development stuck throughout the campaign.

The 1988 presidential election campaign overshadowed the mayor's race somewhat. Elections also were held for a number of county offices. One of those races involved one Richard M. Daley, two-term incumbent, son of the late mayor, and, should he decide to run, the odds-on choice as "white" candidate for mayor.[7]

If Daley was not willing to speak his mayoral dreams during the summer of 1988, others were. Candidates sprang up like dandelions during this springtime of the mayoral election year, and most got little more respect than weeds.

Danny K. Davis, alderman of the West Side 29th Ward, came first. His campaign kickoff merited only a photograph (not a story) in the July 15 *Sun-Times*. Media generally depicted Davis as a well-meaning Don Quixote who would withdraw gracefully once he realized that he could not dislodge Evans or Sawyer as the "black" candidate. That is exactly what happened.

Next in line was Ed Kelly, 47th Ward committeeman and former parks czar, a man whose candidacy generally was considered as eccentric among white voters as Davis's was among blacks. Pundits wondered out loud about Kelly's "real" motivation for his October candidacy announcement. Was it an excuse to raise funds, a means of having a voice in the ultimate "white" candidate, a smokescreen to sidetrack a possible investigation of park district finances during his tenure as parks boss?[8]

The *Sun-Times* did not dally in knocking Kelly out of the box. Shortly after the November elections, a headline story discussed a secret land deal between Kelly and attorney Victor Cacciatorre in which Kelly as park boss netted an estimated $70,000 from the lawyer while steering to him some $428,000 in park district legal fees. Although no one admitted to any impropriety and no charges were ever issued, the story extinguished whatever faint mayoral sparks Kelly's campaign had, and he withdrew shortly afterwards.[9]

Alderman Ed Burke, long-time 14th Ward boss, received even less of a grace period than had Kelly. Immediately following his October 17 entry, the *Trib* described him as a "foot soldier to Byrne and as a tenacious City Council brawler who never was weary of throwing the first, and often the last, rhetorical punch at the late Harold Washington."[10] A *Sun-Times* sidebar recalled Burke's "negative" comments on the Washington administration, reminding readers that Burke "was the architect of the City Council strategy under former mayor Jane M. Byrne and the point man of the 29 opposition votes to former Mayor Harold Washington. In that role, Burke is credited with blocking nearly all of Washington's appointments during his first term."[11] After that first salvo, the media pretty much laid off Burke, figuring (as the candidate himself all but admitted) that he was little more than a stalking horse.

Another contender, Hyde Park alderman Lawrence Bloom, entered the fray in mid-September. A reform alderman in the Dick Simpson–Martin Oberman tradition, Bloom was universally acknowledged to be honest and intelligent—almost too honest and intelligent to be running for mayor. Unlike Davis, Kelly, and Burke, Bloom could not be easily dismissed. He carried none of the "council wars" or personal baggage of Burke or Kelly, and he had no need to dismiss other contenders, as Davis did. But unlike the black or "white ethnic" candidates, he lacked a racial base of voters. These factors—his intelligence, honesty, and lack of base—appeared in almost every story written or broadcast about him.

But these ribbon clerks appeared (and for the most part were portrayed) as minor opening acts. The *real* candidate declared his entry into the race on December 5.

ENTER RICHARD II

Few if any Chicago political observers had accused Richard M. Daley of political rashness. If anything, his performance in the 1983 Democratic mayoral primary contributed to his cautiousness. Daley entered the campaign as a solid favorite against a controversial incumbent (Jane Byrne) and a little-known black man (Harold Washington), yet finished in an embarrassing third place.

Daley's political fortunes had improved considerably since then. He won reelection as state's attorney by a wide margin in 1984 and repeated the victory in 1988. He even carried the black wards against Gainer despite a Tim Evans call for a Daley boycott.

Daley probably harbored no illusions about capturing most of those black votes in a mayoral election against a black candidate. But he would not need them, particularly if Sawyer and Evans continued on their apparent collision course. As for the whites, the field consisted of only a relatively harmless liberal and a couple of minor machine pols who could be chased out by invoking the "spoiler" label (even though both Kelly and Burke preceded Daley into the race, the state's attorney unquestionably was the strongest white guy, and the others would be tagged as spoilers if they stayed in and thus possibly allowed a black man to win the nomination).

Thus the election was Daley's for the taking. All he had to do was refrain from committing outrageous acts from November until April. At the same time, it might have become a "now or never" situation. Any strong white candidate would be a favorite in the election, given the split among blacks. But a victorious white candidate might not be gracious enough to hand over the keys to city hall, should Daley request them in the future. So Richard M. Daley waited a diplomatic amount of time (about a month) after his reelection as state's attorney, and then declared for the job he had craved all along.

The media greeted him with open arms. From the beginning, the coverage was prominent and favorable. The preview story of Daley's announcement, on page 3 of the December 5 *Sun-Times*, received more prominent play than the actual announcements of Davis (page 5), Bloom (page 7), Burke (page 5), or Kelly (page 3).

Almost immediately, the *Sun-Times* gave him a quasi-endorsement. An editorial quoted Daley as saying that people are "sick and tired" of name calling and divisiveness, and that much more could be accomplished by "lowering our voices and raising our sights." That is correct, said the paper in a schoolmarmish tone. "Now if he and the other candidates just keep that in mind we could have the kind of election we haven't had in a long time."[12]

Some—Burke and Kelly—heeded that advice. But Evans and Sawyer, the bad kids at the back of the class, continued their fight. The newspapers were far from neutral.

Newspapers enjoyed trashing Sawyer all summer. But once Tim Evans started his campaign in earnest, an amazing transformation took place. Just as a repulsive caterpillar becomes a beautiful butterfly, Eugene Sawyer evolved from a bumbling and less-than-honest "Mayor Mumbles" into a statesman.

Timothy Evans remained Timothy Evans, a target, and one to be downplayed as much as possible. Evans was still the obvious choice over Sawyer among blacks, and Daley's strongest potential rival. Yet neither major daily saw fit to give Evans's October 30 campaign kick-off front-page coverage (it made page 5 of the *Sun-Times* and page 1 of the *Trib's* Chicagoland section). *Tribune* coverage became critical as early as the second paragraph, which mentioned Evans's attack on the machine and at the same time questioned whether the machine existed at all. In a sarcastic tone, the paper stated "Evans . . . set out to establish himself as reform incarnate."[13]

Evans's supporters hardly aided his cause. Alderman Dorothy Tillman, a city council member known through the years for her loud hats and occasionally louder mouth, added fuel to the anti-Evans campaign when she called Sawyer "a shufflin' Uncle Tom." Never mind that a large number of blacks shared that opinion. Tillman's remarks, and rebuttals from Sawyer ally B. Herbert Martin and racial watchdog group CONDUCT, kept an insult from a person who was not a part of the official Evans campaign team in the spotlight for days. Furthermore, it enabled commentators to attach the Tillman insult to Evans like excess baggage. Mike Royko, in a "Daley versus Evans" *Tribune* column declared "In this corner, wearing the white skin with the happy grin [note—no insult] is Daley. In the other corner, in the dark skin *with Ms. Tillman,* [italics mine] is Ald. Timothy Evans."[14]

Evans had one major ally in the press: Vernon Jarrett, the *Sun-Times* columnist, who made an impassioned plea on Evans's behalf during the memorial service for Harold Washington that preceded the December 1987 city council election.

Jarrett, in a column, told Sawyer, "*You,* as acting mayor, were programmed to play [a role] in the election of Daley, or Burke, or anybody other than the candidate chosen by the people still loyal to the reform movement."[15] He castigated Sawyer for airing radio ads that attacked Evans but ignored white politicians.[16] He even went so far as to criticize Jesse Jackson's "agonizing endorsement of Acting Mayor Sawyer."[17]

For the *Sun-Times,* Vernon Jarrett's column was a godsend, because it sold newspapers to two diverse groups. "Movement" blacks, who saw Tim Evans as the rightful heir to the Washington legacy, hung onto Jarrett's every word throughout the campaign. At the same time, Jarrett provided a convenient lightning rod for anti-Washington, anti-Evans whites. Because other local *Sun-Times* columnists generally espoused conservative views, Vernon Jarrett (a man who went so far as to defend Dorothy Tillman) was far to the left of them. He could be seen as a wild-eyed radical, a journalistic symbol of those who would take power in the event of an Evans victory.

Sawyer announced his candidacy December 11, to general fanfare and front-page coverage by the dailies. The *Sun-Times* opened its story by invoking the magical name among blacks: "Flanked by former Mayor Harold Washington's brothers on Sunday, Mayor Sawyer (not "Eugene" or even "Mayor Eugene," but the more regal "Mayor") vowed to carry on the legacy of his predecessor."[18]

Not long afterwards, the *Tribune* printed a Sunday magazine story that was little more than a puff piece on the mayor. The two major problems of his administration—a $30,000 "finder's fee" he accepted while an alderman and the Steve Cokely affair—were dismissed at the end of the article, which emphasized "Mr. Nice Guy."[19]

Perhaps the most blatant example of the Sawyer-versus-Evans bias involved a third party. Danny Davis gave up his dead-end campaign in mid-December and planned a formal announcement to that effect. The *Sun-Times* on December 13 marked the upcoming concession with a story of questionable veracity and ethics. "Big boost for Sawyer?" read the paper's headline. Davis was likely to endorse Sawyer instead of Evans for mayor, according to unnamed "Democratic sources."[20]

The story had one major flaw: it was patently untrue. Davis had always leaned to Evans over Sawyer, and when he made his concession speech he supported his fellow alderman over the acting mayor. The *Tribune* noted the concession speech but put a Daley spin on the story. Instead of something like "Davis quits, backs Evans," the headline read "Davis sees Daley win if both Sawyer, Evans run."[21]

Sawyer, buoyed by incumbency, campaign contributions that resulted largely from the incumbency, and more favorable press, would not be dislodged from the primary even though Evans had the support of roughly 80 percent of black voters in a direct confrontation between the two. Evans, realizing he was facing an immovable object, decided to form a third party, the Harold Washington party. Both dailies gloated. "Eyeball to eyeball—and Evans blinked," shouted a *Sun-Times* headline.[22] "Ald. Timothy Evans has tried admirably to put a good face on his withdrawal from the mayoral primary, but a setback by any other name is still a setback," declared the *Trib.*[23] The *Tribune* editorial panned Evans for skipping the Democratic primary—something the paper failed to do in 1987 when Daley ally Tom Hynes mounted a third-party campaign.

During the remainder of the primary election, Evans became all but a nonperson. He filed nearly 105,000 petitions for his third-party candidacy—a very impressive number indeed. Where did the papers cover the filing? Second section of the *Trib*, page 48 of the *Sun-Times*.[24]

With Evans out of the way, the dailies could resume their attacks on Sawyer. And they did. Sawyer was the boob who failed to produce income tax returns, allowed overzealous aides to mistakenly count three aldermen in his camp, and permitted another associate to confirm his participation in a debate with Daley, even though there was no such commitment. Sawyer was the dunderhead who unwittingly signed something called the "Hispanic agenda," which supposedly promised Hispanics cabinet-level jobs in ten city departments. Sawyer was the ineffectual clod who could not control provocative and racist statements by "allies" such as Congressman Gus Savage, attorney Tom Todd, and the Reverend Al Sampson (even though all three really were Evans supporters who likely did not care whether they sabotaged Sawyer's campaign).

Sawyer also was the one who supported extension of a controversial contract at O'Hare Airport that would continue the O'Hare Hilton's lease for another thirty years but would open up some adjacent land for immediate development. This deal, strongly supported by Illinois House Speaker Michael Madigan (who acted as a lobbyist for the project and whose law firm stood to gain $5 million from successful completion of the deal) came under continuous fire from the press. Madigan, whose refusal to consider a state income tax increase already had earned him enmity from the major Chicago press, now became "Land Grab Mike," an unscrupulous character to be compared to former attorney general Edwin Meese, the shah of Iran, and former Philippines dictator Ferdinand Marcos. Sawyer was portrayed as his city hall lackey.[25]

There was another primary, by the way. Republicans went through the motions of nominating a sure loser, and the media generally gave that party's efforts all the attention of a dogcatcher race in Beloit. Most attention centered on Jane Byrne, whose name gossip columnists had bandied about for months as a possible GOP standard bearer. Although she might have been the choice of the media (Jane Byrne, after all, remains good copy), there was no shred of proof that the former mayor had any intention of running for the office, especially after her massive setback in the 1988 circuit court clerk primary. As the filing deadline expired, she was somewhere other than the board of elections office. Likewise, the other top Republican hopeful, former Democratic chairman Ed Vrdolyak, took a pass.

That left the Republicans with eleven nobodies filing for mayor, and the media holding the bag. Republican stories appeared infrequently, and when they occurred they focused on the oddballs. Art Jones, an avowed Nazi, got coverage. So did eighty-year-old perennial candidate Frank Ranallo, nineteen-year-old student Jonathan Silverstein, and reputed anti-Semite William Grutzmacher. Had Lar "America First" Daly, the perennial candidate who always campaigned wearing an Uncle Sam suit, been alive, the newspaper, television, and radio might have declared him a frontrunner.

Aside from frequent Lyndon LaRouche candidate Sheila Jones, only two other candidates filed for the Democrats. Juan Soliz received prime coverage upon his entry, but subsequent stories dealt almost exclusively with the 25th Ward alderman's fight against petition challenges that ultimately knocked him off the ballot. James Taylor, the most powerful black politician in the city during the Byrne era but now a political cipher, shared one *Sun-Times* story with Sheila Jones during the campaign.[26] The *Trib*'s only coverage of him was an "about town" feature that was decidedly tongue-in-cheek rather than a serious political effort.[27]

Daley, meanwhile, continued receiving the best treatment possible. When Democratic contenders agreed to two mayoral primary debates (Daley later skipped one of those sessions), the *Sun-Times* did not record "Democrats consent to 2 debates." The headline became "*Daley, other Democrats* [italics mine] consent to 2 debates."[28] On one very rare occasion, all major mayoral candidates showed up at one forum, and all were pictured seated except the one standing at the podium. Who was the candidate shown in the *Tribune* as standing head and shoulders above the others? Hint: it wasn't Evans, Soliz, Sawyer, Taylor, Bloom, or Republican Herb Sohn.[29]

Everything was fair game for positive Daley play—even something as innocuous as the *Sun-Times* Photopinion. This feature, which covers such heated issues as "What's your least favorite color?," on January 31 asked "Will Richard M. Daley get any more votes because of his father?" All four of the respondents pictured answered no.[30] It had to be either a statistical miracle—the paper found the only four people in the city naive enough to believe that Daley's surname had nothing to do with his popularity—or a blatant bit of dishonesty on the part of the *Sun-Times*.

Of course, how honest was the paper on other occasions? The *Sun-Times* held a candidates' forum on January 20, with Bloom, Daley, Sawyer, and Taylor all allowed to speak their piece. Many observers saw a debate in which all candidates fared relatively well, with none breaking new ground.

Not Steve Neal of the *Sun-Times*. He declared in a news analysis that "Daley won decisively on points."[31] However, Neal failed to explain why Daley came out ahead. In fact, a reader who skipped his story's first paragraph might be led to believe that Bloom won the debate, given Neal's description of events. So then why was Daley the winner? Apparently for no other reason than that Neal, whose columns showed him to be a Daley supporter, declared it to be so.

If the Neal analysis was pro-Daley, the "straight" news story following that forum displayed an accompanying anti-Sawyer tone. "Deflecting allegations that he is an ineffective mayor, Eugene Sawyer insisted . . . that he is a 'hands-on' administrator," the article began. Nearly half of the story, which covered a two-hour forum involving four candidates, was devoted to one response— Sawyer's answer covering the O'Hare land deal.[32]

On those rare occasions when Daley received criticism, that criticism always came from opponents and never from the newspaper itself. And even so, the stories often as not were slanted to give a Daley spin. When the Reverend Jesse Jackson attacked Daley on a number of racial issues (such as an alleged "hit list" of black officials and alleged willingness to dismantle quotas), the headline read, not "Jackson blasts Daley on racial charges," but "Jackson distorts my views, Daley charges."[33]

The only criticism of Daley that received more than passing coverage in the dailies dealt with his role in a case involving fraud in 1985 and 1986 concerning petitions for a proposed nonpartisan mayoral election (an issue that Daley reportedly backed). Daley excused himself from the state's attorney's office investigation of the case, but no indictments had come from the case for more than two years. Daley brought in former U.S. Attorney Dan Webb as a special prosecutor, and Webb brought down indictments in less than two months.

Webb announced indictments February 10. How did the major metropolitan newspapers handle the story? The *Tribune* mentioned in the first paragraph of the following day's story that four persons were indicted on petition fraud charges, but mentioned in the very next paragraph that special prosecutor Webb found no evidence of a cover-up by Daley's office.[34] The *Sun-Times* drove the point home even quicker. The story's lead paragraph read "Special prosecutor Dan K. Webb said Friday he found no evidence of a 'cover-up' by State's Attorney Richard M. Daley's staff as four people were charged in an ongoing investigation of petition fraud."[35]

Get the most important message of the story? RICHIE DALEY IS PURE AS THE DRIVEN SNOW! Now, you eggheads who concern yourselves with such trivia as which four saps got indicted and what the charges were may continue reading the rest of the story.

The "major" media throughout Chicago might have shown a strong Daley bias. But the smaller media—community newspapers, ethnic papers, "alternative" papers—displayed a remarkable diversity of opinion during the campaign.

To no one's surprise, the smaller papers largely reflected their constituencies. Community papers along the Northwest and Southwest Sides for the most part refrained from endorsements, but Daley received much more prominent coverage than his opponents.

Of those papers serving predominantly white constituencies, the Lerner newspaper chain was the most prominent to give Daley its endorsement. But it was far from a ringing vote of confidence. The editorial proclaimed "Nagging questions remain over whether Daley has grown enough as a leader to serve all of this diverse city. . . . He must be more accessible. . . . This election pits candidates against other candidates, not against an ideal. Of those running in the primary, Daley is the best choice."[36]

Crain's Chicago Business, a business-oriented paper serving a predominantly white audience, also supported Daley. But as with that of the Lerner newspapers, *Crain's* support registered low on an editorial seismic scale. "It's about time someone came out and said it: Chicago voters are pining for Mayor Daley II because they want some muscle back in City Hall." At the same time, "Our endorsement comes despite Mr. Daley's shortcomings on issues that *Crain's Chicago Business* views as crucial to the city's future economic health. . . . Most surprising, considering his family lineage, is Mr. Daley's ignorance of city finance."[37] As one city reporter put it, "*Crain's* gave an endorsement for muscle in general rather than any candidate in particular."[38]

South and West Side newspapers favored a black candidate—but not the one apparently favored by most community members. Black papers such as the *Chicago Metro News, Chatham Citizen,* and *Chicago Independent Bulletin* came out strongly for Sawyer and heaped scorn upon Evans for failing to offer the acting mayor a primary endorsement.

Hurley Green, *Chicago Independent Bulletin* publisher, summed up the electoral fear held by many Sawyer backers over the impossibility of an Evans win when he declared "If not Sawyer now, it's Daley forever." To that end, he heaped vile criticism upon the alderman: "Evans is not supporting Mayor Sawyer because Evans is a mean, selfish, misguided little person. . . . His all consuming jealousy of Eugene Sawyer has turned him into something less than a black man. . . . Evans' face and stature was never a part of the Chicago political picture; he was just a pawn blown-up to man-size by white media who thought that they could pave the way for a white Mayor, by glamourizing a little, jealous martinet."[39]

Where did the Hispanic press, representing the supposed "swing vote" in Chicago, fall? Squarely in the Sawyer camp—more or less. A number of Hispanic publishers held a press conference to announce that twelve Hispanic papers were declaring an endorsement for Sawyer. However, even though the papers gave a combined Sawyer endorsement, each individual publisher was free to endorse whichever candidate he chose. Why this seeming paradox? One publisher, who was not at the press conference, speculated that the Hispanic publishers were backing Sawyer in hopes of obtaining city advertising should the acting mayor be elected.[40]

The Hispanic press at least provided comic relief in an otherwise drab campaign. Hispanic papers might have been confused over who they were supporting, but one left no doubts who it was attacking. Juan Soliz dropped out of the mayoral race and endorsed Sawyer. But he remained in a heated struggle with 26th Ward alderman Luis Gutierrez, a Daley backer, for the unofficial designation as the city's most important Hispanic politician.

Soliz's wife, Leticia, published a newspaper called the *Hispanic Times.* A cartoonist called "Bandito" decorated one *Hispanic Times* page with a work titled "Pancho Villain," which depicted a lisping "Luisito" (who bore an amazing resemblance to Gutierrez) dressed in women's underwear. Another showed the 26th Ward alderman dressed as Napoleon, with his hand in his crotch, a puppet whose strings were pulled by Richard Daley.[41] Gutierrez objected to the characterizations. That brought about yet another cartoon, which made fun of his reported congressional ambition. This one showed the alderman with his foot in his mouth and flies circling his head, while the offstage voice of Alderman Bernie Stone shouted "You little pipsqueak, the only congressional seat you'll ever see is if Dan Rostenkowski sits on your face!"[42]

Another potential swing group, the gay community, went with Sawyer in its leading publication. The *Windy City Times* boosted Sawyer, mainly for his role in passing a human rights ordinance that foes charged was a thinly disguised gay rights law. Even that endorsement was qualified, stating "many of [Sawyer's] efforts need rethinking and restructuring," particularly over the "city's response or lack of response to AIDS."[43]

Larry Bloom got his best coverage, not surprisingly, in the white liberal alternative press. The *Reader* as early as December printed a highly favorable Bloom story that was tantamount to an endorsement. *Chicago Lawyer* actually endorsed him, claiming that "Bloom stands head, shoulder, and chest above his uninspiring opponents. . . . Bloom is a man of exceptional abilities whose record is one of consistency and principle. Alone among the primary candidates, Bloom clearly articulates a coherent and compelling vision of Chicago's future. . . . In the present campaign, Bloom's position papers have sparkled. Any one of his papers, selected at random, contains more good ideas than all the lackluster offerings of his primary opponents combined."[44]

Mainstream media showed a more mixed attitude toward the reform-minded alderman. The *Tribune* on January 2 stated, "If Chicago's mayoral candidates got voter reaction and campaign contributions based on the wisdom of their ideas, Alderman Lawrence Bloom would be so far ahead of the pack that this race would be a bore."[45] But if his ideas were so good, why weren't they printed? When Bloom released a thirty-page document outlining his public safety program, the news got buried in the last paragraph of a "horse race" *Tribune* story about campaign doings of the contenders.[46] When Bloom promised to bring the police department up to full strength (12,500 members), it was interred in the next-to-last paragraph of a *Sun-Times* story concerning a proposed debate on "Hispanic" issues.[47]

Bloom also received criticism, much of it snide and tasteless commentary at the hands of Steve Neal, the *Sun-Times* political editor. Neal declared "Bloomsbury" to be a comic joke and sunk to personal insults ("the Andy Gump look-alike") while attacking Bloom's "Daley Duck" comic strip, which dared to attack Neal's choice, Rich Daley.[48] Neal even made the laughable assertion that fringe candidate Taylor was closing in on Bloom for third place in the primary (in truth, Bloom got more votes than Taylor in the primary even though he had withdrawn from the race).[49]

The only hope Bloom had of winning depended upon a strong performance in the only televised debate among the three candidates. He did not achieve it. Furthermore, the major media lambasted him afterwards. Bloom labeled Daley the Great White Hope and Sawyer the Great Black Hope during the debate, and the papers threw verbal stones at him for pandering to racial divisiveness. But Bloom merely spoke the truth; for vast numbers of people the election *was* a black-and-white issue, as comparative vote totals for Daley and Sawyer and white and black precincts indicated.

Bloom withdrew a week later, throwing his support to Sawyer, and immediately the major newspapers thrust verbal knives into the electoral corpse. The *Sun-Times* printed a story hinting that Bloom would be offered the job of corporation counsel as a quid pro quo for his withdrawal.[50]

The *Tribune* was more blunt in an editorial. It noted that Bloom had disagreed with Sawyer on numerous occasions in the city council yet now supported him for mayor (without mentioning that Bloom had also on occasion disagreed with State's Attorney Daley and even had run against him once). "What prompted him to link up with Sawyer?" the paper asked. "Oh, well, now that it's established what he really is, his price doesn't matter."[51] That's right; you may have the wisdom of ideas, but endorse a candidate other than Richie Daley, for whatever reason, and you become a whore.

With the debates finished, the newspapers got down to the business of endorsements. It was "a contest matching a respected public official with top legislative and administrative experience (Daley) against an appointed incumbent who, with very short tenure, has performed credibly in some areas, less so in others," according to the *Sun-Times*.[52]

The *Tribune* commented about Daley, "His love of Chicago and his dedication to its progress will take precedence over personal greed and self-interest. His eight years as Cook County prosecutor have established him as someone who not only knows the law but respects it."[53]

Oh? Is this the same State's Attorney Richard Daley described in the January *Chicago Lawyer* as "Son of Boss"? The one who, according to the article, proposed a bill that would give prosecutors the right to call for a jury trial (a decision condemned by the Supreme Court as one that "simply turns the concept of our Bill of Rights on its head")? The one who pushed through the general assembly a law-and-order package described as "a civil libertarian's nightmare"? The one who pursued an "inept, erratic, and ultimately bungled course of conduct" in the trial involving the murder of Little Village community activist Rudy Lozano, the political rival of a Near Southwest Side Daley ally? The state's attorney who, as a supposed consumer ally, gave his assent to a complicated package that would lead to a record Commonwealth Edison price increase, even though he could not possibly have had time to assess the proposal properly before making an endorsement? *That* Richard Daley?[54]

A subsequent *Reader* story, much of its information taken from the *Chicago Lawyer* piece, was only slightly tamer. ''Is Rich Daley ready for Reform?'' The article claimed that the answer was yes, if it is politically convenient, but if there is a conflict, politics will take precedence.[55]

The Republicans? They pared their numbers from eleven down to three. What a group: William Grutzmacher, who led the fight to put a crèche in Daley Plaza and who later was found to have written a tract claiming that the Holocaust never existed; Ken Hurst, a perennial candidate best known for his Scottish hat and his appearance at the 1983 St. Pascal's Church gathering that heckled candidate Harold Washington; and Herbert Sohn, a urologist and a three-time loser for Congress whose Chicago residence was called into question. Where was Ray ''Spanky the Clown'' Wardingley now that the Republicans really needed him?

Sohn, considered the least outrageous of the trio, got the lion's share of their limited collective coverage until February 15. That was the date that Edward Vrdolyak announced his plans to run as a write-in candidate. From then on, Vrdolyak and his write-in chances became the Republican story. The former alderman's belated entry into the race created a situation almost inconceivable to most Chicagoans— a mayoral election in which the Republican primary would be more even and more bitterly contested than the Democratic one.

Still, the Republican primary, no matter how interesting, promised to be nothing more than a sideshow for the more important Democratic election. The *Tribune* took no chances in letting its opinion be known. It published *three* editorials endorsing Daley before the primary: on February 12, the Sunday before the election, and Election Day.

And when Daley won the primary over the hapless Sawyer, the *Sun-Times* celebrated by posting a half-page, full-color portrait of the nominee on the front page—the sort of honor usually reserved for a president-elect.[56]

GENERAL ELECTION: REMARKABLE, THIRD-RATE, AND EVIL

Once the primaries ended, the daily newspapers settled into a firmly established pattern of coverage. They covered Remarkable Daley, Third-rate Evans, and Evil Vrdolyak.

Even before the onset of his campaign for mayor, Ed Vrdolyak drew arrows from the press. In its first Daley endorsement, the *Tribune* referred to the former 10th Ward alderman as "the Count Dracula of Chicago politics, who keeps crawling out of the coffin no matter how often the voters try to put him there."[57]

Afterwards, the insults continued: "Our local [perennial candidate Harold] Stassen" . . . "Past Eddie" . . . "Ol' Rasputin," who "has slithered into the campaign" . . . "Chicago's recurring political nightmare" . . . "Wily eelpout" . . . "a political bully" . . . "a mischievous 'skunk at the garden party' " . . . "rabid" . . . "hysterical." A *Tribune* editorial talked of "kooks, charlatans, bush league Machiavellis and failures hungry for a grudge match. . . . Vrdolyak fits at least three of those categories." Vrdolyak declared his candidacy through a "mouthpiece" (Daley, Sawyer, Bloom et al. had "spokesmen"; Vrdolyak had a "mouthpiece").[58] A Jack Higgins *Sun-Times* cartoon, "Night of the Living Ed," showed Daley jogging past a tombstone marked "Eddie Vrdolyak" as a hand reaches out from the grave and grabs him.[59]

Mostly the dailies handled Vrdolyak (who, it was feared, might attract enough votes from Daley to throw the election to Evans) by giving him as little coverage as possible. The *Tribune* relegated his entry as a write-in candidate to an inside section. When it finally was determined that Vrdolyak defeated party-backed Sohn for the Republican nomination, meaning the Republican candidate might make the mayoral contest a serious race, the *Trib* put Vrdolyak's victory in as unobtrusive a spot as possible on page 1. The top of the page had a story about the possible U.S. giveaway of two tiny Alaskan islands, surely an issue of much more importance to Chicagoans than events that could determine the city's next mayor.[60]

During a March forum about media coverage of the mayoral election, Steve Neal called those who claimed bias in campaign coverage "airheaded."[61] That was quite a charge, coming from the writer who wrote the single most blatantly unfair newspaper story in recent years, the unsubstantiated 1987 story claiming, through a wishy-washy statement by Tom Hynes, that Vrdolyak met with mob boss Joseph Ferriola at a downtown hotel in the middle of his campaign.[62] Neal's story led to a Vrdolyak lawsuit against the *Sun-Times*, and the spectre of the suit affected the paper's coverage of his 1989 campaign (the *Trib*, not the *Sun-Times*, hurled most of the Vrdolyak insults; the latter paper downplayed its coverage of the Republican).

Ironically, Ferriola died during the campaign. Even the coverage of the mobster's death had political undertones. Ferriola, because of the alleged yet unproven meeting with Vrdolyak, was a footnote in Chicago political history. Yet not once did major media mention the incident, which ultimately drew sympathy toward Vrdolyak and away from Daley ally Hynes. After all, something that put a Daley ally in a bad light might reflect badly on the candidate himself.

Statistics watches made by Daley foes suggest that the critics might not have been so "airheaded" after all. Vrdolyak spokesman Larry Horist claimed that during a two-week period in early March, local television news coverage gave Daley a 3 to 2 to 1 advantage in minutes covered over Evans and Vrdolyak; radio gave Daley a 4 to 3 to 2 edge; headlines in the major dailies went 18-6-2 for Daley; the papers gave Daley 85 percent favorable references and only 5 percent unfavorable, while Evans was 52 percent favorable and 21 percent unfavorable, and Vrdolyak only 21 percent favorable and 40 percent unfavorable.[63]

Of course, in Vrdolyak's case, the converse argument could be used. Why should a candidate who never won an election outside his own ward, who garnered only 1.2 percent of the vote in the primary elections, who ran a campaign designed to be a spoiler (his main issues—against abortion, against forced busing, against birth control in schools, against the controversial flag exhibit at the School of the Art Institute—were emotional issues that had little to do with running a city and would alienate large numbers of swing voters, yet would play to a conservative, otherwise pro-Daley constituency) be mentioned in the same breath as others? Michael Miner, *Reader* media columnist, commented that "Vrdolyak was covered the way a LaRouchie would be covered, as a malignant wild card in the election rather than a person of ideas."[64]

Tim Evans, a much more credible candidate in the general election, emerged little better than Vrdolyak in major media coverage. "We didn't get the media to take what we were presenting," complained Evans research director Hal Baron. "They just wouldn't cover the substance that Tim was putting out."[65]

What the major media did cover about Tim Evans fell under two main headings. First there was Evans the "cash-starved" candidate. Hardly a day went by when Evans's monetary woes were not mentioned. In fact, one *Tribune* story managed an unusual two-fer: "If the cash-strapped Evans campaign had any reason to be heartened, it was because of antics involving Republican candidate Ed Vrdolyak." Evans was "cash-strapped" and Vrdolyak had "antics," all in one sentence.[66]

If it was not the lack of funds, it was the rift between Evans and Sawyer, which not even Jesse Jackson could heal. Sawyer once again became a "nice guy." When a handful of Sawyer backers hinted at a write-in campaign for their man (one that would have made Jane Byrne's abortive 1983 write-in campaign look credible by comparison), it became a four-line headline in the March 6 *Sun-Times*. Buried well inside that story was mention of an Evans rally that attracted 4,000 persons, the largest rally thus far of the campaign.[67] (The *Trib* printed a front-page picture of that rally. Who of the 4,000 people did they show with Evans? Alderman Helen Shiller, ally of Uptown activist Slim Coleman, who was considered a radical by many white voters.)[68]

Evans had one important medium working in his behalf: black talk radio, an informal network of support and information within the black community, which *Tribune* columnist James Warren called "a combination of New England town meeting, Bughouse Square debate and intellectual wrestlemania."[69] The medium had influence. Calls from WGCI-AM listeners forced John Johnson, owner of the city's largest black-owned business, to endorse Evans and donate $25,000 to the campaign.

"White" media "discovered" black talk radio in 1989, although such radio had been instrumental even during Harold Washington's 1983 elections. And white media did not like what they heard. Blacks were accusing whites of every sin under the sun ("On a typical morning, you will hear about the white media conspiracy, the white political conspiracy, the white economic conspiracy, and all other forms of white skullduggery," said Mike Royko),[70] and the radio announcers made no attempt to refute the sometimes outrageous charges. CONDUCT was called to investigate black talk radio programs, but no charges were ever filed.

If anything, the furor over black talk radio might have been a first step to racial unity. WVON, a "black" radio station, and "white" public radio station WBEZ combined on a hook-up shortly before the election. On election eve, "black" station WGCI-AM and "white" news station WBBM-AM combined for another joint broadcast. If the experiments changed few votes, at least they got the voters to listen to each other.

Black radio, however, was no match for television in attracting audiences. Local newscasts, particularly those of WLS-TV reporter Hugh Hill, came under fire for their pro-Daley coverage. "Hugh Hill was like [Daley press secretary] Avis LaVelle's assistant," Baron declared.[71] "Every day you saw Uncle Hughie Hill giving what amounted to a Daley commercial," Horist carped.[72]

"I think Daley was given a pass an awful lot," commented *Sun-Times* television critic Daniel Ruth.[73] "You have to give some credit to [Daley press secretary] Avis LaVelle and [campaign strategist] Bill Daley on how he was handled. But if I were a reporter, I would have gone after Daley a lot harder to make him a lot more accountable. Someone should have asked him, what are you going to do about crime, schools, infrastructure—the serious issues.

"At the same time," Ruth continued, "Sawyer and Evans were often given a pass. Maybe it was a lack of courage—no one wanting to report weaknesses of candidates for fear of being called racist. But I don't think Sawyer's record as mayor was ever fully examined. And Evans was allowed by television to assume the Harold Washington mantle without question."

Ruth commented that television coverage was "somewhat lacking." He blamed the transience of local television. "The nature of Chicago television has changed over the years," he claimed. "There used to be a lot of people in Chicago television who were longtime Chicago observers. Now a reporter working in town may be assigned to a campaign without knowing issues. Thus reporting tends to be shallow."

The most thorough television election reporting came from host John Callaway and political correspondent Bruce DuMont on WTTW's "Chicago Tonight." Yet even Callaway admitted to problems in the campaigns from a television point of view.

"We covered the campaign and covered it and covered it, but something interesting was lacking," Callaway said. "In some ways, the candidates were at fault. Take Gene Sawyer—he was so nice, we looked like we were beating him up. Larry Bloom came in for a program carrying little blue cards reminding him to do everything, even smile. And then there was Tim Evans, unrelenting, pontificating."

Part of the perception of a Daley television bias might have been because Daley mastered the medium better than his rivals, Callaway speculated. "He's the master of the short bite. He also has the ability to say something with his face. He is coached on what to say, but how he says it is pure Richie. We got him on "Chicago Tonight," and everytime we asked a question, he'd throw it back to us. We asked, 'How could a guy who lived in Bridgeport be sensitive to the needs of black people?' and he came back with 'This is misjudging Bridgeport, we're not a wealthy neighborhood,' and so forth without once addressing the question. To put it mildly, Richie just beat the shit out of us."

Yet Callaway defended his medium, even while pointing out its limitations. "Interviewing is a very limited form of journalism. If a subject doesn't want to cooperate, he won't. But our coverage was adequate in that you could get a sense of who the candidates were. And if Daley's opponents felt that the press was not relentless enough in attacking his campaign—it's not John Callaway's responsibility to destroy Daley's candidacy. It was theirs, and they didn't do it."

The print media continued to lionize the state's attorney, all but declaring him the winner long before the election. His status in the polls was mentioned so often that children might be forgiven for thinking his first name was "Frontrunner." The *Sun-Times* went so far as to publish a poll before the election asking readers whom they wanted to replace Daley as state's attorney.[73]

No topic better displayed a pro-Daley bias better than the daily papers' attitude toward a mayoral debate. Usually newspapers encouraged debates and belittled those candidates who seek to avoid them. But this time the avoider was Daley, a frontrunner who had the most to lose against sharp-tongued challengers Evans and Vrdolyak.

The *Tribune* could not very well belittle its anointed candidate. Instead, it belittled the debate itself. "Let Count Dracula appear before the cameras," the *Trib* said of Vrdolyak.[74] "That doesn't mean, though, that Richard Daley is obligated to join him." The *Tribune* made its official Daley endorsement before the debate.[75] The day after the debate, a front-page photo showed, not Vrdolyak and Evans squaring off, but Daley at a rally to retire Sawyer's campaign debt. The *Tribune* headline was not "Vrdolyak, Evans attack each other," but "*Daley's opponents* [italics mine] attack each other."[76]

As during the primary campaign, any possible negative Daley story was downplayed. If Evans was hurting for contributions, Daley had money to spare, including more than $600,000 from law firms alone. But these contributions—many from special interest groups—failed to arouse wrath from the downtown press. "When Jane Bryne amassed a multimillion dollar war chest, the media said 'Isn't that obscene?' " commented WBEZ reporter Carolyn Grisko. "When Daley does the same thing, the same people say 'Isn't that amazing?' "[77]

For the most part, the smaller papers held their primary positions. Northwest Side and Southwest Side community papers gave tacit or open support to Daley. Black newspapers on the West and South Sides that had backed Sawyer swallowed their pride and went with Evans. The *Defender*, city's largest black newspaper, which pretty much sat out the primary, gave Evans a last-minute endorsement.

Daley made some gains. Hispanic newspapers, with the exception of the liberal *El Heraldo*, flocked to him. *Windy City Times* printed a Daley endorsement. The black *Independent Bulletin* officially remained neutral, but indicated that Chicago could live with Daley.

The *Reader* continued its Daley assaults. "Is Tim Evans for Real?"[78] the weekly paper asked on March 17 (the answer, several thousand words later, was yes). Cover stories the weekend before the election talked about Daley's fund raising and implied that he was the candidate of fat cats and not of the underclass, who needed representation most.

Local media for the most part provided little self-examination but were quick to criticize out-of-town counterparts. Jim Merriner of the *Sun-Times* derided the Los Angeles *Times* for saying the key issue is "sure to be race," and the Washington *Post* for saying "race again"[79]—

almost a Richard J. Daley attitude of blaming "outside agitators" for the city's racial woes. Yet it was these papers, not the *Tribune* or *Sun-Times*, that cut through the we-know-what and reported the election as it was—at least as indicated by the election results from white and black precincts.

New City contributed the best media commentary of the campaign. The Dearborn Park biweekly, shortly before election day, published on its cover the mock logo of the imaginary *Chicago Sun-Trib* in Irish green ink with the headline "Daley a sure thing; opponents might as well quit now." A photo caption quipped "What a guy! The next mayor, Richard Daley, moves a politically aware, intelligent audience to tears with his vision of the future." Inside appeared "Daley's News," a thoughtful examination of pro-Daley coverage that mentioned everything from favorable photo positioning to coverage of his absence from the debate, "for which he was virtually excused."[80]

To be fair, major media coverage was not entirely a six-month Daley commercial. The *Sun-Times* presented "The Chicago Agenda," a strong series that presented in-depth looks at corruption, health, transportation, race relations and other issues. The *Tribune* simultaneously looked at specific issues and their roles in the campaign.[81] *Tribune* financial columnist William Neikirk expressed irritation with all candidates for ignoring economic issues. Both dailies, as well as the Lerner papers, published good campaign profiles as well as "day-in-the-life" coverage of the major contenders. But even those profiles showed a slant. The *Trib*, for example, portrayed Evans the machine creature rather than Evans the Washington floor leader.[82] Daley, on the other hand, received no substantial criticism for his job as state's attorney.

Did the media coverage make a difference in the campaign? Probably not. Daley had too many other factors working for him: an immovable base of white voters, a competent and experienced campaign team, big-money interests who were all to willing to make generous contributions, a split in the black community, weak opposition. It is questionable whether Daley could have lost even had the media shown a pro-Evans, anti-Daley partisanship.

But as it turned out he had the media—Chicago's Daley news.

NOTES

1. Conversation with Mark Hornung, May 26, 1989.
2. *Skyline*, April 6, 1989.
3. Conversation with Larry Horist, March 31, 1989.
4. Chicago *Tribune*, September 15, 1988.
5. Chicago *Tribune*, December 11, 1988.

6. Chicago *Tribune*, August 30, 1989.
7. Chicago *Sun-Times*, October 29, 1988.
8. *Skyline*, October 2, 1988.
9. Chicago *Sun-Times*, November 17, 1988.
10. Chicago *Tribune*, October 16, 1988.
11. Chicago *Sun-Times*, October 18, 1988.
12. Chicago *Sun-Times*, December 6, 1989.
13. Chicago *Tribune*, October 31, 1989.
14. Chicago *Tribune*, December 6, 1988.
15. Chicago *Sun-Times*, October 27, 1988.
16. Chicago *Sun-Times*, February 28, 1989.
17. Chicago *Sun-Times*, January 29, 1989.
18. Chicago *Sun-Times*, December 12, 1988.
19. Chicago *Tribune*, December 11, 1988.
20. Chicago *Sun-Times*, December 13, 1989.
21. Chicago *Tribune*, December 16, 1988.
22. Chicago *Sun-Times*, December 30, 1988.
23. Chicago *Tribune*, January 3, 1989.
24. Chicago *Tribune* and Chicago *Sun-Times*, January 24, 1989.
25. Chicago *Sun-Times*, January 21, 1989.
26. Chicago *Sun-Times*, February 17, 1989.
27. Chicago *Tribune*, February 16, 1989.
28. Chicago *Sun-Times*, December 8, 1988.
29. Chicago *Tribune*, January 17, 1989.
30. Chicago *Sun-Times*, January 31, 1989.
31. Chicago *Sun-Times*, January 22, 1989.
32. Chicago *Sun-Times*, January 21, 1989.
33. Chicago *Sun-Times*, January 24, 1989.
34. Chicago *Tribune*, February 11, 1989.
35. Chicago *Sun-Times*, February 11, 1989.
36. *Skyline*, February 16, 1989.
37. *Crain's Chicago Business*, February, 20–26, 1989.
38. Interview with a reporter who requested anonymity.
39. *Chicago Independent Bulletin*, February 23, 1989.
40. Interview with *El Heraldo* publisher Joe Garcia, January 27, 1989.
41. *Hispanic Times*, February 1, 1989.
42. *Hispanic Times*, February 22, 1989.
43. *Windy City Times*, February 16, 1989.
44. *Chicago Lawyer*, February, 1989.
45. Chicago *Tribune*, January 2, 1989.
46. Chicago *Tribune*, December 6, 1988.
47. Chicago *Sun-Times*, December 9, 1988.
48. Chicago *Sun-Times*, January 30, 1989.

49. Chicago *Sun-Times*, February 3, 1989.
50. Chicago *Sun-Times*, February 16, 1989.
51. Chicago *Tribune*, February 17, 1989.
52. Chicago *Sun-Times*, February 12, 1989.
53. Chicago *Tribune*, February 12, 1989.
54. *Chicago Lawyer*, January, 1989.
55. *Reader*, February 10, 1989.
56. Chicago *Sun-Times*, March 1, 1989.
57. Chicago *Tribune*, February 12, 1989.
58. Chicago *Tribune*, February 19, 1989.
59. Chicago *Sun-Times*, February 26, 1989.
60. Chicago *Tribune*, March 3, 1989.
61. Steve Neal at "Mayors, Wanna-Be's and the Media" conference, March 9, 1989.
62. Chicago *Sun-Times*, March 23, 1989.
63. Interview with Larry Horist, March 31, 1989.
64. Interview with Mike Miner, May 25, 1989.
65. Interview with Hal Baron, May 26, 1989.
66. Chicago *Tribune*, March 12, 1989.
67. Chicago *Sun-Times*, March 6, 1989.
68. Chicago *Tribune*, March 6, 1989.
69. Chicago *Tribune*, March 23, 1989.
70. Chicago *Tribune*, March 28, 1989.
71. Interview with Hal Baron, May 26, 1989.
72. Interview with Larry Horist, March 31, 1989.
73. Chicago *Sun-Times*, March 29, 1989.
74. Chicago *Tribune*, March 14, 1989.
75. Chicago *Tribune*, March 19, 1989.
76. Chicago *Tribune*, March 22, 1989.
77. Interview with Carolyn Grisko, April 7, 1989.
78. *Reader*, March 31, 1989.
79. Chicago *Sun-Times*, March 30, 1989.
80. *New City*, March 30, 1989.
81. Chicago *Tribune*, January 8, 1989.
82. Chicago *Tribune*, February 3, 1989 (Daley) and March 3, 1989 (Evans).

State's Attorney and Democratic mayoral candidate Richard M. Daley at the City Club of Chicago, stating his support of radical education reform of the Chicago public school system. *(Don Neltnor—City Club)*

In both the primary and the general election contests, Rich Daley *(center)* made periodic campaign stops in African-American neighborhoods. Although he may not have picked up many votes, he did score points with liberals and members of the press. *(Office of the Mayor)*

U.S. Sen. Edward Kennedy *(left)* and Richard M. Daley. Unlike their fathers, Joseph P. Kennedy and Richard J. Daley, who had a close relationship, the sons have had some major political differences. In 1980, Daley supported Jimmy Carter over Kennedy for president; in 1983 Kennedy endorsed Jane Byrne over Daley for mayor of Chicago. In 1989, however, past differences were forgotten (at least temporarily) as the Massachusetts senator went all out in his support of Daley. *(Office of the Mayor)*

Mike Ditka, coach of the Chicago Bears, at his well-known restaurant, endorsing Daley. *(Chicago Sun-Times)*

Candidate Daley *(right)* with his natural political allies, Chicago's blue-collar workers. *(Office of the Mayor)*

A scene from the Democratic Unity Dinner held during the 1989 general mayoral election campaign. The smiling faces are *(left to right)* U.S. Sen Albert Gore, the keynote speaker; national Democratic party chairman Ron Brown; Illinois state party chairman Vince De Muzio; and Democratic mayoral candidate Rich Daley. Brown's support of Daley generated much criticism from Ald. Tim Evans's backers in the African-American community. *(Chicago Sun-Times)*

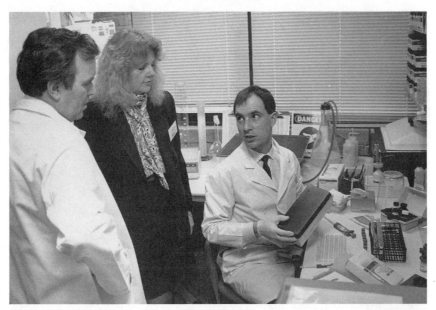

Rich Daley *(left)* being briefed on the AIDS crisis by a technician at Chicago's Howard Brown Clinic. *(Office of the Mayor)*

Rich Daley *(center)* is shown here trying to explain his unfortunate "slip of the lip": his alleged misstatement that Chicago needed a "white"—or was it a "what"?—mayor. For his verbal stumbling, he was censured by a campaign watchdog committee. *(Office of the Mayor)*

Throughout the campaign, Daley played down his deep roots in Chicago's politically powerful Irish-American community. An exception was the night that Daley *(right)* accepted an award from the Limerick Society. *(Office of the Mayor)*

Crucial to Daley's campaign strategy was the building of powerful alliances with Chicago's various ethnic communities. Here Daley *(standing, hatless)* appears at a Chinese New Year celebration at a downtown hotel. *(Office of the Mayor)*

Rich Daley greets people at the Vietnamese Chamber of Congress's New Year's celebration at Tana's Restaurant. *(Office of the Mayor)*

Daley and his close political ally, Northwest Side Ald. Roman Pucinski (41) *(right)*, at a gathering of the Polish National Alliance. *(Office of the Mayor)*

Daley campaigning with Northwest Side Hispanic leaders—and a few non-Hispanic Democratic heavy hitters. (*Office of the Mayor*)

One of the keys to Rich Daley's successful 1989 campaign was his ability to win the support of prominent lakeshore liberals and independents. At a Hyde Park function, Daley posed with his strong supporter, Nobel Prize–winning author Saul Bellow. (*Office of the Mayor*)

CHAPTER 9

Polling in the 1989 Chicago Mayoral Election

Richard Day

Jeff Andreasen

John Ross

INTRODUCTION AND SUMMARY

The mayoral election of 1989 was unique for many reasons. It began with black leaders falling into the same error as had their political brethren before them by learning that " . . . it's easier to share the poverty than the wealth." When Harold Washington died, Timothy Evans, Washington's floor leader, claimed the mantle. Eugene Sawyer, with the backing of white and few black aldermen, was appointed to fill the unexpired term of Washington, or until there was a special election.

The Evans forces pushed for an election to settle the question of who would be the next elected mayor. Chicago was soon faced with the reverse of 1983. In 1989, Chicago was poised to see an election between two blacks (one as the sitting mayor) against a single white challenger by the name of Richard M. Daley.

Although blacks clearly knew it would be foolish to run two blacks against Daley, it became a classic showdown. Sawyer had the office and a million dollar campaign treasury. Evans was held in higher esteem by black voters. The underfunded and poorly organized Evans blinked and allowed Sawyer to take on Daley. Evans decided to wait until the general election, when there would be, he hoped, a more bloodied Daley, a viable Republican, and a better organized Evans.

Daley waited, buoyed by the "forgiveness" of white voters for his having been the "spoiler" in 1983. His strength among Hispanics was also solid. He knew that his white base on the Northwest and Southwest Sides would stay with him solidly. He needed to campaign for the key votes that provided Harold Washington with his margins: white liberals and Hispanics.

Daley did this by campaigning in black and Latino areas of Chicago each day, stressing that his administration would reflect the demographics of the city in 1989, and that he supported affirmative action and fairness. His campaigning in the black parts of Chicago were not as much to get black votes as to show his willingness to reach out, be fair, and run a city that was racially diverse. It worked.

The white liberal/progressives that were the bedrock for Washington were divided. Daley did not appear malevolent enough to focus the opposition energy. Neither Evans nor Sawyer were charismatic enough to attract significant numbers of white voters to their candidacies. As poorly run as Daley's campaign was in 1983, his effort in 1989 was brilliant.

THE PRIMARY

Early Surveys

Surveys conducted months before the primary provided insight into the voters' early perceptions of the candidates.

Since late 1979, Richard Day Research (RDR) has tracked the esteem of numerous public officials on a scale from zero through ten, with five being a neutral score. Figure 1 shows that Rich Daley's esteem rose steadily after his election as Cook County state's attorney in 1980. However, it descended to neutral levels when he became ''the spoiler'' in the 1983 Democratic primary for mayor against incumbent Jane Byrne and challenger Harold Washington.

FIGURE 1   Daley Esteem over Time—Average (Mean) Ratings, 0–10 Scale

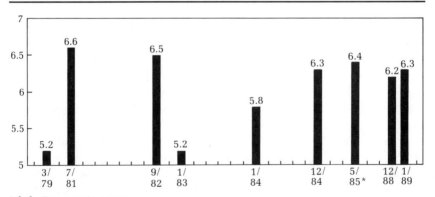

Likely Democratic voters.
* All registered voters (5/85 survey only).

After the 1983 election, Daley carefully avoided the turbulence and chaos of the council wars, and his esteem gradually climbed to its previous high levels. In December 1984, his high esteem (6.3 overall) was consensual across all races (6.4 among whites, 6.0 among blacks, 7.0 among Hispanics and others).

Other early polls showed Daley's strength. A mid-December poll conducted by Richard Day Research (RDR) showed Daley well ahead (47 percent) of a Democratic primary field that included Timothy Evans (23 percent), Eugene Sawyer (16 percent), and Lawrence Bloom (5 percent).

The survey also showed that Sawyer was virtually everybody's second choice. Among Daley supporters and Evans supporters, 46 percent and 36 percent, respectively, said that Sawyer would be their second choice.

A *Tribune* survey conducted in June 1988 showed that both whites (56 percent) and blacks (61 percent) felt that Sawyer had high standards of personal ethics, and that he looked out for the interests in all neighborhoods (50 percent and 57 percent, respectively). A major-

TABLE 1   Polling Done for the Primary Election

Polling Firm	Affiliate	Description of Surveying Done
Richard Day Research	WLS–TV (ABC)	Two preelection surveys in January and February, and an exit poll
	Evans Campaign	Benchmark survey in December
CBS News	WBBM–TV (CBS) and *Southtown Economist*	Three preelection surveys
Gerald Strom	WMAQ–TV (NBC)	One preelection survey
Gallup	Chicago *Sun-Times*, WLS–TV (ABC)	One preelection survey
Market Shares	Chicago *Tribune*	Four preelection surveys
Melman & Lazarus	Daley Campaign	Three preelection surveys, and nightly tracking three weeks before the primary
Martilla–Kiley	Sawyer Campaign	Six preelection surveys

TABLE 2   Polling Done for the General Election

Polling Firm	Affiliate	Description of Surveying Done
Richard Day Research	WLS–TV (ABC)	One preelection survey, one tracking, and exit polling
CBS News	WBBM–TV (CBS) and Southtown Economist	Two preelection surveys
Gerald Strom	WMAQ–TV (NBC)	One preelection survey
Market Shares	Chicago Tribune	One preelection survey
KRC Research	Daley Campaign	One preelection survey and nightly tracking two weeks before election

ity of voters, however, felt that he was not qualified for the office of mayor. Most of their criticism was aimed at his lack of leadership abilities; only 32 percent of both blacks and whites felt he was a good leader. An example was his delaying a week to fire aide Steve Cokely after it was revealed that Cokely had made a number of anti-Semitic remarks. Overall, 52 percent felt that Sawyer should have fired Cokely sooner.

It was apparent from the surveys that Sawyer's low-key manner did not attract strong support from any large bloc of voters. In contrast, Evans's considerably more dynamic style drew support from blacks, but in turn evoked negative feelings in whites and Hispanics.

Evans's support among blacks was strongest early in the campaign. Since Sawyer's tumultuous appointment as mayor, Evans carried himself as the one candidate who would continue the Harold Washington agenda. The effect of this message was evident in a June 1988 Tribune poll which showed that half of the black respondents indicated that only one black candidate should run. The December RDR survey showed that Evans was clearly the choice among blacks (47 percent) over Sawyer (23 percent) in a primary election that included Daley and Bloom.

As the campaign progressed, the division in the black community was made evident by the comments made by Evans's ally Alderman Dorothy Tillman, who called Sawyer a "shufflin' Uncle Tom." The mid-December RDR survey taken just after this comment showed that on an esteem scale from zero through ten, with five being neutral, Tillman received only neutral scores among blacks (5.0), and was held unfavorably by whites (1.3) and Hispanics (3.0).

TABLE 3   Esteem by Race*

	Daley	Sawyer	Evans	Bloom
OVERALL	6.2	5.0	4.6	4.4
Whites	7.1	4.9	2.8	4.1
Blacks	4.8	5.1	6.9	4.8
Hispanics	7.5	5.2	3.5	4.5

*Mid-December 1988 RDR Survey, n = 800 likely Democratic primary voters.

Her comment also hurt Evans in the key north lakefront wards, where a mid-December *Tribune* poll showed that two-thirds of voters felt that her comments were extreme. Two-thirds of the lakefront voters also said that their biggest concern about Evans was his political allies, an apparent reference to Tillman.

Because of the acrimony many blacks felt for Sawyer, Evans could expect to receive most of the black vote. However, the three-way primary race would be a reverse scenario of the 1983 primary—this time, two black candidates would split the black vote, ensuring victory for the single white candidate. By waiting for the general election, Evans risked losing blacks who were "automatic" Democrats. However, he stood to gain with a potentially weaker Daley, a viable Republican, and more time to organize his own effort. In addition, he hoped to avoid the spoiler image among blacks. On December 29th, Evans announced his candidacy as an independent under the Harold Washington party.

The other announced primary candidates received nominal support. In the two mid-December polls, Bloom was unable to break out of the single digits. The December RDR survey also showed that he was unknown to a third of the likely Democratic primary voters.

Juan Soliz proclaimed himself to be the candidate who would represent the Hispanics of Chicago. In reality, however, he was a leader without a following. An RDR survey in mid-January showed that on a zero through ten scale, with five being a neutral score, dislike for Soliz ran across all races: whites (2.9), blacks (4.1), and Hispanics (4.3). Overall, Soliz was unknown to 37 percent of the voters.

Into February

The *Tribune*'s early December survey marked Daley's support at around 60 percent. However, between mid-December and mid-February, virtually all other surveys showed that remained in the area of 40 percent.

During that time, support for Sawyer gradually rose, until he was within 7 percent of Daley two weeks before the election. Support for Bloom during the same period held between 9 percent and 12 percent.

As the election day neared, the increased support for Sawyer apparently came from those who previously had supported Daley or said they were undecided. Table 4 shows that Sawyer's strength among blacks swelled from less that 50 percent in early January to 76 percent six weeks later. During the same period, the percentages of blacks who supported Daley or were undecided were cut in half.

TABLE 4   Media Polls

	CBS Early Jan.	Tribune Mid- Jan.	RDR Mid- Jan.	CBS Early Feb.	Gallup Mid- Feb.	RDR E-Day Exit Poll	Actual Results
% FOR DALEY							
Overall	41	43	48	43	50	53	56
White	57	*	72	68	78	92	
Black	20	15	17	9	11	3	
Hispanic	*	*	64	*	63	85	
% FOR SAWYER							
Overall	27	28	32	33	38	46	43
White	16	*	12	12	12	8	
Black	42	51	59	62	76	97	
Hispanic	*	*	19	*	24	15	
% FOR BLOOM							
Overall	9	10	12	11		1	1
White	10	*	8	9			
Black	8	9	14	14			
Hispanic	*	*	13	*			
% UNDECIDED							
Overall	23	19	8	13	12		
White	17	*	8	11	10		
Black	30	25	10	15	13		
Hispanic	*	*	5	*	13		

The Debate

The only televised debate among the three Democratic mayoral primary candidates was aired on the public television station on February 7. An RDR survey was conducted immediately after the debate had concluded and during the next evening (see table 5). The survey recontacted 586 likely primary voters.

TABLE 5   Voter Response to February 7 Debate

	Saw Debate	Heard/Read About It	Neither Saw nor Heard About It
(overall % of sample)	(29%)	(20%)	(51%)
Who Won Debate?			
Daley	41%	20%	
Sawyer	18	13	
Bloom	32	12	
No one	9	33	
Not sure	0	23	
	100%	100%	

The survey showed that even among likely primary voters, there was little interest in the debate. Half (51 percent) said that they had not seen, read, or heard anything about the debate. Only 29 percent said that they actually saw the debate, and an additional 20 percent missed the debate but heard or read about it the next day.

Those who saw the debate believed the winners to be Daley and Bloom. Most of those who only heard about it the next day could not declare a winner.

Bloom's performance clearly had a favorable impact on those who watched the debate, making it clear why he called repeatedly for more televised discussions.

However, given the low viewership of this debate, Bloom was unable to translate his good showing into support. Table 6 shows that immediately after the debate, Bloom's support rose 5 percent among the viewers, but only 2 percent among voters overall.

Among voters overall, the debate apparently had little effect on their choice for mayor. The RDR survey showed little change in support from before the debate to just afterward, indicating that most voters already had made up their minds.

Blacks and younger voters were least likely to have seen or heard anything about the debate. Although blacks represent 42 percent of the voting population, only 29 percent of the debate viewers were black.

This disinterest among black voters hinted at their low turnout on election day. Not only were they consistently undecided in the predebate surveys, but they also were not inclined to watch or read about the debate. The spark that Harold Washington had generated in 1983 and 1987 had apparently faded.

There were two possible reasons for this disinterest among black voters. The first was that blacks who supported Sawyer felt that he had

TABLE 6   Pre- and Postdebate Trial Heats:
Debate Viewers and Overall Sample

| | Saw Debate (29% of Sample) | | All Respondents | |
	Predebate Trial Heat	Postdebate Trial Heat	Predebate	Postdebate
Daley	53%	53%	49%	47%
Sawyer	23	27	28	29
Bloom	11	16	10	12
Undecided	13	4	13	12
	100%	100%	100%	100%

little chance of winning. The media surveys consistently showed Daley with a substantial lead over Sawyer. The Daley campaign was extremely well organized, and avoided any serious gaffes. The Sawyer campaign, on the other hand, was unsuccessful at attacking the front-runner, and its most critical ad (which showed Daley fumbling and speaking from handwritten note cards) backfired. The RDR postdebate survey showed that only 9 percent of the voters who saw the ads said they helped Sawyer, whereas 37 percent felt they actually helped Daley.

The other reason for disinterest among blacks was a result of the division in the black community. Blacks who supported Evans saw little reason to vote in the primary. Evans refused to endorse a candidate, and his supporters appeared to bypass the primary and wait for the general election.

Bloom Drops Out

Two weeks before the primary, Larry Bloom announced his withdrawal from the race and urged his supporters to back Eugene Sawyer. Surveys taken just before his withdrawal marked Bloom's support at around 12 percent, enough to beat Daley if all or most of his supporters went to the Sawyer camp. The big question, therefore, was where would the Bloom supporters go—to Daley or Sawyer?

In three separate surveys, the answer apparently was "both." An RDR survey taken a few weeks earlier in January indicated that Daley's and Sawyer's esteem among Bloom supporters was identical (3.8 and 3.9, respectively, on a zero through ten scale).

A Gallup survey conducted just after Bloom's departure showed that his supporters were split evenly among Daley (32 percent), Sawyer (34 percent), and undecided (34 percent) in a two-way trial heat for the primary.

Finally, a CBS poll conducted around the same time suggested that although both Daley and Sawyer benefitted from Bloom's withdrawal, Daley may have come out slightly ahead. This survey found that virtually all of Bloom's white supporters moved to the Daley camp. His black supporters, however, were evenly divided between Sawyer and "undecided," again reflecting the lack of interest many black voters had in the primary.

Primary Election Day

Richard Day Research conducted an election day exit poll for WLS-TV. Over 3,100 voters were interviewed as they left their polling places. The results of this exit poll (shown in table 7) provide a profile of the Daley and Sawyer primary voters.

TABLE 7   RDR Exit Poll for WLS–TV: Democratic Primary Results

		Daley	Sawyer
	Actual Results (row %)	55%	43%
	Exit Poll Overall (row %)	53%	46%
Race:			
	White	92%	8%
	Black	3%	97%
	Hispanic	85%	15%
Region:			
	Lakefront	76%	23%
	NW-white	89%	11%
	W-black	18%	82%
	S-black	5%	95%
	SW-white	66%	34%
'87 Mayoral Primary Vote:			
	Washington	23%	77%
	Byrne	95%	5%
	Did not vote	76%	24%

Sawyer's support.   In earlier mayoral races, Harold Washington's formula for victory over a single white candidate was: (1) monolithic support among black voters; (2) high black voter turnout; (3) nearly one-fifth of the white vote; (4) nearly half of the Hispanic vote.

In order to win the 1989 Democratic primary, Sawyer would have needed to duplicate this performance.

RDR's exit poll showed that he was only able to capitalize on the first part of this formula. Virtually all (97 percent) of the black voters who went to the polls supported Sawyer.

Sawyer fell drastically short on the remaining requirements. In the 1987 primary, over 70 percent of the voters in the two predominantly black regions of the city went to the polls. Turnout in these two areas virtually equalled the turnout in the Northwest and lakefront regions.

In 1989, however, barely half of the voters in the two primarily black regions voted. Whereas the citywide drop in turnout was 16 percent less than in 1987, the drop in these two regions was 21 percent.

TABLE 8 Primary Election Turnout for Mayor by Region (1987 and 1989)

	% Turnout		Difference
	1987	1989	1989–1987
Citywide	76%	60%	−16%
Lakefront	69%	54%	−15%
NW, predom. white	77%	67%	−10%
Hispanic	69%	48%	−21%
West, predom. black	71%	50%	−21%
South, predom. black	76%	55%	−21%
SW, predom. white	82%	74%	− 8%

Sawyer's support among whites and Hispanics also fell well below his needed targets. RDR's exit poll for WLS-TV showed that only 8 percent of the white voters and 15 percent of the Hispanic voters supported Sawyer.

The exit poll also asked voters why they supported their candidate. The reasons given most frequently by Sawyer voters were that he had done a good job as mayor (42 percent) and that he deserved more time in office (22 percent); 20 percent supported him because they felt "He would best represent people like me."

Daley's support. Just as low turnout in the black wards hampered Sawyer's chances, the relatively high turnout in the predominantly white wards was the key fact in Daley's victory. Turnout in the Northwest and Southwest areas nearly reached the record high levels of the 1987 and 1983 primaries.

Not only did more than two-thirds of these voters go to the polls, but the RDR exit poll showed that they went overwhelming for Daley, who received 92 percent of the white vote.

In addition, Daley received three-fourths of the racially mixed lakefront vote, as well as 85 percent of Hispanic support. The RDR exit poll also showed that almost one-fourth of those who supported Harold Washington in the 1987 primary supported Daley in the 1989 primary.

The reasons given most often for supporting Daley centered around his leadership skills (35 percent) and approval of his record as state's attorney (35 percent). As with Sawyer voters, one-fifth of the Daley supporters said that their candidate would do a better job "representing people like me" (19 percent).

Even before election day, Daley already had a jump on Sawyer. Normally, the Northwest and Southwest predominantly white wards combine for about 45 percent of the total votes cast in mayoral races. However, in the 1989 primary, two-thirds (66%) of the absentee ballots were cast in these two regions, which went overwhelmingly for Daley.

TABLE 9   Voter Participation

	Historical Vote Contribution in Mayoral Primaries	% of Total Absentee Ballots Cast in 1989 Primary
Southwest (predom. white)	25%	36%
Northwest (predom. white)	20%	30%

Daley won the primary with 56 percent of the vote, the largest margin since his father's reelection in 1975. This wave of support propelled him into the general election against Evans and the Republican write-in winner, Edward Vrdolyak.

THE GENERAL ELECTION

With Ed Vrdolyak's surprise write-in victory in the Republican primary, the general election bore a strong similarity to the 1983 Democratic mayoral primary—two well-known white candidates running against one black candidate.

Given this scenario, a victory for Evans was dependent on three things. First, he needed the united and energized black community that Harold Washington had inspired in 1983. The low black voter turnout that contributed to Sawyer's primary defeat now threatened Evans. Just as Evans supporters skipped the primary, it was possible that Sawyer supporters would retaliate by either foregoing the general or supporting Daley. With near unanimous black support and the kind of turnout that Washington generated in 1983 and 1987, this base would start Evans with about 42 percent of the citywide vote.

Second, Evans would still need approximately 15 to 20 percent of the white vote and about half of the Hispanic vote. This, too, would be difficult. Only 8 percent of the white electorate supported Sawyer in the primary, and Evans was held in very low esteem among nonblack voters. Unlike Washington, Evans apparently could not mobilize His-panic voters and white liberal voters.

Finally, Evans was looking for a strong showing by Vrdolyak to split the remaining white and Hispanic vote.

None of these events were realized. Daley's support was too strong and the rift in the black community was too great for Evans to overcome. In addition, many black voters did not believe that Evans could win.

After the primary election, Daley's support appeared to be stronger than ever among whites and Hispanics. RDR surveys showed his esteem among these two groups had soared a full point since De-cember (see figure 2). In addition, although he never was able to clear a majority in the preprimary polls, virtually all of the March media surveys showed Daley with at least 50 percent. RDR surveys in mid- and late March showed that Daley was the choice of four out of five whites and Hispanics, and that he retained more than 90 percent of his primary supporters. Unlike in the Washington era, the Hispanic vote no longer was divided and now mirrored the white vote in its over-whelming support for Daley.

Daley also continued to receive about 10 percent of the black vote. RDR surveys showed that Daley was strongest among black women and West Side residents.

The March surveys also consistently showed the effects of the di-vided black community. Just as Evans refused to endorse Sawyer in the primary, Sawyer refused to endorse Evans in the general. An RDR poll in mid-March showed that only 71 percent of those who supported Sawyer in the primary indicated that they would vote for Evans in the general. Although Evans had 78 percent of the black vote, 12 percent said they would support Daley, and 10 percent were undecided.

The strong negative feelings that whites had held for Evans did not change after the primary (see figure 2). Even among whites who rated Jesse Jackson favorably, Evans received neutral or unfavorable responses. In the trial heats, only about 5 percent of the white voters supported Evans, far short of his target. His strongest support among whites came from those in the North lakefront wards, the college edu-cated, and those between twenty-five and forty-four years old (about 15 percent from each group).

Throughout the campaign, whites and Hispanics felt that Evans was too pugnacious. These feelings apparently went back to when Evans supporters, protesting Sawyer's appointment as mayor, clogged the streets outside city hall. In addition, Dorothy Tillman's famous

FIGURE 2   Esteem over Time: Overall, by Race

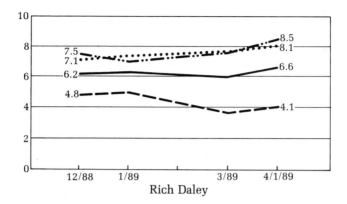

Rich Daley

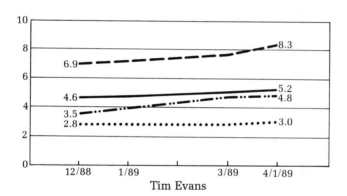

Tim Evans

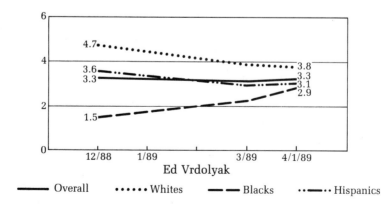

Ed Vrdolyak

———— Overall   •••••• Whites   —— —— Blacks   •••—••• Hispanics

RDR surveys for WLS-TV.
Mean ratings on zero (lowest) through ten (highest) scale.

"shufflin' Uncle Tom" comments about Sawyer (which Evans refused to denounce) may have affirmed these feelings.

It also appeared that Evans was running as the candidate for the black community, whereas Daley worked on his image as the candidate for all groups and areas. Evans rarely campaigned outside the predominantly black wards. Daley, on the other hand, frequently met with black community groups and spoke to black congregations, and received considerable publicity for these appearances.

Most importantly, the surveys showed that Vrdolyak was never a factor. All racial groups held him in low esteem after the primary. His potential "spoiler" status hurt him among whites (although it helped him slightly among blacks). He never received more than 9 percent of the white support. White voters understood that the only way to elect a white candidate for mayor was to vote for Daley.

An RDR survey conducted just before the election showed that whites felt Vrdolyak was opportunistic, racist, divisive, and arrogant. He was also seen as a candidate who is always running and never wins, reflecting on his previous defeats for mayor and Cook County circuit court clerk.

ELECTION DAY

In the RDR general election exit poll for WLS-TV, over 3,200 voters were interviewed. A comparison of the findings from RDR's general and primary election exit polls show very few differences in terms of how different groups and regions voted (see table 11).

Daley matched his primary election victory with 55 percent of the vote. Not only did he keep virtually all of his primary election supporters, but he also was able to attract a third of the Republican primary voters. Daley again carried about one-fifth of the vote in the predominantly black wards on the West Side.

Evans matched Sawyer's primary election numbers. He received nearly all of the black vote and Sawyer's primary supporters. As expected, Evans received less of the white vote in the general (4 percent) than Sawyer had attracted in the primary (8 percent).

Vrdolyak ended up with only 3 percent of the overall vote in the general election, one of the lowest percentages for a Republican in Chicago mayoral election history. His share of the white vote nearly equalled that given to Evans (although he appeared to take away some of Daley's primary election support from the North lakefront wards). In his own 10th Ward, Vrdolyak received fewer votes than either Daley or Evans.

As the campaigns approached the April 4 election, Evans's black support began to solidify. As was seen in the primary, undecided black

TABLE 10   General Election Trial Heat: Mid-
and Late March RDR Surveys for Channel 7

	March 11–15			
	Daley	Evans	Vrdolyak	Undec.
OVERALL	53%	36%	5%	6%
RACE				
White	83%	4%	9%	4%
Black	12	78	2	9
Hispanic	84	15	1	0
REGION				
Lakefront	70	19	4	7
NW-white	81	4	12	4
W-black	22	70	0	9
S-black	12	79	1	8
SW-white	74	13	7	6
PRIMARY VOTE				
Daley	91	4	4	1
Sawyer	14	71	5	10
Didn't Vote	42	49	3	6

	March 29–30			
	Daley	Evans	Vrdolyak	Undec.
OVERALL	51%	40%	5%	4%
RACE				
White	83%	5%	10%	2%
Black	10	84	2	4
Hispanic	89	11	0	0
REGION				
Lakefront	66	25	5	4
NW-white	81	5	11	4
W-black	18	71	2	9
S-black	11	82	1	5
SW-white	80	14	5	1
PRIMARY VOTE				
Daley	92	1	3	4
Sawyer	12	82	3	4
Didn't Vote	40	49	6	5

voters made a last-minute move toward the black candidate. The RDR
survey taken just a few days before election day showed that 84 percent of blacks supported Evans, as well as 82 percent of the Sawyer

supporters in the primary (table 10). Although this late surge among blacks drew Evans up to 40 percent of the overall vote, Daley still enjoyed an 11 percent lead.

TABLE 11   Comparison of the Primary and General Election Vote Based on RDR Exit Polls for WLS-TV

	Primary		General		
	Daley	Sawyer	Daley	Evans	Vrdolyak
OVERALL	55%	44%	55%	41%	3%
RACE					
White	92%	8%	91%	4%	5%
Black	3%	97%	4%	95%	1%
Hispanic	85%	15%	79%	17%	4%
REGION					
Lakefront	76%	23%	68%	25%	7%
NW-white	88%	11%	91%	5%	4%
W-black	18%	82%	18%	82%	0%
S-black	5%	95%	5%	94%	1%
SW-white	66%	34%	71%	26%	3%
PRIMARY VOTE					
Daley			97%	2%	1%
Sawyer			7%	92%	1%
Republican			36%	12%	52%
Didn't Vote			30%	68%	2%

Two other facts ensured Daley of repeating his winning margin from the primary—turnout and absentee ballots.

Citywide, voter turnout in the general election was 7 percent higher than in the primary (see table 12). Virtually every region experienced a similar increase in turnout. This meant that voters in the predominantly black areas were still less likely to go to the polls than voters in the primarily white areas.

As in the primary, Daley again enjoyed a significant lead over his opponents even before the polling places opened on April 4. Of the absentee ballots cast citywide in the general election, 70 percent came from Daley's strongholds of the Northwest and Southwest wards. Historically, these two areas account for about 46 percent of the citywide vote in mayoral elections.

In sum, the mayoral prediction polls for the primary and general were right from the start—it was Daley all the way.

TABLE 12   1989 Primary and General Election Turnout

	Primary	General	General Turnout/ Primary Turnout
Citywide	60%	67%	+ 7%
Lakefront	54%	57%	+ 3%
NW-White	67%	74%	+ 7%
Hispanic	48%	57%	+ 9%
W-Black	50%	57%	+ 7%
S-Black	55%	62%	+ 7%
SW-White	74%	80%	+ 6%

Mr. and Mrs. Daley attending a Greek Fest gathering that featured the famous Billy Goat Tavern mascot. *(Office of the Mayor)*

Daley worked the independent-minded lakefront very hard. Here he campaigns with some of his major lakefront allies *(left to right)*: Ald. Edwin Eisendrath (43), ward committeeman Ann Stepan (43), Daley, State Sen. Bill Marovitz (3), Ald. Bernie Hansen (44), and county board member Chuck Bernadini. *(Office of the Mayor)*

On election day in the 10th Ward, posters abound in front of St. Simeon Serbian Church, a polling place in the heart of Vrdolyak country. Even here, Daley's forces were organized to challenge the once-almighty Vrdolyak in his own back yard. *(Office of the Mayor)*

A subdued Edward Vrdolyak conceding the 1989 mayoral election to Daley. On his right is Northwest Side State Sen. Walter Dudycz (7). *(Chicago Sun-Times)*

Chicago's new mayor, Richard M. Daley, greeting supporters on election night. Mrs. Daley (top left) is in high spirits after the long, successful campaign. (Chicago Sun-Times)

Mayor Daley conferring with his press secretary, Avis LaVelle, before his first city council meeting. LaVelle's appointment as press spokesperson at the outset of the 1989 campaign was considered to be Daley's most adroit political move. A well-respected journalist, LaVelle was not only a first-rate press secretary, but her appointment also sent a message to independents and liberals that Daley would have an open and progressive administration. (*Office of the Mayor*)

Newly elected Mayor Richard M. Daley presenting campaign adversary Ald. Dorothy Tillman (3), with an award for her work on neighborhood enterprise zones. Tillman gained notoriety for her derogatory remarks about Mayor Eugene Sawyer, whom she called a "shuffling Uncle Tom." (Office of the Mayor)

PART FIVE

Back to the Future

By election time in April, it seemed clear that the old Byrne-Washington-Vrdolyak piss and vinegar had been drained at least temporarily out of Chicago politics. . . . A new age of political moderation seemed to be dawning. Low-key Rich Daley took 55 percent of the vote, the biggest mayoral majority since 1979.

Melvin G. Holli (1990)

CHAPTER 10

Daley to Daley

Melvin G. Holli

Nineteen-eighty-nine was a hell of a year. The Berlin Wall was breached; the Iron Curtain was shredded into tatters; a Communist leader was killed by the enraged working classes; and Eastern European Leninists were talking about free-market Marxism. In Chicago the city was still reeling from a decade-long whirligig of historical events that included the election of its first female mayor; the election of its first black mayor; and, equally astonishing, the coalescing of the liberal lakeshore community, the Hispanic community, and the white ethnic community to elect "Son of Boss" Richard M. Daley to fill the last two years of black mayor Harold Washington's unexpired term. Was this the end of history? The lakeshore lamb and the Bridgeport lion had lain together and begat the heir to the mayoralty, Son of Boss. Furthermore, young Daley promised to calm the troubled waters of racism, bring economy and efficiency to the city government, and institute city-manager types of reforms.

And all of this history was crammed into slightly more than a decade, for it had been thirteen years since the death of Boss Richard J. Daley. Rarely in its 150-year political history had the city gone through such a gut-wrenching series of changes and about-faces and turned conventional wisdom on its head and then back on its feet again. Old political alliances were in shambles, new political lines were forming. Hispanics, an important part of the Washington coalition, had defected and joined the Chicago "greens" (read "Irish"). Vertigo was the order of the day. The rate of historical change had moved into overdrive after being blocked for twenty-one years by the old man. The end of Boss Daley was not the end of history; instead, it was the beginning of the history of change.[1]

Twenty-one years of relative political stability with one-man rule and one machine in power had been followed by more than a decade of political instability and what the press had described as "chaosfest," "council wars," and a political carnival played out on the lakeshore of the city the *Wall Street Journal* called "Beirut by the lake."

Chicagoans wondered whether the interregnum of chaos was permanent and whether every election would continue to be a pyrotechnical shootout in a "banana republic" style.

Yet the interregnum of chaos and epic of political instability may have been a necessary historical phase in Chicago's political evolution. Chicago had not passed through a thoroughgoing top-to-bottom progressive reform period. It had not adopted the National Municipal League's 1916 "Model City Charter." It had not embraced a civil service ethos nor adopted citywide elections. Its fifty-ward, fifty-person city council, established in 1923, was an anachronism and out of step with the direction then being taken by most cities, which was toward smaller councils. Even in the 1930s, when urban machines were dying left and right, Chicago installed into office its all-powerful Democratic machine under Anton Cermak–Edward Kelly–Patrick Nash. Chicago's political evolution seemed to move backward or it seemed not to move at all. After 1933 it did not evolve toward modern reform administrations and city managerism, as did most big cities, but instead continued to crank out the old-style machine and boss generation after generation and long after these dinosaurs were past history elsewhere. That also meant that salutary and important changes, such as the election of women and minority mayors, the empowerment of Hispanics, the institution of businesslike practices, and the end of machine-boss patronage came slower than in most of the big cities. The interregnum thus had its positive and beneficial side in that it brought a floodtide of needed change that had been dammed up by twenty-one years of Daleyism.[2]

POLITICAL STABILITY, 1955–1976

Yet to fully appreciate the thirteen-year interregnum of instability and chaos, we should look first at the twenty-one years of the elder Daley era and the stability that characterized it.

What historic and other factors help to account for Richard J. Daley's long-term tenure (1955–1976) as mayor? The times certainly were inauspicious for elected public leaders. The last decade and a half of Daley's career, up until his death in 1976, was a troubled and turbulent period in American history in which the rate of change was faster than normal and there were more kinds of change than ever before. The dynamics of the period were race, gender, ethnicity, a liberal political culture, urban obsolescence, and an economic transformation that was rendering many cities nearly ungovernable. The decade of the 1960s—and its aftershocks that rumbled into the 1970s—was a perilous time for big-city mayors. Ghetto riots, black power, anti-urban renewal protestors, anti-expressway protestors, welfare rights groups, grey panthers, black panthers, and a myriad of other groups all fighting for some special interest cause were turning urban government into one of the most perilous political jobs in America. The afflictions wrought by that age were fatal to the careers of some of the best known and most promising big-city mayors. Detroit's "golden boy" Mayor Jerome Cavanagh's career, for example, was crushed by a 1967 riot. The nation's first big-city black mayor, Carl Stokes, experienced a career-shattering black riot and "shootout" in Cleveland in 1968. New York City's handsome jet-setter, John Lindsay, was ambushed by racial and ethnic conflict over housing and schools that destroyed his career both as mayor and as presidential hopeful. Although wily Los Angeles Mayor Sam Yorty survived the 1964 riots in Watts, he did not survive the decade politically and—like his urban counterpart, Lindsay—saw his try for the presidency collapse ignominiously. Daley almost alone among the prominent big-city mayors survived that career-killing decade.[3]

Why did Daley not only survive but thrive? Important among the factors that contributed to his survival was that he managed a city that actually worked. As *Newsweek* put it in 1971: "Chicago is that most wondrous of exceptions—a major American city that actually works. While breakdowns in essential services have become almost a daily event elsewhere, Chicagoans enjoy virtually an uninterrupted supply of urban amenities. They commute to work on the nation's most ingeniously integrated transportation system. . . . Chicago's streets are probably the cleanest and best-illuminated on the metropolitan scene; its police and fire departments are ranked by professionals as among the most effective in the world." Finally under Daley liberal zoning laws and flexible tax policies prevented the "corporate exodus" then "plaguing New York."[4]

Perhaps even more important, Daley brought a sense of stability to his city during a time of deep troubles in urban America. He projected and often lived up to the image of an in-charge leader whose firm hand on the throttle permitted only orderly and slow change, if it permitted change at all. This effort to slow change to a manageable and controllable pace had a deep and profound appeal to Chicagoans. Chicago's voters—who were heavily Catholic, "corporate" in social outlook, ethnic, blue collar and often hard-hat in occupation, and conservative—were deeply troubled by the long-haired leaders of an ill-mannered generation that ridiculed their occupations, religion, politics, and lifestyles and, furthermore, threatened the existing order of things.

Stability and order above all became Daley's stock in trade for a troubled electorate. "Huge numbers of people in every corner of the city," observed Chicago television newsman Walter Jacobson, "regard

Mayor Daley as a father. He had weathered all the winds of change, and his people look to him for safekeeping." Even Daley's political enemies recognized that. Daley's 1959 GOP opponent, Timothy Sheehan, said he always got a "rise" out of any downstate or suburban audience by referring to "Boss Daley" or "Dictator Daley." "That always worked them up." But after the 1968 riots that did not work any more. "They liked Daley in the most conservative areas and they should. Nobody did the job he did. He didn't let the minority groups have whatever they wanted. He took a stand." A Sindlinger public opinion poll conducted immediately after the 1968 Democratic national convention riots confirmed Sheehan's judgment: Some 71 percent of the public polled found no fault with Chicago's hard-hitting police and 61 percent said Mayor Daley was doing a good job. Another one of Daley's Republican mayoral opponents, Benjamin Adamowski (1963), warned in the 1970s that Chicago was sitting "on a keg of dynamite" and that only Daley, who worked with the black, white, and Hispanic communities, could prevent an explosion. Daley's 1975 vanquished challenger, John Hoellen, after much criticism of Daley's insensitivity, conceded that "He [Daley] has been able to avoid the worst riots, and probably kept the lid on the city from exploding."[5]

Keeping the lid on and stability were also the refrains heard from William Singer, an independent Democrat and challenger in the 1975 primary. In a retrospective on his primary defeat, Singer said that people voted for Daley "not because the precinct captain forced or cajoled them, but because they made a decision that they were for Daley. They felt a great sense of stability in knowledge of what they had . . . . It was an incredible thing. There was an enormous stability factor." Certified reformer and professor William Grimshaw conceded the same with his remark that Daley in his latter years was a "rock of stability. And he was holding the whole thing together."[6] Undoubtedly Daley's ability to control some of the threatening changes and runaway events explains a great deal of his popularity during more than a decade of turbulence and unpredictability for Chicagoans. Stability and order and slow or no change played great roles in Daley's lengthy tenure in a time of national and urban political troubles.

THE INTERREGNUM, 1977–1979

Enter, Exit Michael Bilandic, 1977–1979

Daley's death in 1976 ushered in thirteen years of change that would evolve into political instability and rancorous ethnic squabbling. The slow slide into an interregnum of political disorder began with a racial tiff over who should be interim or acting mayor, a black alderman, Wilson Frost, or a white alderman from Daley's 11th Ward, Michael Bilandic. Unlike most mayors, Bilandic is remembered mostly for his stormy entrance into office and his even stormier exit.

Potent political forces collided during the urgent and secret negotiations just after Daley's death in the days before Christmas 1976 to pick a successor. Frost, the council president, asserted that he was the acting mayor. Backing Frost's mayoral claim was the city's huge black community and its loud-voiced leaders, such as the Reverend Jesse Jackson. Also looking for the city's top job was Northwest Side Alderman Roman C. Pucinski, a sterling son of Polish Chicago, which was irritated over its inability to capture real power in the world's second-largest Polish city. Also entering into the acting-mayor fray was Edward Vrdolyak, a tough, smart Southeast Side alderman. Bilandic was quickly picked by a lopsided 45-to-2 city council vote as interim mayor. Only two lakefront independents opposed the choice, but many in the black community were affronted by what they considered a political snub. The appointed black champion, Wilson Frost, sheepishly explained to his African-American supporters that it would have been "suicide" to go up against a "done-deal" by the remnants of the machine. Bilandic's selection as interim mayor was the old machine's "last hurrah."

Chicago of 1977 was a different city from the one in which a young "Boss" Daley had first come to power in 1955. The black community had swelled by a record-breaking 500,000 people, mostly from southern migration, and their percentage of the city's population had shot up from about 20 percent to 35 percent and was still growing. In addition, the civil rights movement, antipatronage court decisions, the decline of party loyalty, and white flight were steadily eroding the bases for traditional organization power. And the old boys in the organization had been lulled into a false sense of security by the ease with which they had put Bilandic over on the city. In the future they would face stiff resistance on such decisions.

In the mayoral primary scheduled for April 1977, candidate Pucinski unleashed a bitter attack on Acting Mayor Bilandic and the entire closed-door selection process and challenged the mayor to a public debate, which he refused. Then another mayoral contestant jumped into the ring. Underfinanced and underorganized but with overpowering rhetoric, Harold Washington began campaigning vigorously on the South Side, threatening to cut away black voters from the Democratic slate-makers' choice, Bilandic. "There is a sleeping black giant in Chicago," Washington told a South Side Baptist church congregation, "and if this sleeping giant, the potential black vote, ever woke up, we'd control this city."[7] Prophetic words for future elections. Then things really got out of hand when a third unwanted Democratic candidate waded in—discredited State's Attorney Edward Hanrahan (tainted by the 1969 raid on the Black Panthers and the shooting of two Panther leaders). The easy entry of loose cannons such as Hanrahan into the Democratic primary indicated how enfeebled Democratic machine control had become.

Even so, Bilandic went on to an easy victory, carrying slightly more than 50 percent of the vote, although losing seven North and Northwest Side wards and 32 percent of the vote to Pucinski and five middle-class black South Side wards to Washington, signs of weakening party discipline. Three groups—Poles, blacks, and lakefront liberals—had shown their displeasure with the old way of doing things.

Bilandic's short two-year term was not without its achievements. As political scientist Milton Rakove saw it, Bilandic's tenure was one of "accomplishment, continuity, and some forward motion."[8] Bilandic had balanced the city budget, kept the bond rating high, and continued the public service tradition that made the "city that worked." He had also maintained peace in the city council by back-room bargaining and avoiding the public appearance of conflict. Few political commentators saw any storm clouds on the horizon or that Bilandic's upcoming 1979 reelection was in jeopardy.

How then did Bilandic lose—and lose with the last big-city machine backing him? Bilandic's tale of woe began in a record January snowstorm that left the mayor bogged hip-deep in problems he was unprepared to face. The city that supposedly worked stopped working. Garbage piled up in the alleyways and remained uncollected, streets remained impassable, and parking spaces that had been carved out of glacial snow banks were guarded like prime real estate. A cold snap froze the heavy snow that clogged the streets to a concrete-like hardness that snowplows could not even dent. Bilandic's response was to assure the city that all was well. But the city's snow plan, which had been written by a city hall crony, turned into a bad joke. The black community was outraged when the Chicago Transit Authority, which had a limited number of overcrowded trains, began skipping South and West Side stops as white commuters whizzed by, Loop-bound. Other trains ran sporadically, their electric power shorting out on mountains of ice and snow. Buses ran hours behind schedule. Side streets went unplowed. The outrage was widespread and white hot, just the kind of catalyst needed to dump an incumbent.

On Valentine's Day a beleaguered Mayor Bilandic spoke before a huge meeting of precinct captains at a downtown hotel and lapsed into a bizarre and off-the-wall performance. The struggling mayor compared recent criticism of his administration to the crucifixion of Christ, the Nazi persecution of the Jews, and the decline of democracy around the world. His rambling speech concluded with an astonishing outburst: "In the early history of Christianity, you see a leader starting with twelve disciples. They crucified the leader and made martyrs of the others. It is our turn to be in the trenches and see if we are made of the same stuff as the early Christians, the persecuted Jews, the proud Poles, the blacks and Latinos."[9] Some of the audience giggled. Most were embarrassed. The strain was showing.

Even though the Democratic party had not lost a contested primary election since 1911, it was going to lose this one. An outsider named Jane Byrne, diminutive but a bombshell campaigner, unloosed a slam-bang, hell-raising campaign that caught the old boys with their guards down. The anger over the blizzard of 1979 and Bilandic's fumbled handling of it gave three dissident groups the leverage to beat the machine. Byrne won fourteen of the city's sixteen black wards, all seven independent lakefront wards, and several Northwest Side Polish wards.

The tradition of the invincible Democratic machine had been broken. The long and hoary practice whereby machine Democrat begat machine Democrat and Chicago voters queued up at the ballot box like somnambulist proles thumping for the peerless leader was over. Predictability and stability, the great Democratic cynosures, built into the system over a half-century of careful cultivation and polishing, were over. No longer was the Democratic party's choice automatically the people's choice for mayor.

Jane Byrne: "Attila the Hen," 1979–1983

"I beat the whole goddamn Machine singlehanded,"[10] crowed Jane Byrne after her stunning upset of incumbent Mayor Bilandic in the party's February 1979 primary election. It had been a David-and-Goliath contest, pitting a five-foot, three-inch scrappy blonde against the machine political heavyweights and overlords who had not lost such a contest for a half a century. The mighty had fallen, and most of Chicago cheered. The general election that followed in April was a cake walk by comparison, for in one-party Chicago winning the nomination in February had been tantamount to winning the general election in April. Jane Byrne handily beat her Republican opponent, Wallace Johnson, with the largest majority in Chicago's mayoral history, an astounding 82 percent of the vote. Even Richard J. Daley in his masterful triumphs at the polls had never matched that percentage. From all appearances the new mayor had been put into office by a powerful but evanescent mandate.

In her campaign Jane Byrne had caviled endlessly about the evils of machine politics and about the "cabal of evil men" who ran the city. She seemed to promise a new deal in politics and a reshuffling of the structure of power, at least in the city council. Then in a stunning reversal she deserted the reformers who had helped her win and linked up with the "evil cabal" of the council, including Edward "Fast Eddie" Vrdolyak and Edward Burke, permitting them to organize the council and select committee chairmen. Disarray, confusion, and gloom descended upon the dissident communities that had helped elect her. The hopes for political reform had died again at the starting gate.

Grim fiscal realities faced the vibrant new mayor. When Jane Byrne assumed office in 1979, the second destructive wave of OPEC-driven inflation was gnawing at the nation's vitals with 15 to 20 percent interest rates. Cities on the high-risk list had difficulty in selling their bonds, sometimes absorbing massive losses through deep discounts, and some bankers were even looking askance at short-term tax anticipation warrants, which all cities needed to tide them over until taxes were paid. The doubling of interest rates meant that a massive transfer of money that formerly might have gone for raises for city workers would now be needed to borrow money from the bank. No or slow growth and the loss of industrial jobs and plants, a rust belt–wide phenomenon, was felt acutely and exacerbated Chicago's inability to pay its bills.[11]

With the municipal cupboard bare, Jane Byrne resisted the costly demands of public service employees and took on three publicly disruptive and emotionally wrenching strikes. In December it was the transit workers union that struck at the peak of the downtown and Loop Christmas shopping season. In January the teachers union reneged on agreed-upon spending cuts and job trimming and walked out. And in February, in the dead of winter and at the height of the heating season, when citizens most need fire protection, the firemen struck. Byrne was on a strike-a-month schedule. The firemen's walkout was a nasty and messy affair. They brought in an "outsider agitator" to lay out strategy for the union, and he consistently took a belligerent, public-be-damned attitude on the nightly television news. Into this volatile mess Byrne brought strike breakers, some of whom were black. City hall aides to the mayor suggested publicly that some firemen were sabotaging fire protection and that some were even engaging in arson. The firemen capitulated, but the strike disrupted permanently the chummy relationship that had existed between the mayor's office and the firemen.[12]

The urban gravy train, which had richly rewarded such public employees as transit workers and firemen in the inflation-ridden 1960s and 1970s, had come to a halt in the austere, cash-short, deflation-prone 1980s. To her credit, Jane Byrne faced this reality and took on three difficult strikes. To her discredit, Mayor Byrne handled all three strikes in what to the public seemed to be a vacillating, then vindictive, and sometimes mean and small-minded manner. Newsmen and the unions unflatteringly referred to her as "Good Jane, Bad Jane" and "Attila the Hen." Her bombastic rhetoric and her oversell on preparedness to take on the strikes tarnished and diminished the magnitude of her victory over the firefighters union.

Part of the battiness and three-ring circus atmosphere of her administration derived from First Husband Jay McMullen, whom the press took to referring to as "Rasputin in a turtleneck," and who needlessly inflamed relations with the press. He once banished a *Tribune* correspondent from the city hall press room and threatened another group that he would "bloody their noses" if they did not give Mayor Jane better copy. He referred to unfavorable coverage of his wife's administration as "more skunk juice from the Chicago *Tribune*." Part of the perception of "battiness" also came from Jane Byrne's personal style with the press. She was so feisty and combative with reporters that they took to calling their meetings "gang-bang" press conferences. She played fire-away-Flanagan and hurled half-thought-out bombshells at them before disappearing behind an elevator door or exiting in a chauffeured car. She offended friend and foe alike and her administration was, as Robert Davis of the *Tribune* described it, "creative, chaotic, dramatic, devastating, exciting, excruciating . . . historic," although some claimed it was "hysteric."[13]

Fighting Jane had committed soon-to-be fatal blunders during her one administration by turning former black supporters against her. She replaced black appointees with whites on the Chicago Housing Authority and the Chicago Board of Education and petulantly attacked a popular black alderman, targeting him for defeat. She soon became known as "Calamity Jane" who "shot from the lip" and kept Chicago in a state of turmoil with her helter-skelter hiring and firing policies, which became known as the "revolving door" policy.

In the end she obscured many of her achievements. She was in some ways a free spirit, setting Chicago politics afire, a stormy Robespierre ready to chop heads, egged on by her husband, Jay. She ultimately gave way to that powerful force that Chicago politics is at its heart—street theater. Sometimes providing farce, sometimes high drama, and occasionally comic opera, Jane Byrne lightened the civic mood. She clearly had the best act in town. Few politicians in Chicago's history could match Byrne for her zaniness and madcap and daring acts.

CHICAGO'S UGLY RACIAL ELECTION, 1983

The open and unblushing use of racial, ethnic, and religious slurs reached an all-time high in the 1983 Chicago mayoral campaign. That blowout featured incumbent mayor Jane Byrne opposed by black challenger Congressman Harold Washington and State's Attorney Richard

M. Daley in the February Democratic primary. Democratic winner Harold Washington went up against Republican Bernard Epton in the general election for mayor. That campaign unloosed an overload of emotional blockbusters, racial code words, and slurs. Tocsin calls to action, such as "It's our turn now. . . . We want it all, we want it now. . . . It's a racial thing, don't kid yourself. . . . Ditch the bitch and vote for Rich. . . . Go get 'em, Jewboy. . . . Epton! Epton! He's our man. We don't want no Af-ri-can," punctured the heady contest.[14] Harold Washington won the election to become Chicago's first black mayor.

During the four years before the next mayoral election, a new Mayor Harold Washington went through a baptism of fire called "council wars" that amounted to three years of nonstop verbal fisticuffs and rat-a-tat-tat repartee with his white opponents. Bad feelings between the mayor and his white council opponents ran deep. And the conflict was so inflammatory and racially volatile that the eastern press took to calling Chicago "Beirut on the lake." Washington lashed out at his opponents in the language and tone of an irate southern preacher or an Old Testament prophet as he levied a writ of rhetorical fire and sword on the blasphemers who blocked his path or otherwise vexed him by disagreeing with him. The mayor spewed forth barrels of bile and wrath on gainsayers who crossed him. Principal council opponent Edward Vrdolyak was known in inner circles as the "Prince of Darkness," "Darth Vader," or "Mr. V. D." Fast Eddie's twin council commander, Edward Burke, was socked with such epithets as "draft dodger," "twerp," "the pits," and "a pimple on an elephant's butt." The mayoral wrath even reached downstate and arraigned Governor James Thompson for playing "hocus pocus, dominocus" with the voters and for being "a South Africanite," "an aparthedite," a "no good," and a "disaster," and, occasionally, a "nincompoop," and an "S.O.B." For the late mayor Richard J. Daley, Mayor Harold employed a special lexicon of insult, calling him "a racist to the core, from head to toe, from hip to hip," adding "I give no hosannas to a racist, nor do I appreciate or respect his son. . . . He is an insult to common sense and decency." Mayor Washington was an articulate abuser of his real and perceived enemies and got off some of the most intemperate verbal pyrotechnics and *ad hominem* attacks of any mayor in Chicago since Big Bill Thompson, the champion declaimer of bombast, who left the office in 1931. The binge of political name calling exceeded even that of the Jane Byrne administration.[15]

When Washington sought reelection in 1987, that campaign (as hindsight would later show) would reach a crest in ethnic, racial and religious slandering. A new group on the scene, CONDUCT (Committee on Decent, Unbiased Campaign Tactics), directed by John McDermott, helped cool down the smoldering embers of racial conflict. Even so, it was not a squeaky clean, high school–style debate. CONDUCT issued thirteen reprimands related to the mayoral campaign, nine to Washington and his supporters, two to Byrne, and two to Vrdolyak. Ironically, CONDUCT had been set up by liberal types to fight 1983-style white racism but spent more time in 1987 denouncing black racism. The prize for the most inflammatory remark probably belonged to former Appellate Court Judge R. Eugene Pincham, who unleashed an emotional blockbuster at an Operation PUSH meeting in which he threatened, "Any man south of Madison who casts a vote in the February 24 primary and who doesn't cast a vote for Harold Washington ought to be hung. We know who you are. . . ." Despite such egregious blasts, city watchers and campaign observers generally agreed that the free and open use of racial and ethnic attacks had cooled somewhat, probably because of CONDUCT's monitoring.[16]

Harold Washington was reelected in April of 1987 and turned over a new leaf in the book of Chicago mayoral politics. Instead of rubbing salt in the wounds of the vanquished as he had in his 1983 inaugural, he began his term in 1987 on a kinder and gentler note, speaking of a "new spirit of Chicago," the need to work together, and even going out of his way to compliment his hard-working mayoral predecessors who had helped build the downtown. He also excised a section of his campaign speech that cast aspersions on the Democratic machine, and his aldermanic ally David Orr noted that the mayor "didn't challenge them to fight. . . . The mayor's message was we should lower our voices." In October Washington extended an olive branch to his erstwhile enemies, white ethnics, by slating for countywide office a multiethnic, multiracial, gender-diverse slate that included Richard M. Daley, a Polish candidate, Aurelia Pucinski (daughter of Roman Pucinski, one of his bitterest council opponents), and Carol Moseley Braun, a black. This slate "tells people we've gone too far with this acrimony, this negativism, this inability to get along," Washington told the press.[17] This was his famous "dream ticket." But before a racial conciliation could be effected and before Washington could recast Chicago politics in this new rational and pacific mold, he died on November 25.

Like Richard J. Daley before him, Mayor Washington had neither named a successor nor groomed an understudy to take his place. The result was another fight for succession. Beginning on Thursday, Thanksgiving Day, the struggle was on for a new mayor. Jesse Jackson jetted in from a world-class trouble spot, the Persian Gulf, where he had been nursing his presidential ambitions, to support an A.B.C. (Anybody But a Caucasian) successor. In one of the more astute political engineering jobs in recent memory, a white near-majority bloc of twenty-three aldermen joined with a minority black bloc of six aldermen to put over Eugene Sawyer as acting mayor. The event was a stormy one, with the black "movement" posturing alternately like French revolutionaries and bully boys. The spectacular all-night pep rally ended at 4 A.M. When all of the insults had been exchanged and all was said and done, the "movement" people lost to the newly formed black-white alliance of convenience. The new acting mayor, Eugene Sawyer, was a soft-spoken conciliator (so soft-spoken that the press called him "Mayor Mumbles.") A former alderman, Sawyer, who had worked both sides of the street—machine and reform—was acceptable to the ethnics and a small circle of black aldermen.[18]

Acting Mayor Sawyer, who served from December 1987 through April 1989, was an excellent transition figure to ease Chicago out of its brawling past of racial politics and into a new, less rancorous, low-key era where low-decibel politics did not count against you. The new mayor also was a good object lesson in two ways: (1) he demonstrated that a mayor did not have to keep the emotional throttle wide open, always revving up his core constituency with racial politics and thinly disguised honky bashing; and (2) he demonstrated that a mayor whose soft-spoken style was not threatening to white and ethnic Chicagoans could effect cooperation between seemingly irreconcilable whites and recalcitrant blacks.

But "gentleman Gene's" grip on the office began to slip. The "movement" people insisted that Mayor Washington's unexpired term could only be completed by a regularly elected mayor. The courts agreed. Elections were scheduled for February and April, 1989. Then Timothy Evans, the black "movement" candidate, dropped out of the Democratic mayoral primary in December 1988. This permitted two low-key moderates, Richard M. Daley and Eugene Sawyer, to move to center stage. A third candidate, Lawrence Bloom, entered, and when he tried to resurrect the strident tones and polemics of his late friend, Harold Washington, the strategy backfired. After Bloom's intelligently drawn position paper failed to ignite the public, his attacks became more visceral, belittling Daley's intelligence and flaunting his own not inconsiderable abilities. A tactic that had worked for Washington and Byrne flopped badly when reformer Bloom tried it on. However, its failure was less a commentary on Bloom than on how the political climate of Chicago had changed or was changing. A decade of "chaos-fest," "council wars," "Beirut on the lake," and smash-and-grab politics was over. The public had tired of the circus of insult, racial screaming, ghetto ranting, and white demagoguery, and was fed up with the politics of emotionalism and racial battling. Sawyer and Daley were refreshing changes. The overheated and overwrought racial politics of the Byrne-Epton-Washington wars were coming to an end. Only Lawrence Bloom and Timothy Evans were not aware of it. When they tried even tentatively to revive the old "us versus them" style, they appeared to be mean-spirited and anachronistic throwbacks to a little-lamented, conflict-filled racial past. Whites "had learned in their unsuccessful campaigns to stop Washington in 1983 and 1987 that racial campaigns don't work where neither race holds a majority," columnist Clarence Page wrote. "Perhaps now black leaders will learn the same lesson."[19]

Richard M. Daley was ideally suited to exploit the cooling political climate. He campaigned on the argument that the electorate was fed up with the racial polarizers such as Representative Gus Savage, who liked to scream "racist" and shout "Dumb, dumb Daley" when the TV cameras were rolling, or black Alderperson Dorothy Tillman, who attacked Acting Mayor Sawyer as a "shuffling Uncle Tom" for cooperating with whites, or Afro-nationalist Steve Cokely, who poisoned race relations with his venomous slurs that Jewish doctors were injecting the AIDS virus into black babies.

Richard M. promised to calm the troubled waters of Chicago politics. He asked for lowered voices and increased reason. He attacked none of his opponents—only the problems that he identified that needed mayoral attention. He stood up to insult, race baiting, and honky bashing and, following his handlers' advice, returned none in kind. He literally turned the other cheek. Daley rejected the time-tested strategy of the outsider (which had been followed by Byrne, Washington, Vrdolyak, and even Tim Evans) of lambasting the person in power and delivering every other day a bill of particulars about the incumbent mayor's failings. Instead, and ironically, Daley ran like an incumbent rather than an outsider—cool and positive, releasing position papers on numerous subjects, and, above all, underscoring again and again that the city was tired of racial extremism and that he would bring racial healing to the city. In addition, he promised stability and steady leadership. He was businesslike and city-manager-like in tone and substance. He offered no pie-in-the-sky cornucopia of goodies to his followers—in fact, he hinted at austerity and economy in government. He did not say to his followers, as the challengers had in 1983, "It's our turn now. . . . we want it all, we want it now!" Missing was any hint of a classical reward-your-friends-punish-your-enemies sentiment.[20]

By the time the low-key primary ended in February 1989 with Daley's victory, several things had happened. The tone of the campaign had been civil. The only strident voice in the primary, that of Lawrence Bloom, had faded out before the vote was taken. No verbal bomb throwers or flaming incendiaries had excited the campaign. The exchanges were dull, if not boring, and sounded as if they had been prescribed by a League of Women Voters manual on campaign etiquette. Seldom had Chicago seen such well-behaved candidates. There was no eye gouging, ear biting, or hitting below the belt.[21]

The general election campaign was only a tad more exciting, and pitted Democratic Daley against Timothy Evans of the Harold Washington party. Underfinanced and poorly directed, Evans was so ineffectual he looked like a rabbit caught in the headlights of a car on a country road. He did not know which way to run. His campaign tried to exploit the "Son of Boss" theme and "plantation politics," but it floundered and got nowhere. When Evans tried to resurrect the stridency of his mentor, that too fell flat. He failed to rev up the black community, where he did most of his campaigning. When race baiters and honky bashers such as Tillman and Savage tarnished his candidacy, he seemed genuinely surprised over his loss of liberal lakefront supporters.

By election time in April, it seemed clear that the old Byrne-Washington-Vrdolyak piss and vinegar had been drained at least temporarily out of Chicago politics. The ice age of nasty racial code words, harsh honky bashing, and Jew baiting were being left behind with the machine. The city had passed through violent contractions with the death of the machine and was experiencing the birth of a new age. The city's political system, halted in its tracks for a quarter of a century, was beginning to evolve again. A new age of political moderation seemed to be dawning. Low-keyed Rich Daley took 55 percent of the vote, the biggest mayoral majority since 1979.

NOTES

1. Paul M. Green and Melvin G. Holli, eds., *The Mayors: The Chicago Political Tradition* (Carbondale, 1987), 33 ff., 144 ff.
2. Melvin G. Holli and Paul M. Green, *Bashing Chicago Traditions: Harold Washington's Last Campaign* (Grand Rapids, 1989), 169–172.
3. See mayoral biographies in Melvin G. Holli and Peter d'A. Jones, eds., *Biographical Dictionary of American Mayors, 1820–1980* (Westport, Ct., 1981).
4. "Chicago's Daley," *Newsweek*, April 5, 1971, 80.
5. Walter Jacobson, "Daley," *Chicago Tribune Magazine*, March 28, 1971, 27; Sheehan quoted in Mike Royko, *Boss: Richard J. Daley of Chicago* (New York, 1971), 190; Adamowski quoted in Milton Rakove, *We Don't Want Nobody Sent* (Bloomington, 1979), 278; Hoellen cited in Rakove, 278.
6. Singer cited in Rakove, We Don't Want Nobody . . . , 373; Grimshaw quoted in William Braden, "Daley Remembered," Chicago Sun-Times (spec. reprint, December 9, 1986).

7. Washington cited in "Michael Bilandic: The Last of the Machine Regulars," in Green and Holli, *The Mayors* . . . , 167.
8. Ibid., 168.
9. Ibid., 169.
10. Byrne quoted in "Jane M. Byrne: To Think the Unthinkable and Do the Undoable," in Green and Holli, *The Mayors* . . . , 172. See also Bill and Lori Granger, *Fighting Jane . . . and the Chicago Machine* (New York, 1980), 19.
11. Interview with Jane Byrne, March 4, 1986; Alfredo Lanier, "Jane Byrne's High Hopes and Hard Times," *Chicago* (December 1981), 198.
12. Interview with Byrne, March 4, 1986; Bob Wiedrich, "Byrne's Strident Strike Rhetoric," Chicago *Tribune*, December 2, 1979; "Byrne Halts Strike," Chicago *Tribune*, February 19, 1980.
13. McMullen cited in "Byrne, McMullen Hit Abusive Press," Chicago *Tribune*, January 19, 1980; Robert Davis, "Byrne Crusade," Chicago *Tribune*, April 5, 1981.
14. For campaign coverage, see Melvin G. Holli and Paul M. Green, eds., *The Making of the Mayor, Chicago, 1983* (Grand Rapids, 1984.) Personal interviews with Bernard Epton, June 10 and August 9, 1984.
15. Washington quoted in Holli and Green, *Bashing Chicago Traditions* . . . , 143–144.
16. Interview with John McDermott, November 19, 1987; Nancy Isserman, "Conduct Press Releases and Numerical Summary of Complaints," (Staff report, Chicago, 1987).
17. WBBM-TV news, November 18, 1987; T. Hardy, "Mayor Keeps Byrne Off Democratic Slate," Chicago *Tribune*, November 19, 1987.
18. William Raspberry, "Jesse Jackson's Selective Application of His Fairness Principle," Chicago *Tribune*, March 28, 1989; WMAQ-TV news, December 2, 1987; L. Gorov, "Long Night Was Hard to Stomach," and R. Feder, "480,000 Homes Maintained a TV Vigilance," Chicago *Sun-Times*, April 5, 1989.
19. Clarence Page, "A Racial Campaign that Didn't Work," Chicago *Tribune*, April 9, 1989; Jim Merriner and Fran Spielman, "Evans Never Had a Chance, Chicago *Sun-Times*, April 5, 1989.
20. Interview with David Axelrod, February 7, 1990.
21. Ibid.; "Daley Turns Down Chicago's Fire" *Insight*, September 11, 1989, 23; John McDermott, "Our New, Positive Racial Politics," Chicago *Tribune*, March 14, 1989.

Index

Abernathy, Ralph, 100
Ackerman, Sam, 38
Adamowski, Benjamin, 196
Adams, Bob, 77
African-American political community, "splits" in, 3, 18; politics of, x
African-American population in Chicago, 197
Anti-Semitism, ix, 7; *see also* Cokely, Steve
Austin, Jerry, 12
Axelrod, David, x, 10, 11, 47, 63, 75, 76, 77, 78, 79, 80, 134; on Evans, 69; on lakefront vote, 70

Barefield, Ernest, 96, 97, 127
Baron, Hal, 154
Bilandic, Michael, 5, 6, 78; as mayor, 196–99
Black political coalition, x; vote turnout, 116; voting and ethnicity, 112
Bloom, Lawrence, 6; as mayoral candidate, 12, 17, 20, 21, 22, 23, 68, 75, 76, 77, 78, 142, 143, 147, 150, 173, 175, 177, 204, 205; supports Evans, 38; supports Sawyer, 151, 176
Booth, Heather, 38
Braun, Carol Moseley, 203
Burke, Edward, 12, 103, 112–13, 120, 135, 141, 142, 143, 200, 202
Burris, Roland, 15
Byrne, Jane, x, 6, 10, 13, 67, 71, 199–202

Callaway, John, 137, 156
Carey, Bernard, 74
Carter, Marlene, 37
Cavanagh, Jerome, 195
Chicago city council, 199–200
Chicago, "city of neighborhoods," 3
Chicago Defender, 18, 157
Chicago Democratic convention riots, 196
Chicago Federation of Labor, 39–40
Chicago Independent Bulletin, 149, 157

Chicago Lawyer, 150, 151, 152
Chicago *Metro News*, 149
Chicago voter registration, 124–25
Chicago's political evolution, 193 ff
Claypool, Forrest, 23
Cokely, Steve, 7, 104–06, 121–23, 172, 205
Coleman, Slim, 78, 155
CONDUCT, 23, 24, 144, 155, 202–03
Crain's Chicago Business, 14, 139, 148–49

Daley, Richard J., vii, xii, 30, 41, 139, 158, 199, 202; as mayor, 74, 133, 193–96, 203
Daley, Richard M., 3, 48, 65, 68, 134, 203; in 1983 campaign, 66, 75, 169; in 1989 campaign, 34–35, 39–42, 115, 126–127, 139, 142, 204; campaign contributors of, 19; campaign style of, 205; "capital-intensive" campaign of, 118; and debates, 21; "dreaded tongue slip" of, 23, 24; formula for victory of, 66; future of, ix; and Hispanic vote, 19 ff, 50–51; issues and, 35; and lakefront vote, 20; political image of, 128, 205–06; political strategy of, 19; use of TV by, 10
Daley, William, 11, 23, 41, 134, 155
Daly, Lar, 146
Davis, Danny, 48, 122, 141, 142, 143, 144–45
Davis, Robert, 201
Dawson, William, 67
Degnan, Timothy, 11
Drake, Tim, 77
DuMont, Bruce, 111, 156
Dunne, Finley Peter, vii
Dunne, George, 101, 123, 128
Dvorak, James, 13, 24, 43

Elections: 1977 mayoral candidates,